Dial Detective
Investigation with the 90° Dial
2017 Edition

**An Illustrated Introduction to
Cosmobiology and Uranian Astrology**

DIAL DETECTIVE

Investigation with the 90° Dial

2017 Edition

*An Illustrated Introduction to
Cosmobiology and Uranian Astrology*

MARIA KAY SIMMS

ACS Publications
Starcrafts LLC
Epping, New Hampshire

Other books by Maria Kay Simms

Twelve Wings of the Eagle, ACS 1988

Search for the Christmas Star (with Neil F. Michelsen), ACS 1989

Your Magical Child, 1st Edition, ACS 1994; 2nd Edition 1997,
Expanded 3rd Edition 2011

The Witch's Circle (formerly Circle of the Cosmic Muse, Llewellyn 1996

Future Signs, ACS 1996

Millenium: Fears, Fantasies and Facts
(with Maritha Pottenger, Zipporah Dobyns and Kim Rogers Gallagher),
ACS 1999

A Time for Magic, Llewellyn 2001

Dial Detective, First Edition, ACS 1989, **Revised Second Edition** 2001

Astrology and the Power of Eight
1st Edition 2014, 2015,   2nd Edition 2017

2017 Edition, ACS Publications, an imprint of Starcrafts LLC, Epping, New Hampshire

Second Edition, 2001, Cosmic Muse Publications, an imprint of
Starcrafts Publishing, Exeter, NH 03833

First Edition, 1989, ACS Publications, San Diego, CA.

Front cover drawing, illustrations and book design by Maria Kay Simms.
Cover design and interior production design by Daryl Fuller.

ISBN 978-9781934976661
Printed in the United States of America

ACS Publications
is an imprint of
Starcrafts LLC
PO Box 446, Exeter, NH 03833
Our website: *www.astrocom.com*
24 Hour toll free order line: 866-953-8458   FAX: 603-734-4311
Mail orders: Astro Computing Services, 68-A Fogg Rd., Epping, NH 03042
Office phone: 603-734-4300 Monday-Friday 10am - 4pm EST

Dedication and in Memorium

Since **Dial Detective** was first published two of the gentlemen whom I especially acknowledged in my First Edition and the Revised Second Editon have passed away into worlds beyond. I honor their memory by dedicating this 2017 Edition to them, in loving gratitude for their vast influence on all of my work in astrology, and especially as it led to my initial creation of this book

Charles Emerson
July 6, 1923 — September 19, 1992

Charles was a well-known Uranian astrologer and teacher in New York City. He was widely respected as a founding father of the National Council for Geocosmic Research, Inc., in which he worked tirelessly for the growth and the success of the organization. Charles was my primary teacher and my mentor in my early years as a professional astrologer and as a member, then officer of NCCR. He was always informative, encouraging and inspiring to me, as well as to many others in the astrological community.

Egon Eckert
May 3, 1906 — September 17, 1992

Egon, a retired engineer who had immigrated to the USA from Germany, continued to be actively engaged in research, as he also served as a loving caregiver for his ailing wife and disabled daughter. While a younger man in Germany, he had studied astrology with the Hamburg school.

Egon became my good friend during the late 1970s and the early 1980s after he joined my classes as a student. I am quite sure that I learned far more from him than he from me. Astrology, for Egon, was primarily a hobby, but his vast knowledge of Uranian techniques was, I daresay, far beyond many professional practictioners. Egon's tips and ancedotes from his training in Germany, plus his translations from his German Cosmobiology books and the Lexikon during my classes, contiributed greatly to class activities and to my own knowledge. I am grateful to Egon for having provided data and permisson for some of the case studies in this book, and for editing portions of my manuscript, as I prepared it for the first edition of this book.

Acknowledgements

Most of the first edition of **Dial Detective** was written during the very early 1980s when I lived in Connecticut and held a weekly Urarian workshop in my home. That workshop started in 1977 at Mystic Arts, my metaphysical bookstore in New Milford, then "followed" me when I moved to Newtown in 1979, and continued right up until left Connecticut in mid 1985. Some came and went, but a few people continued through those years. Without the stimulation and contributions from that "core group" I might not have even tried some of the charts that became the case studies in this book. I will always remember that class with a great deal of pleasure. In addition to Egon, whose valuable contributions are noted on the dedication page, may thanks to my "core group," Patti Skiff, Pat Miske, Louise Patrick and Tom Canfield.

The original idea to do a picture book about the 90° dial came out of group discussions among myself, Mary Downing, Arlene Nimark and Brita Okin. We planned to collaborate on a project to publish some easy "how to" books on astrological techniques, and I was assigned the task of doing a dial book. , but various interferences from our personal lives got in the way of the realization of our project. I moved from Connecticut to Illinois to Florida to San Diego during 1985 and 1986, and with all those changes, the dial book moved to low priority. Still, I am very grateful to Mary, Arlene and Brita for motivating me to start this book and for their encouragement and comments on the intial draft of my manuscript.

Very special thanks also to Gary Christen, noted Uranian astrologer, lecturer, Astrolabe partner and a fellow board member in NCGR. Gary generously permitted me, back when I began serious work on the illustations for my first edition, to copy his graphic design for the 90* dial. The dial Gary had designed for Astrolabe, had been first developed by Wayne Booher, a prominent Uranian astrologer from New York City. I had used their durable hard plastic dial for years and favored it above all others I'd tried. My dial s not quite so closely calibrated as Gary's—I used 7-1/2' increments rather than 5', in order to make my smaller illustrations read well with the available programs of the time. Although newer programs would have allowed the use of Gary's dial, and indeed a redesign throughout this book, I have decided for consistency as well as in the interests of getting this 2017 edition completed faster, to use my original dial for the additional illustrations, and to update pages from the older edition only in the case of text references that are no longer valid. Gary's more precisely drawn dial has since become available in a hard plastic edition from Astrolabe. Find contact information in the Bibliography and Resource Guide.

Dial Detective was first published in 1989. At the time, I was Art Director for ACS Publications in San Diego and was blessed with both the time and the equipment needed to turn my projects into reality. I was also assisted by the supportive staff, and by the encouragement and a moral support of the late Neil Michelsen, who was then ACS President and my husband. I am also grateful to Maritha Pottenger, Anna Mathews,, Kristeen Roberts and Spencer See for their help with my 1st edition. Special thanks sldo to Kathryn Fuller for proofreading and Daryl Fuller for helping me through my learning curve on new programs, his production advice, and for updating my 2nd editon front cover and redesigning the back cover.

Last and certainly not least, special thanks to my daughters, Shannon, Molly and Liz, to my Mom, and to Mrs and Mrs. Egon Eckert for permission to use their charts in this book.

Also, thank you to my personal friends whose correct or full names are not revealed, who gave me permission to use their charts within various case studies.

Contents

Introduction

First I must tell you that I am not an "orthodox" Uranian astrologer or Cosmbiologist. I am an eclectic, mixing what I first learned of these two systems with other techniques. I've not attempted to teach all aspects of either system within this book, but instead to show you the parts that I have found to be most useful. In some cases I have mixed in a few ideas that have come from other systems or from my own experience.

In my opinion, the best thing in Cosmobiology and Uranian astrology is the 90° rotating dial and it is the use of this valuable tool that is the main theme of this book. My primary reason for creating *Dial Detective* was becuase my graphic arts ability afforded me a way to save others fhe frustration I had experienced when I began learning the dial in relative isolation, with no availabe teacher, from books that were mostly text with very few pictures.

Dial technique truly proves that old adage that, "a picture is worth a thousand words." This is why I created *Dial Detective* for those who are eager to learn dial technique, but have no ready access to a live teacher. It can also provide a useful workbook supplement for those who are fortunate to work with a teacher. Indeed, I have hear that some teachers use it with classes and recommend it to their students.

The dial is not at all difficult to use, and in fact I have found that it helps beginning students learn astrology faster. Although explaining or understanding the dial is not easy with words alone, this very visual technique is quite easy to learn if you can see it demonstrated. It is probably not for everyone, however. An analogy that I like is one I once heard Gary Christen use: "Some people are oriented toward digital clocks and some people like the clock faces better. The dial is for clock-face-people. If you like to scan through computer lists, figure precise mathematicale orbs of aspect, and do other primarily "left-brain" things like that, you probably prefer digital clocks and may not "take to" this technique. But if you are visually oriented, you are going to love it! A turn of the dial will reveal pictures of symmetry that will "speak" to you, and open up new doors of astrological interpretation.Once you have tried it, I am sure that a great, great many of you are going to agree that it is an indispensible tool for a thorough investigation of any chart.

I have successfully taught the dial to people who had only recently begun their study of astrology. Sometimes it has even proven to be easier for a novice to learn the dial because he or she is not yet too "locked in" to a different tradition. But astrologers who have become very advanced in other methods sometimes find it difficult to "shift gears" and therefore they perceive the dial to be complicated. It most definitely is not!

Although I say the dial is for beginners, I do not mean absolute beginners, who are still learning the basic alphabet of astrolgy. The text of this book is written with the assumption that you at least know basic keyword meanings for planets, signs and houses (athough signs and houses are mentioned only slightly), and that you can easily recognize astrological glyphs.

It is also assumed that you are at least somewhat familiar with transits, directions progressions, composite charts, solar returns and relocation charts. Simple definitions for these techniques are given as each one is introduced and then used to demonstrate its application to dial case studies, but the techniques themselves are not explained in detail.

This book is intended to be used as workbook. The pages are 8-1/2 x 11 in order to allow larger than usual type and large illustrations so that you can lay the book out on a table, set up your own dial and follow along with the case studies. **A paper dial for you to cut out and use can be found on page 93.** It is true that pictures are a lot better than just words in learning to use the dial, but you will understand the techniques much more easily and thoroughly with actual "hands on" experience. **It is highly important that you do each exercise in sequence, for the techniques taught in each one builds upon what has already been demonstrated.** I have found that students having trouble with this book have invariably been "skipping around."

Since I did not want to clutter up the illustrations by including the degrees, signs and minutes for each planetary position, I didn't included other than for one example on page 4. I don't put the numbers on the dial chart in my own work; I just keep a "regular chart" nearby to refer to if I want. **Lists of the birth date and planetary positions for each of the charts appear in Appendix I. Data for charts that were added to the 2nd edition appear with the charts.**

Appendix II lists all of the **planetary pictures** that are used in the text, pus quite a few extras, **in alphabetical order by delineation.** That means, for example, that you would look under "M" for marriage to find the combinations of the astrological factors that indicate marriage in the Uranian system.

Appendix III lists by astrological factor all the planetary picture formulae given in Appendix II by astrological factor that refer to dire and drastic events and suggests alternative delineations. Some of the alternatives come from the Uranian tradition, but many are derived from my conviction that no astrological actor is inherently "bad." All astrological factors symbolize energies that have the potential for positive manifestation through the choice of the individual.

Appendix IV is a potpourri of Uranian tips and terminology that are not covered in the main text. It includes 360° dial techniques. You will find caution "flags" waving throughout the text. A major source of some peoples' fascinations with Cosmobiology and Uranian Astrology—and at the same time a major potential danger—is the fact that specific formulas are given for specific events. Some astrologers who are primarily oriented toward contemporary astro-psychology may well question if I should be teaching event-oriented systems which dare to pinpoint events of death and destruction.

I have seen cases of self-induced anxiety in people who, with a little bit of knowledge of Uranian Astrology, after being impressed with a conference lecture or attending a few classes, will buy a book with interpretation guidelines and start "doing' their own charts. They "hook into" a configuration that has a dire textbook delineation and start imaging the worst. I did something of this nature to myself when I was first learning the system, and I tell you about that in Chapter 5 that is titled "Caution!"

Destructive things do happen in the world—that can't be denied, no matter how much we might prefer. It's truly amazing how planetary pictures correlate with events, as you will see in the page ahead. It seems to me that it is best to confront the full range of possible manifestations of planetary pictures, how they work and then put them into perspective that allows for the use of this system for strategic planning. I believe in a large amount of free choice—with room for a little humor. (You'll see how you can "write off" some of those nasty configurations as a wild idea of fiction or even a past life memory!"

It is my hope that this book will encourage a great many of you to use the 90° dial, for I think it is an extremely useful tool for any astrologer, no matter what your philosophy.

For those of you who are attracted to the systems of Cosmobiology and Uranian astrology, may *Dial Detective* help you to learn them thoughfully, at your own pace, and that you will maintain a healthy, positive perspective .

It IS Elementary, Dear Watson!

As a tool for the investigation of events the 90° dial is unbeatable.

"But not for beginners," you may protest, "I must thoroughly learn the basics of astrology before I attempt to use such a complicated tool."

Not true! The dial IS basic—quite elementary. Of course, you should know the language of astrology, the glyphs and the meanings of the planets and signs, before you use the dial.

Beyond that you will discover that the dial can help you progress in understanding the dynamics of any chart you want to investigate.

Why 90 Degrees?

90° is 1/4 of the whole 360° circle. Four has always been thought to symbolize material manifestation. Four is the physical world. It is measured in time and space. When we investigate a chart with the 90° dial we are primarily interested in the answers to the questions: What happened?

What will happen? Other methods of astrological investigation may contribute to the understanding of one's deep psychological or spiritual motivations. That is not what we are doing with our 90° dial. We want hard, practical information. We want to know where the action is!

Let's set up a dial and begin:

1. Here is a standard 360° chart wheel divided into 12 signs. Let's for fun color the cardinal signs light and bright, the fixed signs solid and murky, and the mutable signs scattered with dots.

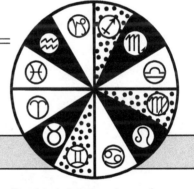

2. Now let's stack up all the cardinal brights on top of Aries, all the solid fixed signs on top of Taurus, and all the scattered mutables on top of Gemini. All 12 signs are now in 1/4 of the wheel—90 degrees!

3. This 90° triangle, however, would be a very unwieldy tool. Let's stretch it out, then, into a nice smooth circle.

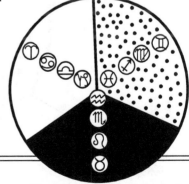

Now turn the page to see your new tool for the investigation of charts!

Quite so! Now we can dial our way to greater insight into the workings of the planets involved in each case we want to investigate. Various designs for the 90° dial are available, and you will find information on sources in the bibliography in the back of this book.

So that you will be able to practice immediately and follow along with the examples as you read, a paper dial is provided on page 93. Cut out the dial carefully. You might choose to have the dial laminated. If not, at least reinforce the center of the dial with a small piece of transparent tape. Center your dial on a piece of plain paper. Carefully punch a thumb tack through the center dot, including the paper beneath. Remove the tack, and then from the back, push the point through the holes you have already punctured in paper and dial. To avoid pricked fingers while you work, you could cover the tack point with an eraser, or perhaps with a cap from a tie pin or pierced earring. Now your dial will turn freely.

Holding the dial steady, place a straight edge along the line of the pointer arrow and draw a line on the paper. (Even nicer, if you can find or make one, is a thin, transparent plastic ruler with a hole in one end to fit over the tack.) Label the line with the glyph for Aries. This line represents the beginning of all four cardinal signs. In the same manner, draw a line to represent the beginning of the fixed signs, labeling it with the glyph for Taurus, and a line to represent the beginning of the mutable signs, labeling it with the glyph for Gemini. I also like to draw a line at 15° fixed, which is the opposite end of the pointer arrow from Aries. As you begin to enter planetary positions for a chart it will be important to line the dial up precisely with these lines you have drawn on the paper. Some people like to anchor the dial with a bit of scotch tape while they are entering chart factors. This is unnecessary so long as you always note the precision of your line-up before entering each new factor. The dial is now ready for our first case.

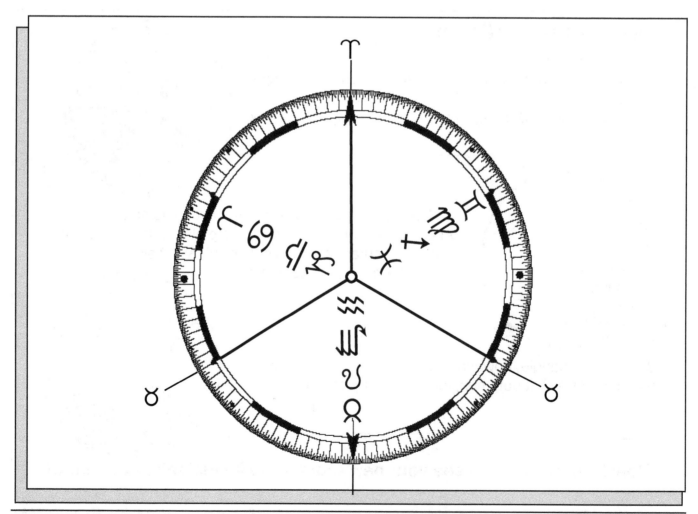

The Adventures of Sherlock Holmes

And why not? After shamelessly borrowing a classic phrase of the famed detective, it is only fitting to accord him a place of honor.

Sherlock Holmes is the creation of Sir Arthur Conan Doyle, who was born May 22,1859 in Edinburgh, Scotland. A physician, Sir Arthur gave up the practice of medicine to write full time after the publication of *The Adventures of Sherlock Holmes* brought great recognition. He is considered to be the creator of the modern detective story. His ingenious methods for Sherlock's detection of crime contributed to the progress of the science of criminology.

Lois Rodden, in *AstroDataBank*, now confirms 4:55 AM LMT as "AA" data for Sir Arthur.[1] Exact positions (the same as in my First Editon) are:

☉	00 ♊ 33	♅	03 ♊ 21
☽	00 ♒ 46	♆	26 ♓ 45
☿	05 ♉ 25	♀	07 ♉ 35
♀	27 ♈ 07	☊	23 ♒ 57
♂	18 ♊ 29	M	10 ♒ 36
♃	25 ♊ 49	A	23 ♊ 13
♄	07 ♌ 10		

Setting Up the Dial Chart

Note that each five degrees on the dial is marked by alternating black and white bands. This makes the counting of degrees easier. Each single degree section contains a long 30 minute line, slightly shorter lines to indicate 15 minutes and 45 minutes, and very short lines to indicate each 7-1/2 minutes of arc (1/2 of 15 minutes). If you enter each factor precisely, you will be able to see very close orbs of aspect. As Sherlock has said, "It has long been an axiom of mine that little things are infinitely the most important." The time you take in the careful drawing of the chart will be greatly rewarded in the later ease of your investigation.

Some dial designs include numbers for the degrees, but this is unnecessary. With a little practice you will find the counting of degrees will become easy and you will appreciate the clean, uncluttered design of this dial.

To enter the position of Sir Arthur's Sun, locate the beginning of Gemini—an easy task since you've already marked and labeled it! The Sun's position is 0 and 33 minutes, so you must draw the line at the halfway mark of that first degree. Always use a straight edge to make sure your lines are drawn radiating out from the center of the dial. Draw the glyphs BIG so they are easy to see. Use a pencil at first, so you won't worry about mistakes.

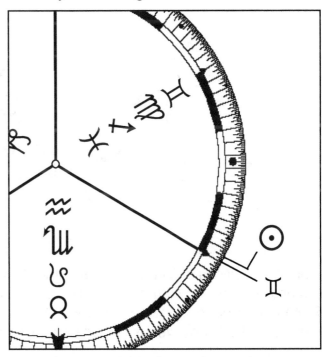

Now enter the rest of the chart factors.
Your result should look like this:

Look at the close 1 degree orb between Jupiter and Neptune. On the dial they appear as if they are in conjunction, but actually they are in square. The Gemini sector, remember, represents all of the mutable signs. Jupiter is in Gemini and Neptune is in Pisces.

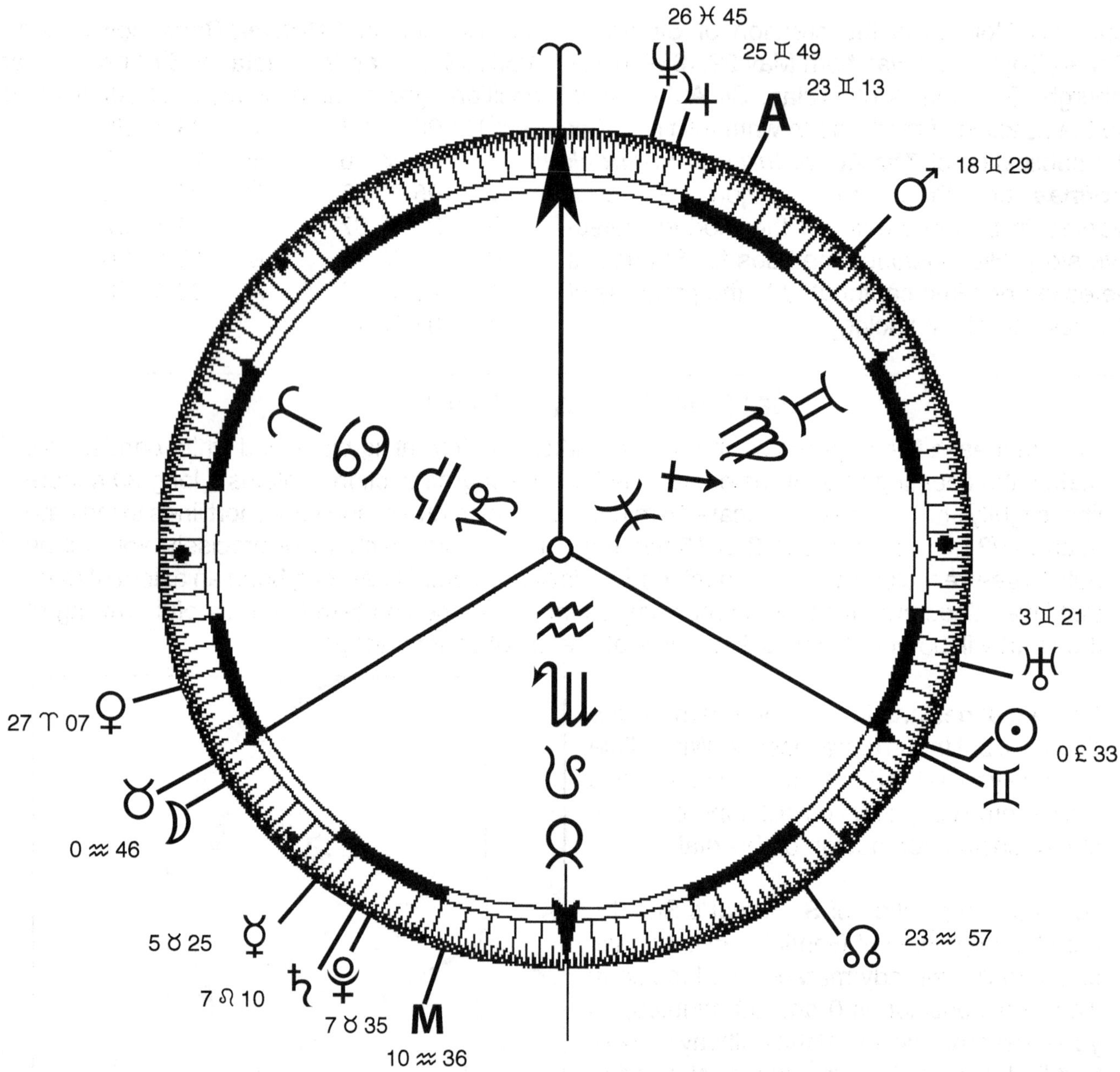

Note the positions of Mercury, Saturn, and Pluto. Mercury and Pluto are conjunct in Taurus, but both are square Saturn in Leo. The Midheaven (M), in Aquarius, is square Mercury and Pluto and in opposition to Saturn. For 90° dial work the 3° to 5° orb of aspects of these planets to the Midheaven is considered quite wide.[2]

Look at the arrow directly opposite the pointer and you will find Jupiter. Jupiter at 25° is in a 135°or sesquiquadrate (⬦), aspect to **M**, with an orb of less than 15' of arc. Factors in ⬦ and ∠ (semi-square, 45° aspects) can be immediately recognized by their placement opposite the factor to which the arrow points. Neptune, at 26 ♓, is ∠ **M** with an orb of slightly more than 1°.

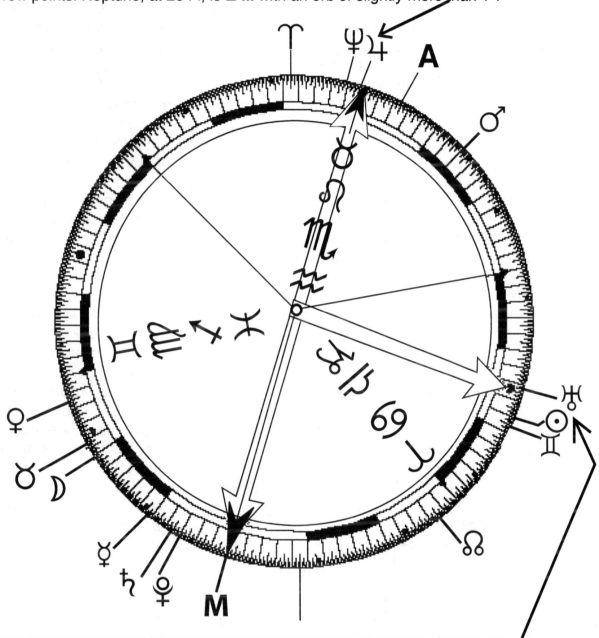

Look, now, to the right, to the large black dot half-way between the pointer arrow and its opposite arrow. Here you find Uranus. The dot marks 22°30' from the pointer, or half of a semi-square. All of these aspects, derived from the square, symbolize ACTION. They relate to FOUR and tell us how the energies symbolized by the planets may ACT in the physical world.

Astrologers who do not use the 90° dial often ignore the 135°, 45°, and 22°30' aspects, and many textbooks refer to them as "minor" aspects. This is most likely because on a traditional 12 house chart wheel these aspects are difficult to spot without tediously counting degrees. On the 90° dial they can be spotted instantly, with no counting. Astrologers who use the 90° dial do not consider them to be "minor" aspects at all. For example, suppose that Midheaven in this chart is activated by a transit or direction. It is easy to see in Doyle's chart that Jupiter and Uranus are "hit" at almost exactly the same time. These three factors, Midheave, Jupiter and Uranus, in such tight orbs of aspect, work closely together. You can scarcely consider the action of one without the others.

Turn your dial, now, so that the pointer is on Uranus. Notice that Jupiter and Midheaven are each just a smidgin past the 22°30' dots from the pointer. The arcs from Uranus to Jupiter, and from Uranus to Midheaven are equal. Here's another way to say it: **Uranus aspects the midpoint of Jupiter and Midheaven.** If you want to know what

aspect, look at the signs. ⛢ is sesquiquadrate the midpoint of ♃ and M. This is called an **indirect** midpoint. If one planet is conjunct or opposite the midpoint of two others, it is called a **direct** midpoint. Direct midpoints are said to be stronger than indirect midpoints. For all practical purposes, however, you do not have to look up the aspect. **A configuration this close in orb works.** You may be sure of that—indirect or not. "Equals" is substituted for "aspect" to note in glyphs:

(Uranus aspects Jupiter/Midheaven)

$$⛢ = ♃/M$$

"Interesting." you may remark, "but what does it **mean**?" Let's pause, then, to consider what clues we have already collected in our investigation of the life and works of the creator of Sherlock Holmes. Important guidelines for our interpretation can be found in the book, **Combination of Stellar Influences by Reinhold Ebertin**.[3] This book is usually called the **CSI** for short, and that is how I will refer to it in future examples. At the top of page 183 of **CSI** we find ♃/M, and beneath it are listed interpretations for each factor on the midpoint of ♃/M. After Uranus (the Ebertin books use German glyph ⛢ instead of ⛢) we find *"a lucky hand in enterprise... the ability to utilize the right moment...sudden successes, recognition."* We then know that this is a potential in the life of Sir Arthur Conan Doyle.

Also observe the conjunction of Mercury and Pluto in Taurus, square Saturn and also widely square Midheaven. Of the conjunction Ebertin says: *"The wielding of influence through speaking or writing."* The sign position of Mercury, and also the Mercury–Pluto–Saturn configuration indicate a person who is logical and extremely thorough, patient, reserved, and very organized.

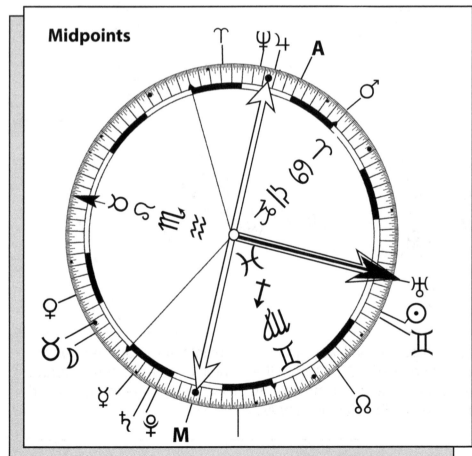

Midpoints

Such a person is also likely to be quite suspicious and skeptical. That these characteristics would influence career is shown by a link to Midheaven. More could be said, of course, but this is enough to suggest important attributes of our famous detective and, it appears, of his creator.

An obvious question that now arises is–when? **When** might the thorough, self-disiplined work of this potential writer be expected to pay off in the "sudden recognition" of ♅=♃/M?

Look again at the dial with pointer on Uranus. Count the degrees clockwise to Pluto, Saturn and Mercury. They are from 25-1/2° to 27-1/2° from Uranus. Now count counter-clockwise from Uranus. You will find that the Aries point is about 27° from Uranus.

It appears that twenty-seven degrees could represent an important *time* in Sir Arthur's life direction.

Why do I say that? Because in the form of prediction most commonly used in dial technique 1° symbolically represents approximately 1 year. At approximately the age of 27, then,Sir Arthur's ♅ =♃/M "success configuration" will also be in contact with his ☿-♄-♀ (and all that **they** mean) *and* the ♈ point, which symbolizes his connection with the **world** in general. Before we continue you will want to know how to calculate these directions, which are called:

SOLAR ARC DIRECTIONS

Solar arc is simply the difference between the secondary (day-for-a-year) progressed Sun and the natal Sun. All factors in the chart are directed forward according to the arc of the Sun. You don't have to know a person's exact secondary progressed Sun position. **Any** ephemeris for any year can be used.

Count forward from the birthday one day for each year of age. From the Sun position of the resulting day, subtract the position of the Sun that is given on the birthday. The result is the solar arc for the age on the birthday of the directed year. If the desired solar arc is for an event that occurs at some point in the year after the birthday, add 5 minutes of arc for each additional month, and one minute of arc for each additional 8 days. The directed position of any factor is the natal position plus the solar arc.

> **SOLAR ARC is the form of prediction most commonly used in dial technique**

Here is an example of solar arc calculation: In **The American Ephemeris for the 20th Century**[4] look at May 22 (Sir Arthur's birthday) for 1986. (1986!! Remember—any year will do.) The Sun position is 0 ♊ 37 (you can round off the seconds). On his 1887 birthday, Sir Arthur was 28 years of age. Counting May 22,1986, as zero, count forward 28 days. That brings you to June 19 with a Sun position of 27 ♊ 26.

$$27 \text{ ♊ } 26$$
$$- \ 00 \text{ ♊ } 37$$
$$\overline{26 \text{ ♊ } 49}$$

The difference between the Sun positions is **26° 49'**–only 11 minutes short of **27°**. This is the solar arc on the **28th** birthday of **any** person born in **any year** on **May 22**.

27° is also the arc that we found visually when we counted around the dial from Uranus to Aries. Even though Sir Arthur was actually **28** years of age on his birthday in 1887, his **age by solar arc** at that time was about **26 and 3/4**. This is because the apparent motion of the Sun is faster in the northern hemisphere winter than in the summer.

People born in spring and summer will have solar arcs less than their actual age, while people born in winter have solar arcs slightly "older."

If Sir Arthur had been born with Sun in Sagittarius instead of Gemini—say on November 23—you would find that his calculated solar arc for his 28th birthday would be 28°25'—almost 28-1/2!)

A Study in Scarlet, the first of Sir Arthur's many stories about Sherlock Holmes was published in the 1887 *Beeton's Christmas Annual*. It was very well received by the public.[5] During the time period that Sir Arthur's ♅ came to ♈ by solar arc (about 27°) and his solar arc directed ♀, closely followed by ♄ and then ☿, came to ♅ (from 26° to 28°) his thorough and organized (♄) writing ability (☿-♀) paid off in success and recognition (♅=♃/M) throughout the world (♈).

We don't know for sure just when this first story actually reached the public. It was probably some months before Christmas. It would be a fair guess that the ♄ and ♀ directions were active when the work was being prepared for publication, the ♅ "hit" ♈ at the time of publication, and as the ☿ direction became active, the news of his public acclaim was being received.

The techniques that you have practiced so far in this book are basic to Cosmobiology, which is an astrological method that was first publicized by Reinhold Ebertin. The 90° dial was invented by Alfred Witte, founder of the Hamburg School of Astrology. Witte's method was introduced in the United States by Hans Niggeman, who called it Uranian Astrology.

Changes from the First Edition

At this point, in first edition of *Dial Detective*, I took the reader right to an introduction to Uranian Astrology. In the years since, after working with many more students, I've come to realize that decision was unwise. Most people benefit from more practice in 90° dial work with only the limited factors of Sun, Moon, the angles, the eight planets, their natal midpoints and the solar arcs, before going on to add any of the extra bodies or the additional complexities of the Uranian method.

The elegantly simple methods of *Cosmobiology* give the "big picture." Adding Uranian techniques provides fascinating confirming detail. But when one adds the detail before understanding the big picture, it is all too easy to be misled into finding what one wants to find rather than what is actually there. It's a classic example of the old adage of missing the forest by being too busy examining the bark on one tree. For this reason, this 2nd edition has a new chapter for practice charts using *Cosmobiology* techniques only. I recommend you thoroughly practice using the 90° dial techniques shown in this chapter and the next one before you go on to the remaining chapters on Uranian Astrology.

Notes:

Rodden, Lois, *The American Book of Charts*, San Diego, ACS Publications, 1980, was the reference for the first edition of *Dial Detective.* At that time Lois rated the data as "C" for Caution, which meant the time was speculative. In preparing this second edition, I decided to check AstroDataBank software for the Doyle chart. There I found that Rodden has apprarently discovered confirming data for this chart, for the rating is now given as "AA", which means based on birth records. *AstroDataBank* is an extremely valuable research tool for any astrologer. Contact information is in the Bibliography.

[2] Very tight orbs are used in natal dial work. For natal analysis, some will recommend up to 5 degrees, but I am inclined to consider only up to 2 unless the planet under consideration is part of a stellium. For midpoints use an orb of up to 1-1/2° from the axis. For timing I want to see no orb—visually on the dial, the direction appears exact. More on this in the next chapter.

[3] Ebertin, Reinhold, *Combination of Stellar Influences,* Ebertin-Verlag 7080, Aalen, Germany, 1972. The CSI is a "must have" book for working with Cosmobiology. If you don't find it easily in a store, American Federation of Astrologers will have it. Order phone is 888-301-7630.

[4] Michelsen, Neil F., *The American Ephemeris for the 20th Century 1900 to 2000* at Midnight or at Noon, San Diego: ACS Publications, 1983.
   Since Neil's passing in 1990, Rique Pottenger has continued Neil's work in programming, so new versions of the ephemerides, such as *The American Ephemeris for the 21st Century, 2000-2050*, in both midnight and noon versions by Neil F. Michelsen and Rique Pottenger are now also available, with the new planets Ceres and Eris included.

[5] *The Encyclopedia Americana*, Vol. 9, Danbury, CT: Grolier, Inc.. 1987

COSMOBIOLOGY ②

Cosmobiology is best known through the book **Combination of Stellar Influences**, written by Reinhold Ebertin. It was first published in 1940 in Germany, and continues to be widely used by astrologers in the United States, as well as internationally. You will find a much more detailed background on the system in that book, as well as others by Ebertin, most specifically the **CSI's** companion textbook, **Applied Cosmobiology**.

Ebertin, his father Baldor Ebertin, and other astrologers, along with professors and medical professionals, developed Cosmobiology. They were thoroughly knowledgeable in the methods of the earlier Hamburg School (more commonly known as Uranian Astrology), which flourished in Germany circa World War I. Although they used some facets of Uranian, most notably the use of the 90° dial, they vastly simplified their system.

The word "Cosmobiology" was first coined by an Austrian physician named Dr. Feerhow, with the intent of designating an astrology based on scientific foundations and keyed to the natural sciences, as differentiated from the popular astrological tradition which had become tainted as superstition or dismissed as "entertainment."

After extensive study, the Cosmobiologists determined which astrological factors could be most scientifically relied upon for accuracy, and then limited their methodology to those factors only, as follows:

1. The Sun, Moon and eight planets: Mercury, Venus, Mars, Jupiter, Saturn, Uranus, Neptune and Pluto, plus the Moon's Nodes.

2. The Midheaven and Ascendant (as degree points, derived from unequal house system calculations—the Cosmobiologists used the Koch system for this).

3. The angular relationships between the above factors (lights, planets, lunar nodes and angles), including midpoints.

4. The tropical zodiac signs of the planets

That's it—that's all. Those readers accustomed to most commonly used methods of astrology will immediately notice: "No houses?" Yes, no houses. The Cosmobiologists felt that since the comparative accuracy of the various competing house systems could not be scientifically proven, it was best not to rely on them.

Although I am admittedly eclectic, I do not pretend to be a scientist and I do like to consider the classic house chart for some types of my astrological work, I will concede the Cosmobiologists their point as to the unprovable nature of which house system is best. A few astrologers have technical reasons valid to them for choosing one house system over another, and I have studied some of these, while also asking questions and hearing many opinions expressed. So far, I'm unimpressed by any clear evidence of a "winner." All things considered, it is my belief that if you "scratch the surface," the primary reasons for the majority of astrologers' choice of which house system to use boils down to one of two: 1. "My favorite teacher used that system," or 2. "I like my own chart best in it." All of the unequal house systems result in the same degrees for Midheaven and Ascendant. Since other than for the degrees of M and A, houses are not used at all in Cosmobiology, then which unequal house system you choose matters very little.

(What is my preference for house system? When I use houses in chart reading, I prefer Koch. Why? Because I started out in the German systems, Dr. Koch is among the developers of Cosmobiology system...and I also like my own chart best with Koch houses!

It's the uncertainty of houses that calls attention to one thing I like most about Cosmobiology—the amount of information you can get from it if you do NOT use houses. More could be said beyond this simplified explanation, but for the purposes of this book, it will be sufficient. For further study, see Ebertin's **Applied Cosmobiology**.

Although the system that was originated by the Cosmobiologists seems to have remained quite pure within the work of its adherents, the new word they coined never quite caught on as a wide-spread community substitute for astrology. Gradually, over time, professional astrologers are edging toward regained acceptance of their ancient art/science under its age-old title of astrology. Today, at least in the USA, Cosmobiology is generally understood to denote a specialty system of chart interpretation that focuses on the 90° dial as a primary tool, and on the importance of midpoints. I have noticed that the primary elements of the system, midpoints and dial work, are used by many astrologers who would not necessarily consider themselves Cosmobiologists, but have nevertheless seen the value of using its tools in combination with other techniques.

In my opinion, Cosmobiology is a system that deserves much more widespread attention, for it often yields information about a chart that cannot be as easily discovered with other methods. I will demonstrate that for you with two example charts of public figures, one for whom birth time is not known, and another for whom accurate birth data has been widely published.

Advantages of Cosmobiology for Studying Charts with Unknown Birth Time

It can seem very limiting to work with a chart where the birth time is unknown, but if you must, the midpoint system of Cosmobiology allows you a decided advantage. I pointed this out in the footnotes to the Sir Arthur Conan Doyle chart in the first edition of **Dial Detective**. At that time, I referenced Lois Rodden's **American Book of Charts**, which listed Sir Arthur Conan Doyle's data as "caution" (source unknown). In explaining

why I chose to use speculative data for my first example chart, I pointed out that, of course, it was partially because I wanted to play off Sherlock Holmes for my book's title—but I also wanted to make the point that Cosmobiology offers a lot of information without necessarily having to use a timed chart. Now, thanks to Lois Rodden's latest, wonderful and invaluable **AstroDataBank** software (that she developed with programmer Mark McDonough), I already know that the Doyle data is "AA," so I will show you another example chart to show you how a time can be found when correct recorded data is not available. In my search for potential biographies, one of the best examples with dramatic events was Mike Tyson, the heavyweight boxing champion who served prison time after a rape conviction. I tried the birth date given for Tyson and it worked great! Maybe I was a bit lucky, but I'll bet that you can get more accurate info with the dial than with any other methods for a chart with unknown birth time. So, for your practice in Cosmobiology, we'll look at the Tyson chart, and then another celebrity case study for which accurate time has been published.

For your practice in Cosmobiology, let's first look at the Tyson chart, and then another celebrity case study for which the accurate birth time has been extensively published. I will refer to interpretations directly from Ebertin's **Combination of Stellar Influences** for Tyson, and for the second study I'll refer also to Michael Munkasey's **Midpoints: Unleashing the Power of the Planets.**[1]

To learn Cosmobiology well, you should obtain a copy of the "CSI" and, if possible, also the Munkasey book as an additional good guide for learning interpretation.

As you progress in your studies, you will also form your own interpretations, based on the basic meanings of planetary combinations and, of course, from your own observations. But for the student, the guidebooks are very valuable.

For now, To borrow from the Munkasey book's subtitle, let's...

Unleash the Power of Midpoints!
More Practice with Cosmobiology

Famous boxer Mike Tyson, was born June 30, 1966 in Catskill, NY. Since we do not know his birth time, his planetary positions show are for for noon on his birthday. The chart shown has solar houses, since we do not have his time of birth. Planetary positions for noon EDT are:

☉	08	♋	24		♄	29	♓	14
☽	12	♐	53		♅	16	♍	07
☿	04	♌	07		♆	19	♏	40 R
♀	04	♊	56		♇	16	♍	05
♂	22	♊	53		☊	23	♉	05
♃	11	♋	59					

In the illustration of the Tyson chart shown below, solar houses are used with the planet degrees rounded off, since we do not have accurate birth time. The chart is calulated for noon, and by that we know that only the Moon would be more than about 1/2 degree befor or after these positions, depending on what Tyson's birth time may be.

Since Moon moves 12-15 degrees in a day, and is about 13° Sagittarius at noon, we can be reasonably sure of its sign, but we can't rely on Moon aspects, unless we allow very big orbs, which reduces us to pure guesswork. There are a few close orb aspects among these planets, but what shows what we know of Tyson's public life? Yes, there is a t-square of Mars square Saturn and also square the Uranus-Pluto conjunction, but the orbs are quite wide—too wide for a Cosmobiologist. Still, the T-square seems an appropriate one for Tyson...or, what else do you see?

Just for fun, with your best sense of objectivity, why not just take a few minutes looking at the chart this way and jot down whatever potential characteristics it suggests to you for this individual. Then compare it to what can be found with Cosmobiology. On the next page we'll look at the same planetary postions, all but the unreliable Moon, on the 90° dial.

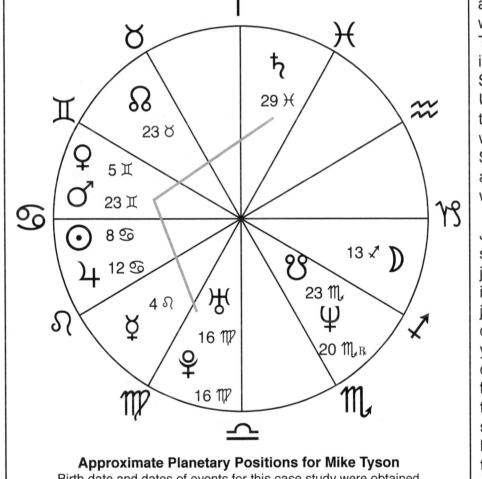

Approximate Planetary Positions for Mike Tyson
Birth date and dates of events for this case study were obtained from **AstroDatabank** software.

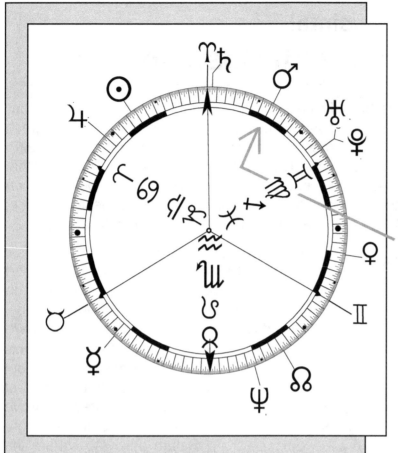

Leaving out the Moon, we can look at the remaining planets using the tight orb that are standard for dial work: 1-1/2° for midpoints with 2° (some will use 3°) for Sun, Moon, Midheaven and Ascendant. For aspects between two planest, use only up to 3° orb (some will allow 5°), unless perhaps for a stellium for which you might allow a bit more. In all the factors in the configuration, I think the tighter the orb, the more significant, so I generally stick to the 1-1/2° to 2° rule, and I find I get the most reliable information from those configurations that are very close in orb.

Without moving the pointer off Aries, a glance at this dial chart draws one's attention to the same T-square factors as we saw, with wide orbs, on the classic chart. Now, though, we see that Mars appears to be on the midpoint of Saturn/Uranus and Saturn/Pluto! Let's look that up and see what Ebertin's interpretation is. Under the heading Saturn/Uranus (page 185, **CSI**), move down to find Mars, and we see:

> "An act of violence, the occasionally wrong use of extraordinary energy, undergoing great efforts and toil... the stage of challenging others for a decisive contest or fight..."

Ah, ha! Good start. Under Saturn/Pluto (page 189), Mars on the midpoint:

> "Brutality, assault or violence, ruthlessness — The necessity to fight for one's existence or life, maltreatment."

When the dial is rotated to point directly at Mars, we see that the midpoints Saturn/Uranus and Saturn/Pluto are virtually without orb — visually on, forming a perfect symmetry. Less obvious, perhaps, if you are a beginner at this technique, is that Mars is also within acceptable orb of the midpoint of Venus and Jupiter. Not sure? If you rotate the dial just a bit to the left so that the arrow is directly on Venus/Jupiter, you'll see that Mars is less than one degree from the exact midpoint.

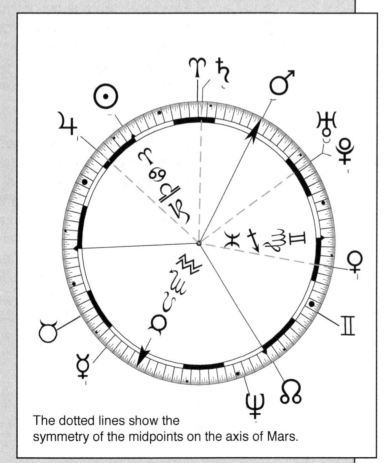

The dotted lines show the symmetry of the midpoints on the axis of Mars.

Let's try another one. If I hadn't spotted that very obvious Mars configuration, my first step in looking at a chart like this would have been to start with the Sun.

The illustration to the right shows the pointer turned to Sun. Note that directly across the dial, right on the axis of the Sun, is North Node. This means (as was explained in the earlier Sir Arthur Conan Doyle chart) that Node is in either a semi-square or sequiquadrate aspect to Sun. More significantly, for the purpose of dial interpretation, think of factors on the same axis as working together. The same midpoints are on the axis of both Sun and Node. When a solar arc direction or transit comes to one, it also comes to the other one simultaneously. When one of them moves by solar arc, the other one, along with all midpoints on the axis, moves right along with it.

Now, it is not nearly as immediately apparent what midpoints are within orb of the Sun-Node axis. When you're not sure, rotate the dial in one direction (up to 1-1/2°, perhaps 2° for Sun),

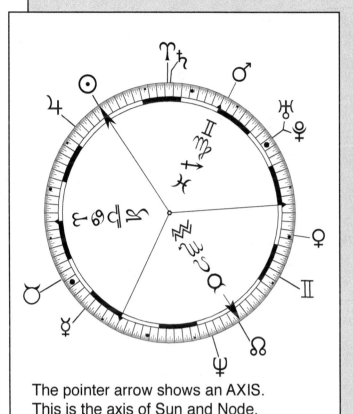

The pointer arrow shows an AXIS.
This is the axis of Sun and Node.

and then the other, to see what midpoints will line up. With the pointer rotated a bit over 1-1/2 degrees to the left of the Sun, as shown, notice the pointer is on the Sun/Jupiter midpoint and that Mercury and Uranus-Pluto are now equidistant from the pointer—equal arcs. This means, of course, that ☉ = ☿/♅ and ☿/♀ by an orb of 1-1/2 degrees. Moving the pointer a little less than two degrees to the right of the Sun would show equal arcs to Neptune and the Node: ☉ = ♆/☊.

Keeping track of these midpoints and just what they mean is much easier if you make the little diagrams that are commonly called "trees." The next page shows you trees!

Not sure? If you rotate the dial just a bit to the left so that the arrow is directly on Venus/ Jupiter, you'll see that Mars is less than one degree from the exact midpoint.

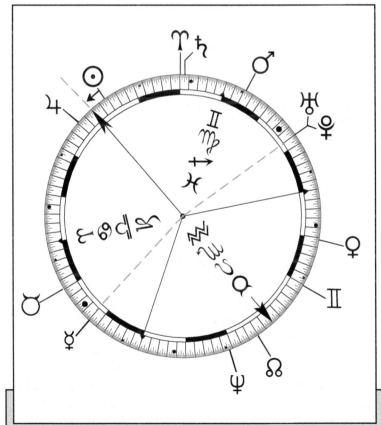

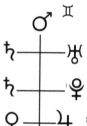

challenging others for decisive contest or fight; violence; occasional wrong use of energy

brutality, ruthlessness, violence; the necessity to fight for one's life

sex—strong powers of wishing; procreation/birth

aggressive, fighter, competitive may be violent, strong sex drive

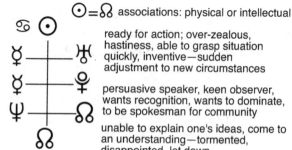

☉=☊ associations: physical or intellectual

ready for action; over-zealous, hastiness, able to grasp situation quickly, inventive—sudden adjustment to new circumstances

persuasive speaker, keen observer, wants recognition, wants to dominate, to be spokesman for community

unable to explain one's ideas, come to an understanding—tormented, disappointed, let down

has many contacts, gains recognition, smart, but might cause self problems through misunderstandings, hastiness

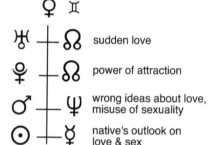

sudden love

power of attraction

wrong ideas about love, misuse of sexuality

native's outlook on love & sex

highly sexual, powers of attraction may come on too strong, though

acts independently, nervous energy, tests of power carried out calculatingly, exessively irritated nerves

desire to realize plans fanatically, excessive nervous irritation

insists on his own ideas, his own way, nervous, high-strung, independent

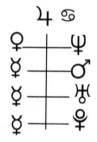

imaginative, romantic reverie

sound judgment, one who is able to make his way successfully, celebrated speaker

optimism, confidence—a fortunate turn

able to persuade, teach—recognition by the masses, great success— crook, swindler

confidence; capable of strong success, gaining of recognition, persuasive

one-sided, obstinate, sometimes suddenly inhibited—sudden losses

inhibitions in development, unable to progress— separation

obstructions in vitality, difficulties in profession— defeat in a fight or contest

shyness in talking with others— terminating associations

this axis likely to be active at times of defeat or disappointment; obstinance; may experience sudden feelings of inhibitions in normally aggressive personality

transformation: sudden, revolutionary

urge for success at all cost— sudden upsets uses compulsion on others, wants to influence the masses

experience of the contrast between fantasy and reality—coming down to earth with a bump

unreasonable plans, speculations—a great loss

drive for success to the point of compulsion, risk-taker, may be unrealistic in expectations and bring on problems

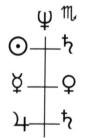

inhibited mental development inner peculiarities—crisis

fantasy, inspiration, odd attitude to art, lack of tact

pessimistic, tends to begrudge others good fortune —feels abandoned

inner insecurities and big dreams, unlikely to handle disappointment well; may feel very alone inside

Here are "trees" of all reliable factors for the Tyson chart; ☽, M & A omitted because birth time is unknown. Even so, a lot of information is revealed. Next to each midpoint is a short paraphrase of the ***CSI*** interpretation. A good way for beginners to learn is to look up each planet-midpoint like this, and then summarize it in your own words, as shown by the bold type phrases below each tree. As you progress, you will begin to **define** your own ideas for each midpoint and rely less on guidebook interpretations.

Most anyone would have to say that dial work yields an impressive amount of information for a chart with no birth time, no Moon, no Midheaven, no Ascendant, no houses, and using only orbs of 2° or less. In this demonstration, we didn't even consider the signs! But—helpful as the guidebooks may be, they do not save you from having to synthesize the information, and use common sense in placing it in context. So...what do we have here, supposing we did not already know this was the chart of a champion boxer, who also has created serious trouble for himself?

The "rule of three" is a commonly held adage for astrologers of varied traditions, and it's a good one. If a chart tells you the same or very similar information three different ways, it's important. If you only see a theme suggested once, it may not be that significant.

Although this untimed chart offers no specific details that confirm what we know of Tyson from public record, we can see some of the significant characteristics that explain how his life might have unfolded as it has. For example, if you scan the textbook interpretations for the midpoint trees, it is easy to find more than three indicators of one who will fight hard, and perhaps fanatically, for what he wants. Although there are more than three indicators that he could lose a fight, or be disappointed, there are also more than three that indicate he could achieve significant success and recognition in life. Additionally, we see more than three suggestions of a strong sexuality, which coupled with his very abundant drive to fight for what he wants, could possibly lead him into trouble.

The purpose of this book is primarily to demonstrate a method of investigation, so I will leave it to other books to deal with how a counselor reading Tyson's chart for him, at any point in his life, might have offered him guidance. Let's next go on to observe just how the potentials in this particular chart were activated by solar arcs at just a few of the most significant published events in Tyson's life.

Moving the chart ahead via solar arc moves the entire axis of each planet. You can examine each solar arc planet to see which natal planets and midpoints it contacts, and you can also look at each natal planet to see which solar arc midpoints have now come to be on its axis.

Considering Tyson's midpoint trees, we can expect that a strongly successful event in his career would almost surely involve Jupiter, and it would also very likely involve the axis of Sun-Node. The axes of Mars and of Uranus-Pluto should also be noted, for they include significant indicators of Tyson's strong will to succeed at all cost. Let's first investigate Jupiter.

Directed Sun came to Jupiter at about 4°. Jupiter won't move by direction around to the Node end of the Sun axis until about 41°, past Tyson's age at this writing. Looking for a more logical Jupiter event, it is easy to see that Mars will move to Jupiter at a solar arc of about 19°. Let's try directed Jupiter at that same arc. It will come to the Uranus-Pluto axis. Jupiter's connections with Mars and with Uranus-Pluto are significant in Tyson's career. He became the undisputed heavyweight champion shortly after his 19th birthday, when on June 28, 1985, he knocked out the previously unbeaten champ in round one.

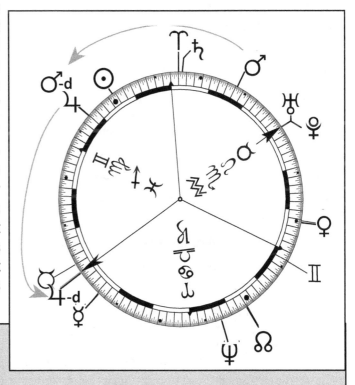

♂-d = ♃ is a success combination in itself. ***CSI***, under "Probable Manifestations" says, "successful results in one's profession."

♃-d = ♅/♇: attainment of immense success
♃-d = ☉/☊: recognition...successes in public

Looking at the trees, notice that while the Sun-Node and Uranus-Pluto axes include success potential, they also both include the potential of loss and disappointment. The Mars axis is also problematic, as is that of Saturn. The Venus axis carries the potential of misuse of sexuality.

In February of 1992, Tyson was convicted and imprisoned for having raped a Miss Black America contestant the previous summer. His solar arc at the time of his conviction was 24.26. Extraordinary tensions that led to his imprisonment may have begun at around the time Tyson's Uranus-Pluto conjunction and his Sun-Node axis connected by solar arcs of about 23 degrees.

One way to look solar arc "hits" for a particular time is to enter the directed positions onto the dial chart in a second color. In the illustration, the solar arcs are shown in gray. Set up your practice dial and try the pointer on each of the directed "hits" listed to the left of the dial illustration. You will see that all of these configurations become active in the order listed within a solar arc range of about 23°-25° which is the time frame from shortly prior to the rape through the time of the conviction, to his imprisonment. (I am not attempting to be exact here, because we are not certain of the exact planetary positions. With an accurately timed chart, we can be amazingly exact, as you shall see.

Interpretations for Tyson are either excerpted or paraphrased from the ***Combination of Stellar Influences***, and of course there are alternative things that each of them could mean. That is why looking ahead is a considerably more challenging prospect than to investigate something that has already happened. Still, it is through investigations of past events that we learn. (More about looking into the future with this method later.)

Range of Solar Arc aspects for the months prior to and including conviction and imprisonment.

♅-♇-d = ☉/♃ speculating; the expectation of good luck; pursuit of wealth

☿-d = ♀/♆ disappointed hopes; trouble cause through mis-directed love sensations

♀/☊-d = ♂ passionate urge for love

♄-d = ☿/♃ and ♂/☊ uncertainty in decisions; breaking off negotiations; desire to withdraw; problems with others, reserve, inhibition

♂-d= ☿/♄ tendency to treat others badly, disputes, bring about separation by force

♆-d = ♀/♂ abnormal craving in sex; an inclination to perversity

♀-d = ♄ suffering through love

And at the solar arc of about 25, after the conviction & in prison:

♂-d = ♅/♆ and ♆/♇ paralysis, sadness, to succumb to external forces, lack of energy (shown by pointer)

Interpretations paraphrased from CSI.

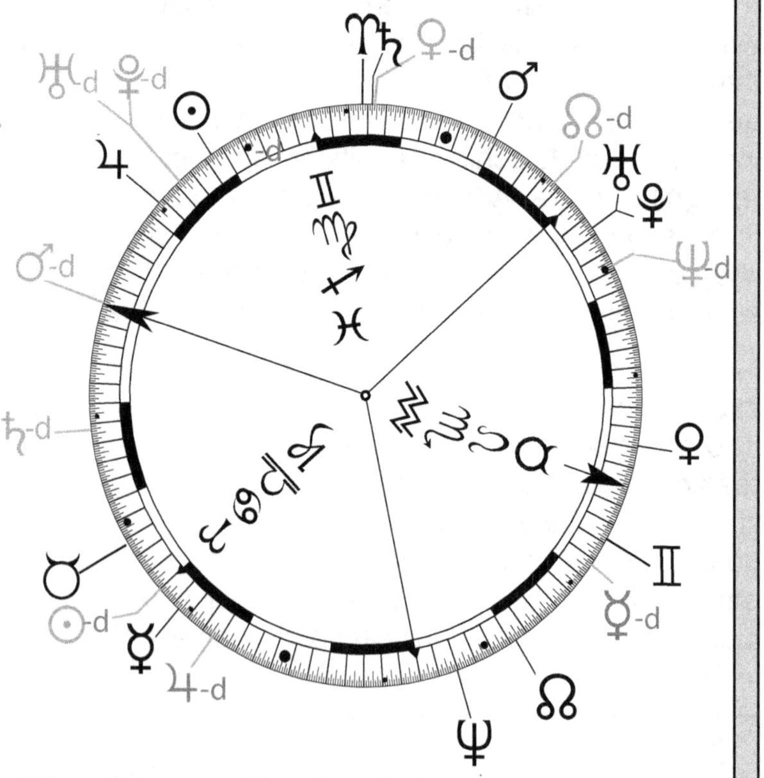

Solar arc positions shown in gray.

In November of 1996, after having made a successful comeback as a fighter following his release from prison, Tyson infamously bit off a piece of the ear of his opponent during a fight. This was the time, at a solar arc of 28.58, that his directed Sun came to Mars, which is on the midpoints Saturn/Uranus and Saturn/Pluto, thus bringing together his Sun tendency to over-zealously seek to dominate others, with his very tense and potentially violent Mars axis.

For practice in looking at accurately timed charts, there is no more dramatic example with which all

The Power of Midpoints with an Accurately Timed Chart...
The Clinton Scandal

readers should be familiar than that of former President Clinton. His data has been widely published, and is classified in AstroDataBank as "A."

Here you will first see how to notice a highly significant complex of factors within a natal chart, and what the potential of those factors might be. Then you will see how, one-by-one, the planets in the configuration moved by precise solar arc timing to show the significant stages during the scandals of second term of his presidency which ultimately led to his impeachment trial.

Natal Sun in Leo, 11th house, is suggestive of this politician's great charisma. It is not so obvious, though, why this Sun has also been prominently activated at times of his major scandals—until you add one key midpoint.

Look at the illustration of Clinton's chart on the dial. Notice how closely Sun is on the midpoint of Saturn/Uranus. Venus is also on the Sun axis, and the only other close midpoint is Mercury/Node.

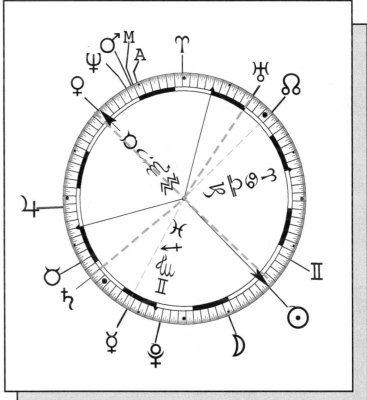

Interpretations of ♄/♅ = ☉ and ♀ from the CSI include: ☉—*severe tests of strength; power of resistance, rebellion, inflexibility;* ♀—*tensions or strains in love life often leading to separation.*

For this case study, I will compare the **CSI** with excerpts from the delineations offered in Michael Munkasey's book, ***Midpoints: Unleashing the Power of the Planets***. Munkasey, in researching and writing his interpretations, sought to bring them more into line with contemporary USA culture, and he also made a point of showing the potential "upsides" of each combination. His is a more psychological approach.

With President Clinton's chart I found that the Munkasey text shows quite well the talents that seem to coexist so closely with the flaws in this complex personality.

It will be well worthwhile to acquire Munkasey's book, too, if you can. It is my intent to help see that it is soon in print and available again.

Munkasey hits quite well on the talents we know this politician to have, thus showing the ways in which his Saturn/Uranus = Sun and Venus work positively: ☉—*finds effective ways of reconciling forces for change with demands to uphold tradition. Determined to introduce the new to those who remain conservative, prestige through invoking radical reform;* ♀—*introduces change in a more acceptable way; satisfaction with new ways of showing affection, appeasement of those demanding change. (The* ☿/☊ *midpoint, in both references, of course, indicates communication skills.)*

Still, Munkasey agrees that this combination spells tension. Rebelliousness and inflexibility may be an advantage at some times, but at other times, quite the contrary. **How** a natal con-figuration might manifest when activated can often be reflective of the **planet** that activates it.

Just as when looking at traditional natal charts, it is important to notice major aspect configurations, iand in dial work to notice which axes are most complex, having more than one planet together. Such axes are sure to figure significantly in the lifetime, and as you investigate many charts,

you will see just how effectively their movement by solar arc directions will reflect the most life-changing events.

Look again at Clinton's chart and notice how close M, A, ♂ and Ψ are together on the dial. Also note that in terms of the counterclockwise solar arc movement of the planets, Ψ leads the train. Now, what do you suppose might happen when that particular train crosses ☉, ♀ and then theh ♄/♅ midpoint, one by one?

I offer you the following chronicle, using events taken from the Starr report to Congress, to demonstrate how very simply and explicitly the events of the Clinton scandals culminating in the impeachment trial were ticked off by the solar arc movement of the Ψ-♂-M-A complex over the ☉-♀-♄/♅ axis.

If you count back from the Sun, you will see that Neptune would cross it by solar arc at around the age of 49. Clinton was 49 the year that his infamous affair with Monica began, but because he is summer-born, his solar arc is "younger" than his chronological age. At his first meeting with Monica in November 1995, his solar arc was 47.48, Neptune was bearing down. At that exact

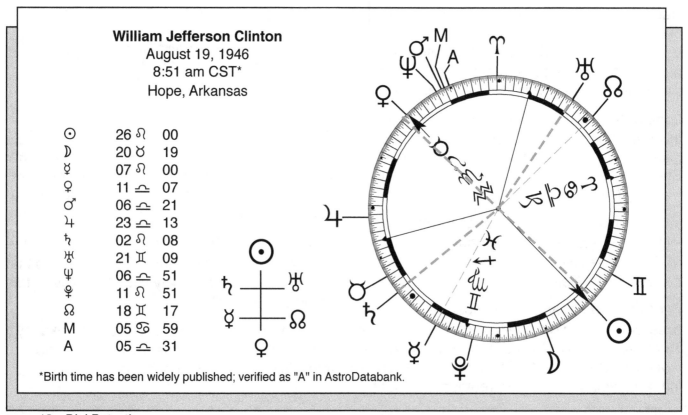

William Jefferson Clinton
August 19, 1946
8:51 am CST*
Hope, Arkansas

☉	26 ♌	00
☽	20 ♉	19
☿	07 ♌	00
♀	11 ♎	07
♂	06 ♎	21
♃	23 ♎	13
♄	02 ♌	08
♅	21 ♊	09
♆	06 ♎	51
♇	11 ♌	51
☊	18 ♊	17
M	05 ♋	59
A	05 ♎	31

*Birth time has been widely published; verified as "A" in AstroDatabank.

time, M=♀/♆ (**CSI**: ***romantic reveling...illusion***)

All event dates that follow are taken from the published Starr report to Congress.[2]

Neptune came to Sun at the solar arc of 49.08, just as Clinton's second term of office began in January 1997. ♆-d=♀ (49.16) was exact within 2 minutes of Clinton's actual solar arc (49.14) on the 2/23/97 occasion of his first act of perjury, and exact within 3 minutes of his final intimate encounter with Monica (49.19). In the next several months ♂-d crossed Sun and Venus, and the scandals over campaign finance, the Paula Jones case, Whitewater and Monica began to build. At a solar arc of 49.47, Neptune came to ♄/♅. Here, let's look at the guidebooks for interpretation:

♆=♄/♅—***CSI***: *inability to face emotional stress; falsehood or malice caused through weakness; resign self to inevitable, mourning*

Munkasey: *masked changes designed to break traditional roles; delusion that change will operate to improve.*

On 12/28/97, (50.04), just as M-d=☉ (50.02), Clinton called Monica in to instruct her how to handle the Jones subpoena. On 1/17/98 (50.07), he is questioned under oath in the Paula Jones case, and the next day he queried his secretary prior to her Grand Jury testimony. Mars was about to cross ♄/♅ (50.17 exact).

From the ***CSI:*** *wrong use of extraordinary energy; violent or forced release from tension; challenging others for a decisive fight; deprivation of freedom.*

From **Munkasey**: *increased irritation with changes; impatience with radicals who insist on new ways; struggles to impose changes.*

As the scandal continued to build, A-d had now moved up to ☉ (50.30) and then to ♀ (50.37). In mid-August of 1998, at a solar arc of 50.41, Clinton made his T.V. apology to the nation. At the exact solar arc of 50.40, M-d hit ♄/♅. For that ***CSI*** speaks of: *making the highest demands on one's strength, and of rebellion and provocation.*

Munkasey's more psychological approach has: *accepting change, removing old habits & benefiting, altering personal goals due to changes in work, releasing old ideas which no longer work.*

But the culmination is still to come! And here is the one factor in the Neptune train complex that you might not have yet noticed. Look at the Moon. Is it not also part of this? Yes, right on the Ascendant axis, and well within orb of being on the midpoint of every factor in the complex. On the next page you will find a tree for the Moon showing the very large number of midpoint combinations that can be derived from this complex axis.

Note that the closeness of orbs means that ☽, ♆, ♂, M and A are all on the ♃/☊ midpoint. Also, ☽ = M/A, ♂/A, ♂/M, ♂/♆, ♆/M and ♆/A. Also M = ♂/A and ♆/A, ♂=♆/M and ♆/A, and even the outer factors, ♆ and A are within a degree of orb to count as being on the midpoints of the others: ♆=♂/A , ♂/M, M/A and A = ♂/♆, ♆/M and ♂/M.

If you look up all of these midpoints in the ***CSI*** and also in ***Midpoints*** by Munkasey, you will find an amazing amount of detail relating to both strengths and weaknesses in this man's complex personality. Within this axis alone, we can also see his charismatic ability to relate to

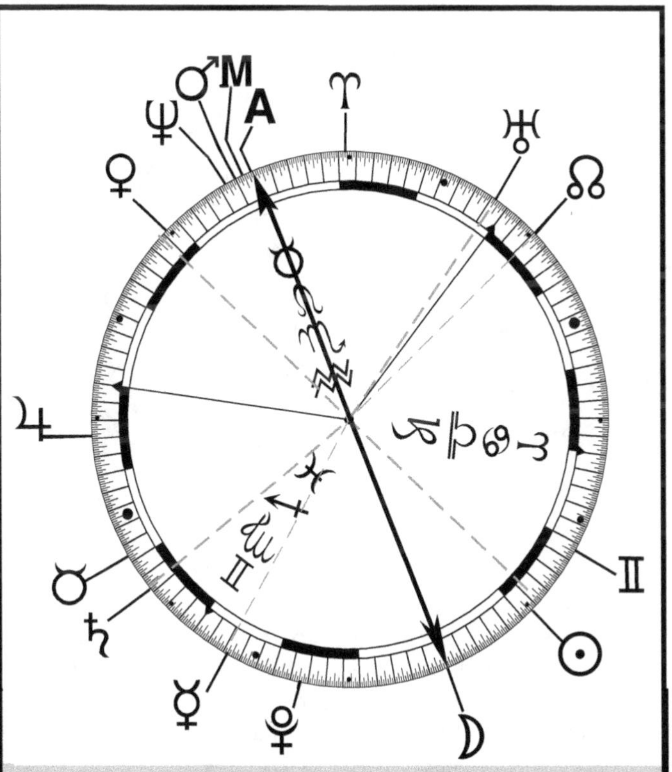

people emotionally and gain recognition as their leader, and we also see the emotional insecurities, the impulsiveness, the lack of self-control and the tendency toward deception and pretense.

If you count degrees of solar arc counterclockwise from the Moon, you'll see that Moon moves around to the Venus end of the Sun axis at about 51°. To be exact: ☽-d comes to ☉ at 50.41, to ♀ at 50.48,

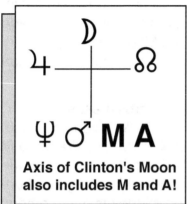

Axis of Clinton's Moon also includes M and A!

and to the midpoint ♄/♅ at 51.19. A-d =♄/♅ at 51.08.

The events are as follows, with the exact solar arcs for the dates that they occurred.

9/9/98—50.45 The Starr report was

sent to Congress. 12/11/98—51 The Articles of Impeachment are approved.

02/12/99, 51.13—President Clinton is acquitted in the Senate impeachment trial.

2/24/99, 51.13 —NBC's interview with Juanita

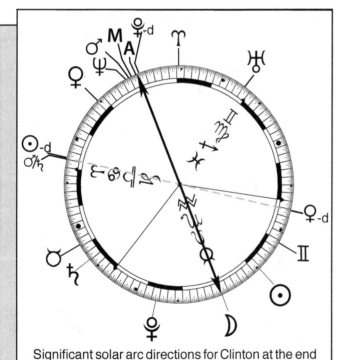

Significant solar arc directions for Clinton at the end of his Presidency are shown above. Note that Pluto is just beginning to aspect his Moon, Midheaven, Ascendant, Mars and Neptune complex.

Broaddrick, who had accused Clinton of raping her years before. On 4/1/99, 51.18 Clinton was interviewed by Dan Rather on CBS, and said that the impeachment was not a badge of shame, not warranted, not right. The people should let it go.

As Clinton left office in January of 2001, his reluctance to let go was reflected by ☉-d and ♀-d on the midpoint ♂/♄. Directed Pluto was just minutes of solar arc from Ascendant and on the axis of Moon. Over most of the next two years it continued on to cross M, ♂ and ♆ in turn. January and February brought more scandal over last minute pardons which many, even in his own party, found unacceptable due to the financial implications of those pardons, and once again, over women.

The former president seemed unlikely to accept a background seat to anyone in the attention of the public. It will be interesting to see what future events might correspond to the transformative theme of Pluto moving by solar arc through this major configuration in his natal chart as he tries to finds a niche as the youngest ex-president.

Look up all the midpoints with Pluto and try your hand at forecasting! Speculate, as you do, on the probable manifestations of Neptune being the "caboose" (last planet to be aspected), rather than the leader of the train, as it was in the events we've just studied.

How to figure out exactly when Solar Arc Directions will become "Right On"

In the Clinton example I cited exact solar arcs for ~~several events. Psychological correspondences~~ to directions may be evident at a considerably wider orb. I would consider it reasonable to use 1 degree applying and at least one half degree separating. For known events, though, I look on the dial for a time when there is no visible orb, and if I want to check it for sure, I find the exact solar arc with simple math, or with the help of a computer program.

Nearly always I find solar arcs that appropriately reflect an event are exact within just a few minutes on the actual date of the event. A range of directions closely reflecting the general theme will

President Clinton.—solar arcs for 1998				Start: 50.04
Jan-Mar	Apr-Jun	July-Sep	Oct-Dec	Beg 1999
M-d = ☉	♂-d = ♄/♅	A-d = ☉	☽-d = ☉	A-d = ♄/♅
M-d = ♀		A-d = ♀	☽-d = ♀	☽-d = ♄/♅
		M-d = ♄/♅		
	♃-d = ☽/♆		☉-d = ♅/♇	☉-d = ♀/♃
A/♆-d = ☉		♄-d = ☿	☿-d = A/ ♅	☿-d = M/ ♅

occur shortly before or after the event.

It is easy enough to find a person's solar arc for a specific date. Review page 7 for that, or just calculate the directed chart for the person on the computer software that most of you probably use by now, and then subtract the position of the natal planet from that of the directed one.

Some software will also make it even easier for you by providing a list of the dates when solar arc directions are exact. However, not many of them allow you to do the dates for when directed midpoints are exact, and even if I can extract that information from my computer, I usually find it is faster to just do the very simple math.

It is easy enough, often faster than going into my computer and, believe me, if I can do this, so can you. Despite the rather technical nature of this book, I am primarily right-brained and math phobic. Prior to finding astrology in my mid-30s, my background and education had been focused on art. I went from art teacher to a substantial career as a painter, then to commercial art, and eventually in my mid-40s to ACS as Art Director.

Surely this background has much to do with why, when I did begin studying astrology, I took to the dial so readily. I am visually oriented, and the dial is like a mandala, in which I can see pictures of elegant symmetry.

Still, sometimes I am still very curious about just how close to the actual events those visually exact or almost exact directions that I can see on the dial when studying an event. Following are some thoughts on how you can best figure such things out.

First, Think of the Circle as a Whole

Learn to think of the circle of the zodiac in terms of 360 degrees, with each sign having a section within the whole, and the prospect of adding and subtracting planetary positions will become much, much easier. It takes a bit of memorizing, but you'll be surprised how fast you learn to think this way if you just try it a few times. Memorize the beginning degree of each sign, as shown in the box below. Once you have the beginning degree of each sign in mind,then adding in your head to find the whole number for each degree will follow quite easily. For example: 26° Gemini 25' will be 86.25, 22°, Leo 37' becomes 142.37, 16° Libra 47' becomes 196.47, 28° Aquarius 03' becomes 328.03, 10° Cancer becomes 100, and so on. Remember when working with the degrees and the minutes, you must translate any minutes over 59 into a degree. If you come up with a number over 360, you'll have to subtract 360 to be back within the zodiac circle!

Aries	♈	0
Taurus	♉	30
Gemini	♊	60
Cancer	♋	90
Leo	♌	120
Virgo	♍	150
Libra	♎	180
Scorpio	♏	210
Sagittarius	♐	240
Capricorn	♑	270
Aquarius	♒	300
Pisces	♓	330

When figuring exact "hits" involving directed midpoints on the 90° dial, you will likely run into a few additional potential complications. Let's look at some live examples based on the Clinton chart:

236.43	26° Scorpio 43'
+189.33	09° Libra 43'
425.76	Too much! More than a circle
–360.00	Subtract one full circle of 360°
65.76	Still too many minutes...1°=60'
– .60	Subtact 60 minutes; add it to the degrees
66.16	Result translated into sign: 6° Gemini 16'

Question: How did I determine the exact solar arc for when Clinton's directed Moon came into his Saturn/Uranus during the final term of his presidency? We can see visually from the dial that Moon-d would come to Sun axis at about 5-3/4° of solar arc. Obviously, we are looking for the latter. First we must find the exact position of the Saturn/Uranus midpoint, and then exactly how many degrees and minutes it takes for the Moon to move into that position. We learn that the mathematical position of Saturn/Uranus is actually on the Venus end of the Sun axis, at 11 Cancer 38, and would aspect Sun from Venus end of the axis at between 50° and 51° of solar arc. Obviously we are looking for the latter. So, first we have to find the exact position of the Saturn/Uranus midpoint.

Question: How did I determine the exact solar arc for when Clinton's directed Moon came into his Saturn/Uranus during the final term of his presidency?

We can see visually from the dial illustration on page 20, that Moon-d would come to the Sun-Venus axis in about 5-3/4° and would aspect Sun

122.08	♄ 2 ♌ 08
+81.09	♅ 21 ♊ 09
203.17	♄ + ♅
101.38	Divide the sum of ♄ + ♅
2/203.17	by 2 to get the half-sum or midpoint ♄/♅
101.38	♄/♅
-50.19	☽ 20 ♉ 19
51.19	Exact solar arc for ☽-d = ♄/♅

with one less step because Moon traveled exactly into the mathematical midpoint. If we had been looking for ☽-d = ♄/♅ for when Clinton was about age 6, we'd have had one more step to account for the fact that the "hit" would be by semi-sqare or sesquiquadrate.

To find exact timing for a solar arc aspect when your initial math leaves you on the wrong side of the dial, you must add or subtract 45.° For an example of this, let's look at that Clinton dial chart again and find at what solar arc age ♄/♅-d will aspect Mars. The earliest age would be by 45° aspect.

An easy way to do that is to first subtract 45° from the position of Mars to find that point on the dial. Then subtract ♄/♅ as shown:

186. 21	♂
− 45. 00	
141. 21	215 21
−101. 38	♄/♅
39. 43	exact solar arc for ♄/♅-d = ♂

The math is easy, if you first just think through where you are on the dial.

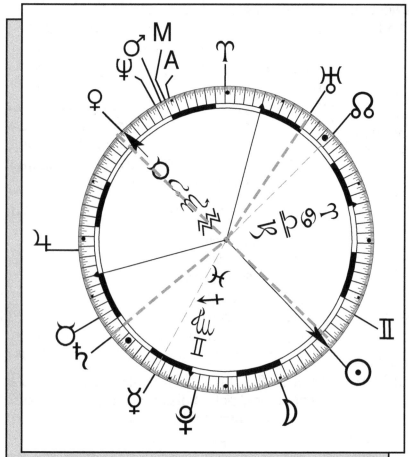

Dial Your Year Ahead

Using Cosmobiology and the Dial for an Annual Personal Forecast

If you've come this far without first stopping to try something out on your own chart or the chart of someone close to you, I'd be very surprised! So, before we go on to Uranian, I'll share with you the most basic things I do for an annual update.

First of all, never do directions until you have familiarized yourself with the natal chart. If you do not first understand the natal potential, you are more than likely to misjudge what the current patterns will mean.

Next, (I told you, I'm eclectic), I take a look at the traditional chart with Koch houses, with attention to an overview of the major transit cycles. Then I computer-calculate a secondary progressed chart for the birthday and a solar return, using the location where I (or the person whose chart I am doing) will be on the birthday. The solar arc is easily found by subtracting the natal Sun from the Progressed Sun. The additional advantage of having the progressed chart is to notice any signficant progressions, and especially the phase of the progressed Moon. (Although I didn't include progressions in this book, since it is solar arcs that are central to the systems the book was designed to teach, I do consider progressions significant, especially the progressed lunar phases.)

After my quick overview, I do a dial chart. I've tried using computer programs with a moving dial pointer, but I just don't find them as satisfying as using my own dial on paper. I can get the feel of what is happening better that way. Still, I do often run computer dial charts. The Astro Computing Services[3] dial charts are, in my opinion, the cleanest and easiest to use. Tthey are not available on home software yet, although a software designed for that purpose is being prepared. As for chart formats that I like to look at frequently, I get one ACS dial chart and then photocopy a bunch of

them. Then I can pop my dial on one any time I like, jot in directions, transits, margin notes and then toss it when I'm through. Some home computer programs will do a nice dial chart that just fits a 6" dial such as that on page 93 of this book. For quick dial charts, I have used my home computer with Solar Fire software[4], and these charts also fit my laminated 6" dial. (You still need to know how to enter factors on the dial by hand so you can jot in transits, midpoints and such—so if you skipped over that first lesson on Sir Arthur's chart, go back and do it!)

Let's get started...

With natal chart on the dial, and solar arc for the birthday in mind, enter each directed factor with a colored fine-line marking pen. Hold the dial with the pointer on the natal planet, count out the solar arc counter-clockwise around the dial and enter the directed position. If your marker is one that you can easily rub off the dial, you can put a dot on it to mark the solar arc count from the pointer so you don't have to count. Once all of the directed positions are entered, you can easily point to any

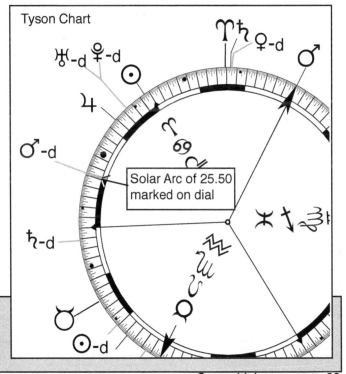

Tyson Chart

Solar Arc of 25.50 marked on dial

directed planet and see all the natal planets and midpoints on its axis. Also, you can point to each natal planet to see the directed midpoints on its axis.

I like to make a rough graph, as shown below. Divide the year by quarters, and then jot down the directions within the quarter when they become exact. Those that are visually exact go in the first quarter. Directions that will form 15–30 minutes ahead go in the second quarter, 30–45 minutes in the 3rd quarter, and 45 minutes–1 degree in last quarter. A scan down the page tells you quite a bit about the relative importance of each direction. Multiple directions with similar themes and time frame call for attention.

I have found that transits can be misleading if there are no directions of similar theme. Too often people tend to expect transits to be more dramatic than they turn out to be. If there are underlying directions that are also critical, indeed the transit may be a significant timing trigger. But if no strong directions repeat a similar theme, the transit period may go by with much less impact than anticipated.

After looking at the directions, enter the outer planet transits on the dial. You can draw in the range and note the dates of stations. Also enter positions of eclipses. These are very important transits.

By now, with directions and transits plus your knowledge of the natal chart and the environment (natal chart, plus something of what is going on in the native's life currently) you should be developing a good idea of the potentials of the year ahead.

At this point I like to look at the Solar Return chart. Some details of how you might do that are in Chapter 6, but for now I will say that almost invariably, I find the tree of the Sun with solar return midpoints to be very descriptive of major themes for the year. Other personal point axes add detail. Return charts put transits into a context, and transits act as timing triggers.

Sometimes if I am really trying to zero in on a significant time (judging from all I've seen so far), I will scan through the Koch chart lunar returns for the year, looking for the really strong ones—those that have planets right on angles, or that have angles or planets in same degree as natal planets. I'll also note lunations and eclipses on the dial. New Moon and Lunar Return assist in more closely timing when themes suggested by the solar arc directions are most likely to manifest into events.

Objectivity? Tough, when it's YOUR year!

You've heard, I am sure at one time or another, the caveats about a lawyer pleading his or her own case, or a doctor doing self-diagnosis...
Well, there is also wisdom in your asking another astrologer to look at your chart, especially if you are at all inclined to take your unobjective look at it and imagine the worst! If it isn't tough enough to be objective about yourself, try it with one of your children! I've learned over years to handle that fairly well...mostly by avoidance in reading their charts, at least not very often. But, there are times...one of which came up in the year 2000. It involved the only daughter I had not previously embarrassed (with prior permission, mind you) by using her chart in the first edition of this book. She was a small child then, but now (just prior to work toward completing this second edition) she was 22, and a recent honors graduate of New York University. So, with Liz's permission, I'll share with you a "live" example of looking at your "own" worries with astrology...for what it may be worth in terms of perspective, and also in regard to times when you may be trying to be objective, but in truth are not feeling one bit objective about the situation at hand and any decision you might need to make about it.

President Clinton — solar arcs for 1998 Start: 50.04

Jan–Mar	Apr-Jun	July-Sep	Oct-Dec	Beg
1999				
M-d = ☉	♂-d = ♄/♅	A-d = ☉	☽-d = ☉	A-d = ♄/♅
M-d = ☉		A-d = ♀	☽-d = ☉	☽-d = ♄/♅
		M-d = ♄/♅		
	♃-d = ☽/♆		☉-d = ♅/♇	☉-d = ♀/♃

How Worried Should Mom and Dad be about Liz's Trip?

What Liz wanted more than anything else or her college graduation gift was a trip to the middle eastern countries. Her university major was very focused on art and religious studies. Earlier she had already traveled in India for an independent study, and previous through several European countries. Visiting Turkey, Israel and Egypt were important to her for obvious reasons, and even more so, for her strong interest in her study and her performance of middle eastern dance. So, we agreed to gift her with the trip, which she planned for the autumn following her graduation. Guess when that turned out to be? Yes, October and November of 2000. She left at the beginning of October for Turkey, where she would then be for her Solar Return. This was, of course, BEFORE the outbreak of violence in Israel.

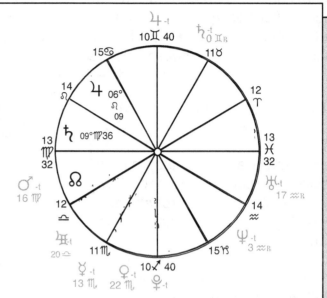

Liz's natal chart; transits for 2000 birthday in gray.
10/13/1978, 4:04 am, Danbury, CT, Birth Record

I had already looked and assured myself that Liz's transits and directions were quite good for the period of this trip, Indeed the Jupiter-Pluto opposition on her M axis seemed a wonderful indicator of the educational and spiritual opportunities offered to her in visiting the many sacred sites in the middle east. Of course, when the violence broke out and we realized she was scheduled to fly into Israel to be with her good friend from high school, Tamar, an Israeli national who is now in college in Jerusalem, Mom and Dad were just a little bit worried, to say the least. I dug out the charts to look again, glad I had this tool, and with also much gratitude to Liz's father for his insistence that she take with her a special international cell phone through which we could call her and be called easily. Did we attempt to dissuade her from flying into Israel as scheduled? Of course, but knowing my daughter, I really knew better than to think she wouldn't go. She flew into Tel Aviv on the day of the big summit meeting.

First and most important: the current patterns must be seen in context of knowing the natal chart. To the right is Liz's dial chart with pointer to her Moon axis, a complex of personal points, which I knew had been activated at just about every major event

of her life. Though it had fairly recently been activated by Mars/Uranus (count solar arc back from pointer). That was past, and accounted for by a minor surgery months ago. Nothing was "right on" for this trip, except the Vertex, which I don't always use but am aware of for charts I look at frequently. The "fated" Vertex axis, which is also

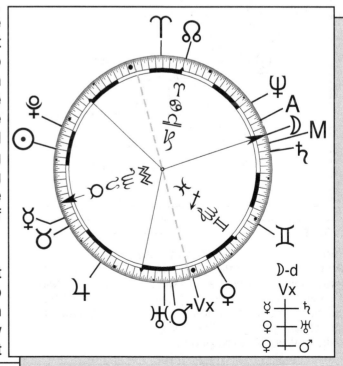

Moon-d, on the midpoints of Mercury/Saturn, Venus/Uranus and Venus/Mars, sounds of no more concern than what we'd already teased her about after noting her transits. It was her Venus return. Also, the Solar Return for Kayseri, Turkey, showed a strong 7th house emphasis. so: "Don't fall for someone over there and decide to stay!"

The Sun axis of the Solar Return (more on this later in "Have Dial, Will Travel") is shown below. In summary, it also indicates strong relationship potential (Turns out he's here, not there—solar return chart heralds the year, no matter where you travel during it.) Also shown are potential changes in or of the place, hard work and some difficulties. Self-discipline and restructuring indicators are not surprising for a

recent graduate entering the "real world." M/☽ indicates rich inner soul or spiritual ties. All this was reassuring to parents at home, although I'll admit some detailed looks at transits, even while telling myself they can be pretty mild unless the directions back up a stronger theme. I paused for a hard look during the November days when

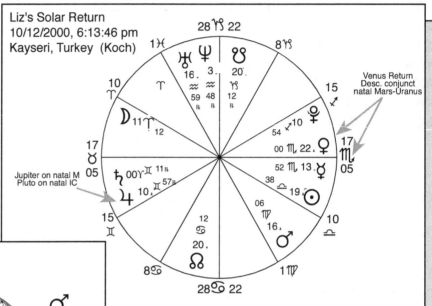

Liz's Solar Return
10/12/2000, 6:13:46 pm
Kayseri, Turkey (Koch)

Venus Return
Desc. conjunct
natal Mars-Uranus

Jupiter on natal M
Pluto on natal IC

Sun Axis of Dial
Solar Return

transiting Mars-Uranus was crossing over her Moon complex. She was in Egypt then, and had a minor illness which she handled competently by going to a good clinic and taking it easy for a couple of days.

Back in Jerusalem for the last weeks of her tour, the situation had calmed such that she was safely able to visit both Christian and Jewish Holy Land sites; sadly, still not the Islamic—so this turned out to be her only disappointment on what was an otherwise a very good trip.

Mom and Dad were, of course, very glad to see her come home!

Notes:

[1] Michael Munkasey, **Midpoints: Unleashing the Power of the Planets**, ACS Publications, 1991, is unfortunately out-of-print at this writing. If you can obtain a copy, try to do so. Its interpretations are a valuable supplement to those in the **CSI**. It is currently available as pdf files through Online College of Astrology, www.astrocollege.com

[2] **The Starr Report**, Public affairs pb, 9/15/98, and the Library of Congress web site, icreport.loc.gov/icreport/

[3] **Astro Computing Services** 1-866-953-8458 (toll free order line Fax: 603-734-4311

[4] **Solar Fire**, by Esoteric Technologies of Australia, is published in the US by Astrolabe, -848-6682.

With this chapter, we enter the realm of Uranian Astrology, the more complex predecessor to the Cosmobiology systerm. As the first step, there are eight new "planets" to consider...

The Uranian Planets

Commonly referred to in the United States as "the Uranians," the eight hypothetical planets of the Hamburg School are more properly called the Trans-Neptunian planets or TNPs. Many years ago in Germany, circa World War 1, Alfred Witte observed that energies seemed to come from places where there were no known planets. After extensive study he began to calculate ephemerides for places from which he believed energy emitted, and/or from where unknown planets might exist. Witte completed the first four TNPs and his protégé, Fredrich Sieggrün, added four more.

No one really knows if there are undiscovered planets out in space that correspond to the TNPs. Perhaps they are only mathematical points, like nodes, that reflect combinations of energies. It can only be said that after over eighty years of observation Uranian astrologers are convinced that they work, and that is reason enough to use them. The case studies in this book will demonstrate ways in which the Uranians work, adding fascinating detail to our investigations that we would not otherwise find.

As you add Uranian planets to your dial work you will want to own a copy of the Witte-Lefeldt *Rules for Planetary Pictures*.[1] As in the *CSI*, "*Rules*" (as it shall hereafter be called) contains a page heading for each two-factor combination, followed by a delineation for each possible third factor. *Rules* adds interpretations for all combinations that include the Uranian Planets. Briefly, the 8 hypothetical planets of Uranian Astrology are:

CUPIDO has to do with small group associations like family and community. It also relates to matters of art. The meaning is colored in combination with other factors. For example: Jupiter/Cupido could be a happy marriage, while Saturn/Cupido means separation of marriage.

HADES means all sorts of vile things like poverty, garbage, dirt, sickness, and crime. Nothing in astrology, however, is ALL bad! Hades has to do with the ancient past and secrets, so in some combinations it can even represent the study of ancient sciences, such as astrology. It has positive meanings in the charts of people who deal with Hades matters constructively. For example, members of the medical profession usually have strong Hades combinations because they treat the sick.

ZEUS shows fire, leadership and creativity. Venus/Zeus is sexy, which often results in the creative activity of procreation. Mars/Zeus could relate to that, too, but aggressive Mars combined with fiery Zeus could also symbolize shooting flames, or firearms.The Jupiter/Zeus midpoint is successful creative activity, while the Saturn/Zeus midpoint suggests blocks and obstacles that could cause anxiety and require great perseverance to achieve the success that one is seeking.

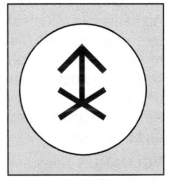

KRONOS represents everything that is above average—or that is high up. Kronos combinations can refer to things literally high up, such as airplanes or mountains, or they may be figuratively high up, such as government

authorities. In a personal chart Sun/Kronos might mean the father, or in a mundane chart, it mght refer to the president or the ruler.

APOLLON means that which is greatly expansive. It symbolizes commerce, science, peace and success.

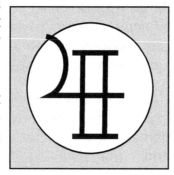

Used in combination with other energies, Apollon adds the meaning "lots of." Jupiter/Apollon is lots of money or success. Saturn/Apollon could mean "many separate", but remember, Saturn teaches important lessons, too. Saturn/Apollon can also means a method of education, or the teacher.

ADMETOS is extremely intense.Wherever it appears, something is likely to be blocked, or at a standstill. In the positive combinatons, then Admetos can take matters to the depths, as in total concentration.

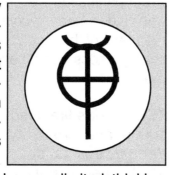

Mercury/Admetos could mean limited thinking, or it could mean very profound thinking. Venus/ Admetos could be the end of love, or a very deep and true love.

VULCANUS relates to great energy, power, and force.Combined with other factors Vulcanus adds the adjective "mighty". A few examples might be:

Venus/Vulcanus—mighty love or passion; Mars/ Vulcanus—mighty activity; Jupiter/Vulcanus— mighty luck; Saturn/Vulcanus—mighty hindrance or caution.

POSEIDON is about mind, spirit, and ideas. Mercury/Poseidon means spiritual perception. Venus/Poseidon refers to faith or platonic love. Ethics and moral behavior is symbolized by Mars/

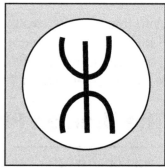

Poseidon (acting ♂ with honor ♓). The midpoint of Uranus/Poseidon could mean a sudden flash of enlightenment.

"Rules" gives further guidelines in interpretation of the Uranian Planets. Please keep in mind, though, that the very short delineations given in **Rules** are very brief and should be taken as guidelines only, and NOT as literal, exclusive truth. As with all methods of astrology, the art of synthesis is very important. Unfortunate misunderstandings can result when one combination is isolated from the whole of the chart, and given more importance than it deserves. Significant mistakes can be made, or at best, nuances can be missed if you take the delineations as they are written in **Rules** to be the only possible way to "read" a particular combination.

Rules for Planetary Pictures was written in Germany during the first World War and the "**CSI**" (**Combination of Stellar Influences**) was first published toward the end of World War II. Some of the delineations are, therefore, very grim compared to how the same configurations might be interpreted within the context of contemporary peace time society. Reading both sources will yield extra information, especially valuable to the beginner. Still, though, keep this in mind: your own intuition and common sense should be used to combine the meanings of whatever factors you are investigating with the chart as a whole—and with the circumstances and the environment of the person to whom the chart belongs.

Let's look at a few of the ways in which the Uranian planets add to our investigation of Sir Arthur Conan Doyle. The illustration shows the Uranian planets added to the dial, with the pointer on Aries. We can see a great deal without even turning the dial.

Aries represents the four cardinal points of the earth. The Uranian astrologer considers factors on the axis of Aries to be very important because they show the connection of the native to the world in general.

Longitude of TNPs for this chart and full data for **First Edition** charts used in this book are in Appendix I

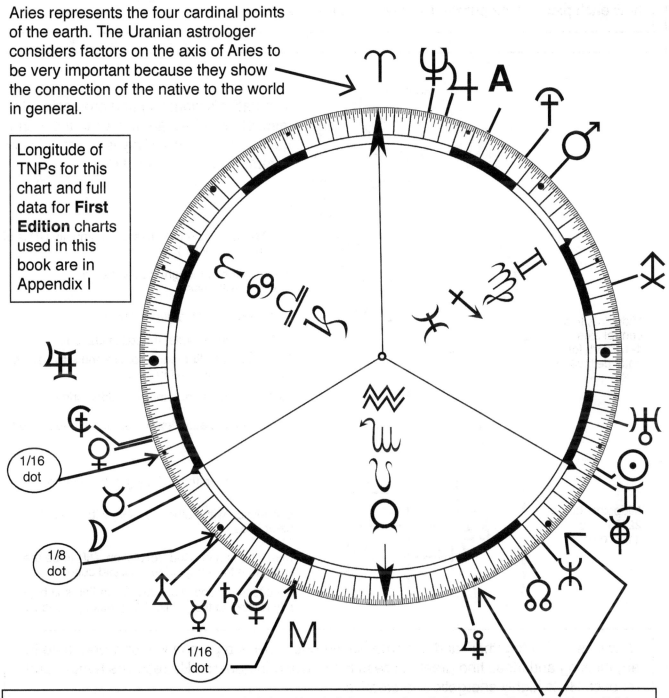

1/16 dot

1/8 dot

1/16 dot

M

Notice that between the pointer and the 22° 30' dots on the dial are smaller dots that divide that 22°30' sector in half. They indicate sectors that are 1/8th of the dial. Now notice that each 1/8th sector is divided in half by a tiny dot showing a 1/16th division of the dial. We are still dealing with derivatives of the square, the number four—ACTION in the physical world. If a planet appears within a very small orb of a dot (1/2° or less), we will consider that it relates to the axis of whatever factor the pointer is on—in this case, the Aries axis.

With the pointer on Aries, we find connections to Mars, Apollon, and Vulcanus. This native's mighty (Vulcanus) work (Mars) was very commercial (Apollon). We are only just beginning. To make interpretive notes about a particular axis it is handy to draw a "tree." Draw a diagram of the axis and jot down notes alongside. When you've finished you'll find it much easier to get a sense of the whole axis. You'll be better able to weigh relative importance and to see how each piece of the puzzle fits. I will demonstrate:

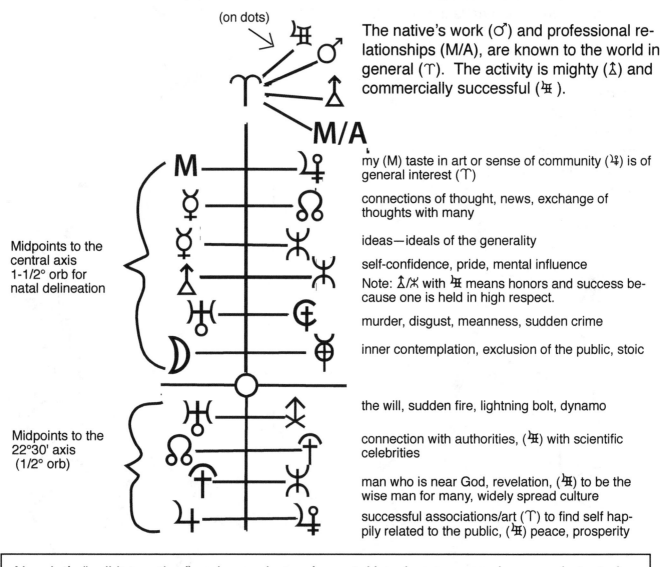

(on dots)

The native's work (♂) and professional relationships (M/A), are known to the world in general (♈). The activity is mighty (⚼) and commercially successful (♏).

M/A

my (M) taste in art or sense of community (♃) is of general interest (♈)

connections of thought, news, exchange of thoughts with many

ideas—ideals of the generality

self-confidence, pride, mental influence

Note: ⚼/✶ with ♏ means honors and success because one is held in high respect.

murder, disgust, meanness, sudden crime

inner contemplation, exclusion of the public, stoic

Midpoints to the central axis 1-1/2° orb for natal delineation

Midpoints to the 22°30' axis (1/2° orb)

the will, sudden fire, lightning bolt, dynamo

connection with authorities, (♏) with scientific celebrities

man who is near God, revelation, (♏) to be the wise man for many, widely spread culture

successful associations/art (♈) to find self happily related to the public, (♏) peace, prosperity

Now let's "pull it together" and see what we've got. Here is a person whose work, taste in art, thinking and ideas find great success in the world in general. He receives honors and respect. He is highly energetic and creative.

What I have said so far is the all-over sense of the axis—the theme that is repeated. "But what of the other pieces?" you might ask. "What of midpoints like Uranus/Hades?"

We know, of course, that Sir Arthur wrote about crime. Suppose, however, you were investigating a similar axis in the chart of someone whose background you did not know.

How would you "weigh" such a murderous combination? Remember, it is only ONE statement among many others that reflect success and honor. It would be foolish, in studying such an axis, to conclude that the native is either a murderer or a criminal. **(Remember, also, that astrology is not everything.)** Choices and environment count, too. Similar configurations might manifest as criminal—or police officer; as psychologist or psychotic.) The problem of relative "weight" will be clearer to you if Sir Arthur's chart is compared with the chart of an actual murderer. Below is the Aries "tree" for the chart of Lee Harvey Oswald, who was famed for his assassination of President Kennedy. Each factor on the dots can, by itself, have a "good" meaning. However, all of them together in contact with Aries does not bode well for this native's connection to the world in general.

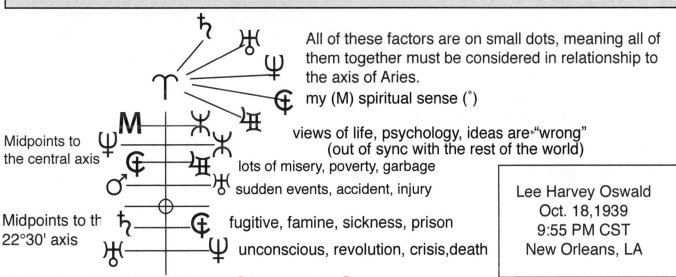

All of these factors are on small dots, meaning all of them together must be considered in relationship to the axis of Aries.

my (M) spiritual sense (°)

Midpoints to the central axis

views of life, psychology, ideas are "wrong" (out of sync with the rest of the world)

lots of misery, poverty, garbage

sudden events, accident, injury

Midpoints to the 22°30' axis

fugitive, famine, sickness, prison

unconscious, revolution, crisis, death

Lee Harvey Oswald
Oct. 18, 1939
9:55 PM CST
New Orleans, LA

PLANETARY PICTURES

Symmetrical arrangements of planets and points around a common axis are called **planetary pictures**. In the illustration of Oswald's chart, the pointer is on the midpoints Saturn/Hades and Uranus/Neptune. Notice **equal arcs** from the pointer to the factors on each side. Within very tight orbs of only a few minutes, the arrangement is symmetrical.

Below is one way to notate the picture illustrated: is

$$ ♄/♇ = ♅/♆ $$

Another way is:

$$ ♅ + ♆ - ♇ = ♄ $$

Rules interprets $♅ + ♆ - ♇ = ♄$ to mean "assassination!" A planetary picture needs a connection with a personal point to be significant. Here a close Midheaven-Neptune conjunction is applicable.

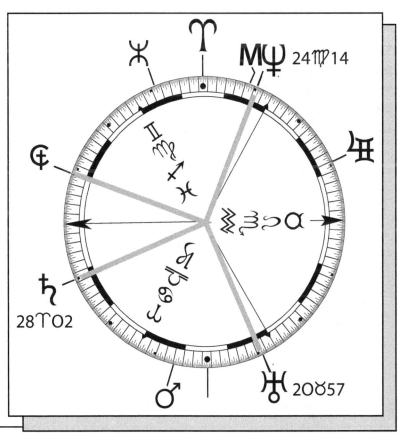

24♍14

28♈02

20♉57

The personal points in Uranian Astrology are M ("I" the ego). A (others, the place), ♈ (the world in general), ☉ (vitality, the body, males), ☽ (emotions, women, public), and ☊ (connections). Planetary pictures must involve a personal point to be important.[3] The assassination picture aspects ♈ by 22°30'. M and ♅ are found on small dots. "Successful Apollon, in this example, could be taken to mean "a successful assassination."

SENSITIVE POINTS

If we work out the formula ♅ + ♆ - ₵ mathematically we will find out that it does indeed fall in the same degree of the dial as ♄. You will seldom ever have to figure formulas mathematically unless you just enjoy that kind of thing, or are being picky about a recification. The following math demonstation will merely "prove" a point that can much more easily be seen by just looking at the dial.

It is easier to add and subtract degrees and minutes if you use absolute longitude—the whole circle. (See page 21 for a list of beginning degrees for each sign.) ♅ is 20 ♉ 57. The first degree of ♉ is 30, so in absolute longitude 20° ♉ is 50.

♅	20 ♉ 57, or	50.57
+♆	24 ♍ 14, or	<u>174.14</u>
		224.71
- ₵	17 ♈ 31, or	<u>17.31</u>
		207.40, or 27 ♎ 40
		Oswald's is 28 ♈ 02 ℞

The assassination formula was also completed by Kennedy's Saturn at 27 ♋ 10. The important Sun/Moon midpoint in the Kennedy chart also falls in that degree: 27 ♋ 32. Here is just one more (I promise!) math demonstration that uses the transits for the exact moment of the assassination.

♅-t	09 ♍ 49, or	159.49
+♆-t	15 ♏ 56, or	<u>225.56</u>
		384.105
- ₵-t	11 ♉ 46, or	<u>41. 46</u>
		343.59, or 13 ♓ 59

Let's see how the **transiting formula** is found just by looking at the dial.

The pointer is set at the midpoint of the first two factors in the formula, ♅/♆

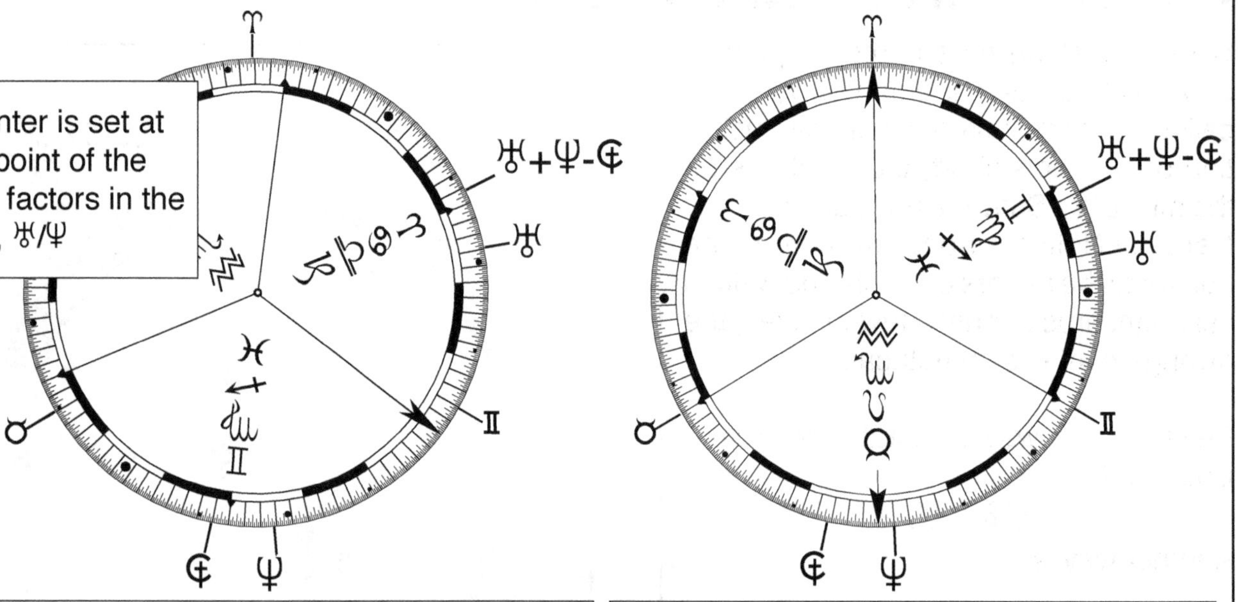

Look for the third factor, ₵. How far is it from the pointer? Mark the position of the sensitive point ♅ + ♆ - ₵ at exactly the same distance in the opposite direction from the pointer.

If we swing the pointer back to ♈ you can see that we've found 13°59' of a mutable sign. We did not need to do any math at all at all to find this ♅+♆-₵ formula.

For most purposes, there is no need to do the math—just turn the dial and look!

One final picture of the assassination formula shows how the transiting ♅ + ♆ - ⚷ in transits is completed by Saturn in both Oswald's and Kennedy's charts.

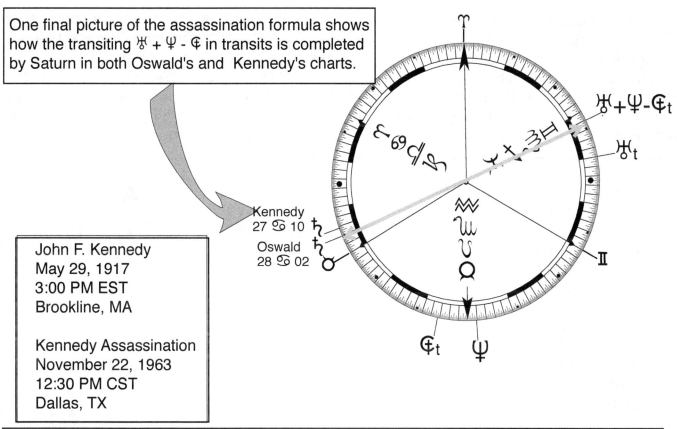

John F. Kennedy
May 29, 1917
3:00 PM EST
Brookline, MA

Kennedy Assassination
November 22, 1963
12:30 PM CST
Dallas, TX

For one more practice run at working with sensitive points we will return to the chart of Sir Arthur Conan Doyle, where we can expect that the formula for "the successful author," ☉+♅-☿, should "work."

Here the pointer is on the midpoint of ☉/♅. Mercury is found at the small dot to the left.

Midheaven is within 1 degree of the pointer, and Jupiter is at the other end of the axis. Already we see the potential for success as an author without even turning the dial.

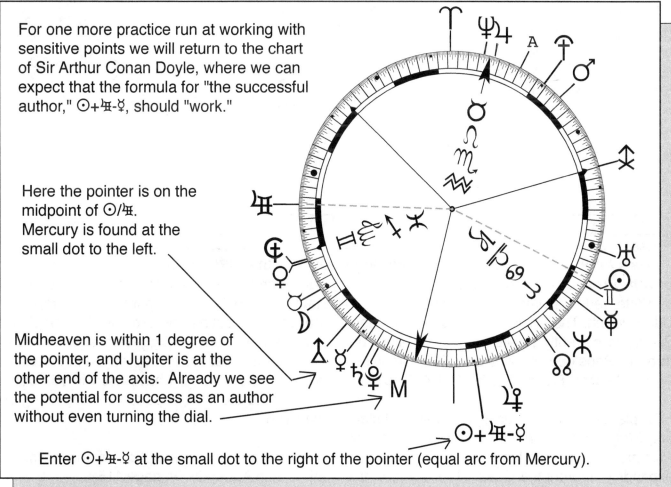

Enter ☉+♅-☿ at the small dot to the right of the pointer (equal arc from Mercury).

Now turn the dial arrow to the sensitive point $\odot + \text{♅} - \text{☿}$. Remember how directed $\odot$ came to Sir Arthur's ♅ success configuration at about 28°, just as he was probably receiving the public recognition for his first Sherlock Holmes story? Was the formula for the successful author also activated at that time? Yes, indeed!

Count the degrees from the arrow opposite the formula to $\text{☽}-28°$! The formula contacts a **personal point,** Moon, by solar arc. Isn't this fun? Congratulations, dear Watson! You've just practiced some elementary dial techniques that are usually billed as advanced. **You're well on your way to becoming a Dial Detective!**

Pointer is on the sensitive point. Solar arc is counted from the opposite end. Yes, this is perfectly valid. It is an easy way—without turning the dial—of seeing what you would see if you directed the position of the senstive point 28°, entered that position on the dial, and then turned the pointer there. You would see that solar arc directed $\odot + \text{♅} - \text{☿}$ is on the axis of ☽. Or, we could say:

$\odot + \text{♅} - \text{☿}$ directed = ☽-natal

Notes:

[1] **Rules for Planetary Pictures: The Astrology of Tomorrow,** by Rudolph Ludwig, first pubished by Witte-Verlag, Hamburg, Germany, in1928, © Udo Rudoph. The English translation by Richard Svehla is currently published by and available through Penelope Publications, 927 Crestview Circle, Weston, Florida 33327, 954-475-1014.

[2] For planetary pictures using the classical planets, **Midpoints: Unleashing the Power of the Planets**, by Michael Munkasey is also helpful in expanding interpretive ideas. This book, in the style of the **CSI,** contains interpretations often more appropriate to contemporary life in the United States. There is no comparable contemporary book that also delineates all of the Uranian planet combinations. I have suggested alternatives to some of the most "grim" delineation in **Rules** for the planetary pictures I have used in this book. You will find them in Appendix III, beginning on page 106.

[3] A more detailed description of the personal points is in Appendix IV, page 115.

URANIAN CASE STUDIES

A Case of Surgery

Of all the charts I encountered in my first year of astrological study, the one that most sparked my enthusiasm for "dial detecting" was this case of surgery. My daughter, then 6 years old, had frequent urinary infections. From my self-study of Cosmobiology I deduced that surgery might soon be necessary. (Yes, I bought the Ebertin books and began to work with them just a few months after I was first introduced to astrology back in 1973. I was working largely on my own with no one to tell me that the 90° dial was not for beginners!)

The likelihood that surgery could result from health problems is most certainly suggested with A on the midpoint of Mars/Uranus and M right on the midpoint of Saturn/Uranus.

My concern for the year ahead was easy to see by counting degrees between Saturn and Uranus and also between the Sun and Uranus. Both arcs are a little less than 7 degrees.

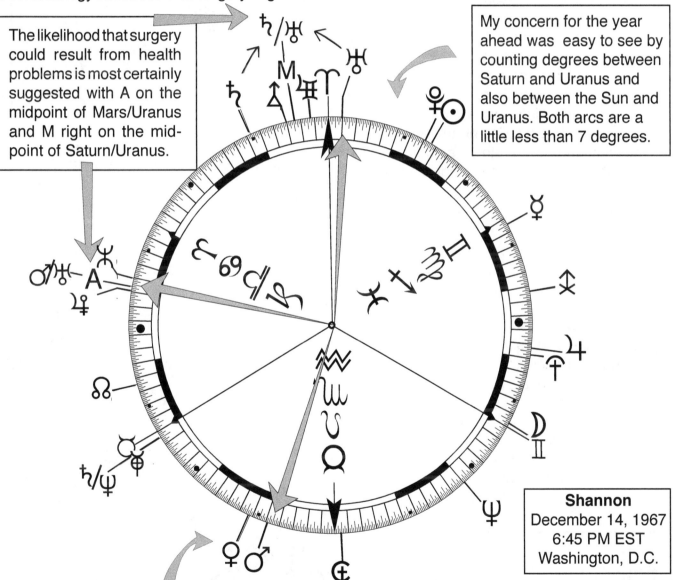

Shannon
December 14, 1967
6:45 PM EST
Washington, D.C.

My daughter's chart has a close square between Venus at 8 ♏ 48 and Mars at 10 ♒ 11. Under biological correspondence, P.136, *Combination of Stellar Influences*, you can see that the aspect could be identified with a kidney ailment.

It was not until a few months after my daughter's surgery, that I became fully impressed and excited about the precision with which astrology could show the details of the event. We moved east and I began to take my first formal classes in astrology. In Charles Emerson's class, "Medical and Psychological Astrology," I offered my daughter's chart for class discussion. Charles gave us xerox copies of the Mary Vohryzek translations of the Ebertin list of anatomical correspondences to each degree of the zodiac. (The list is currently available through NCGR, Inc.).[1] Look at at the position of Saturn/Neptune, at 0°24' fixed. Admetos is precisely to the minute square. Saturn/Neptune, we were told by Charles, is the weak point in the body where an organic problem could likely occur. Admetos means blockage. My daughter's left ureter was incompetent, probably from birth. The passage of urine from kidney to bladder was blocked, causing urine to reflux back into the kidney. A surgery called uretal vesicul reflux (reimplantation of the ureter) was necessary to avoid further damage to the kidney. Imagine the points scored for astrology in Charles' class that day when we discovered that the zero degree of Scorpio is that of the left ureter!

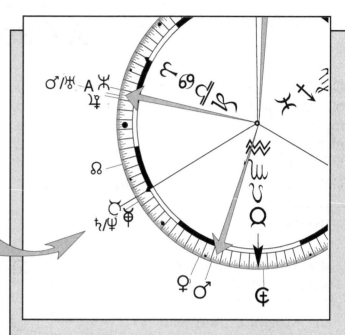

The solar eclipse prior to surgery, June 20, 1974, at 28 ♊ 30, fell on the axis of Uranus.

Point the dial arrow to ♂/♅ (key midpoint for surgery) and make a sensitive point using 0°24' fixed as the third factor. The solar arc directed Midheaven activates that sensitive point at 6°35', which is only 10' from the exact solar arc (6¥45') for my daughter at the time of her surgery on August 9, 1974.

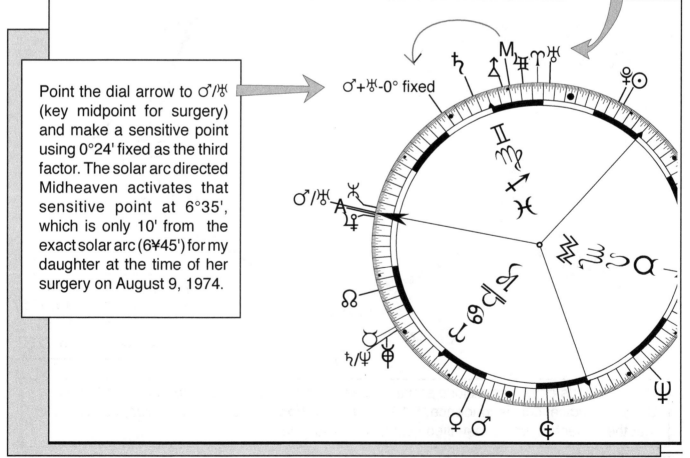

♂ + ♅ - ☿ is the surgery formula that specifically reflects the skill of the doctor (☿). For success in surgery there should be a contact with Jupiter. Transiting Jupiter is exactly 22°30'. Note that natal Jupiter is on the 11-1/4° dot, indicating the natal potential for successful surgery. The surgery was indeed successful. Within the following year tests showed that all damage to the kidney had completely healed.

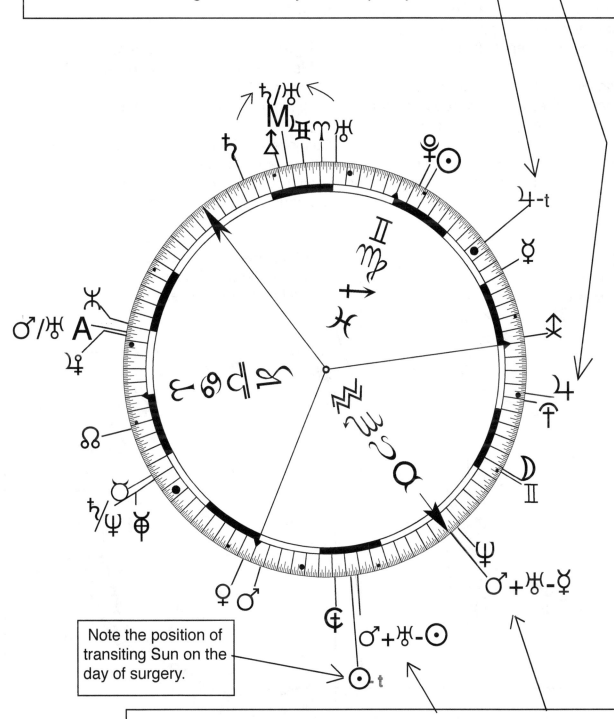

Note the position of transiting Sun on the day of surgery.

Two important surgery configurations are ♂ + ♅ - ☉ and ♂ + ♅ - ☿. Note that one of them comes to the other by solar arc direction in about 7°. ♂ + ♅ - ☉ is on the axis of natal M.

The Prize-Winning Mystery

A favorite activity of my Uranian workshop (a group that met weekly at my home from 1979 to about the middle of 1985) was "mystery charts." At each class session one person would present a challenge for the others to figure out.

A prize example of our "mysteries" comes from the evening that Egon asked us to guess what had happened to him during the past week.

As was our usual practice, everyone set up the charts on the dial and worked independently for about a half hour. It was our practice to enter the natal chart in one color and the chart of the event in a different color.

Egon	Event
May 3, 1906	June 4, 1983
8:45 AM MEZ	4:00 pm EDT
Berlin, Germany	Danbury, CT

We looked first for a general idea of the nature of the event, and then for confirming details. Soon the guessing began. "The transits are goo good." "Obviously this must be a favorable event."

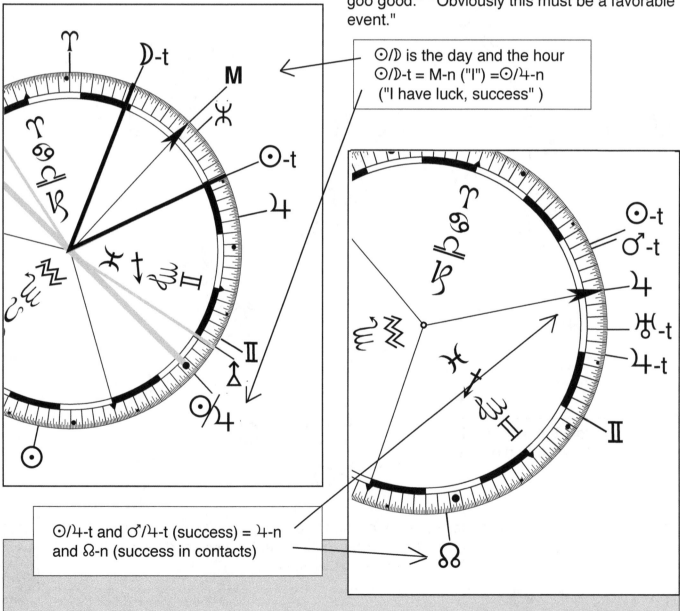

$\odot/\mathrm{D}$ is the day and the hour
$\odot/\mathrm{D}\text{-t} = \mathrm{M\text{-}n}$ ("I") $= \odot/\mathrm{4\text{-}n}$
("I have luck, success")

$\odot/4\text{-t}$ and $\sigma/4\text{-t}$ (success) $= 4\text{-n}$
and $\Omega\text{-n}$ (success in contacts)

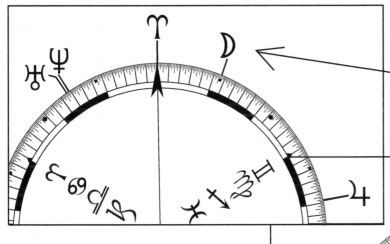

"You were lucky! Did you win something?

D-t (the hour) = ♃/♅ (sudden luck)
= ♃/♆ (speculation)

☉/♅-t and ♂/♅-t (sudden event) = ♃-n
(is successful)

"Yes, you're right!", said our challenger. "But now you must tell me what I won!"

"How can the chart show that?"

"In this case it does. Keep looking."

After some general grumbling a suggestion came:

"Uranus/Poseidon combinations can have to do with propaganda and media things. That Sun-Mars/Uranus-transit = Jupiter-natal combination has Poseidon on the other end, and also M/A for 'the moment in the place.' "

One person guessed, "Transiting Sun/Moon (day and hour) has natal Poseidon, too and Mercury/Uranus [which can mean sudden news] and then also Uranus/Vulcanus can mean electrical energy."

Another offered a guess—"Could you have won a camera?"

Egon shook his head, "No, try again."

"A T.V. set? "

"Yes! And it shows even more specifically than you've found. There's a formula for television!"

"You're kidding! T.V. wasn't even invented yet when Witte thought up those formulas. Maybe he and his collaborators were not only astrologers but prophets!"

"Well, someone thought of it. I was surprised, too. It's there! Look it up in your 'Key'."

Key to Planetary Pictures is Hans Niggeman's translation of Witte's **Lexikon**.[2] This book is an alphabetical listing of topics or situations, each with their corresponding formulas alongside. The book has been out of print and unobtainable for years. Some of my students have resorted to xeroxing my entire copy of it!

All of the formulas are in **Rules,** and it is often very handy to be able to look up the delineation alphabetically, instead of only from lists of the formulae. Hopefully one day soon someone will do a new and updated translation of the **Lexikon**.

Our class had the very special extra advantage of having Egon bring his **Lexikon** to our classes and then translate from the German for us.

"Sure enough! There it is: television—Neptune + Poseidon - Ascendant = Midheaven!"

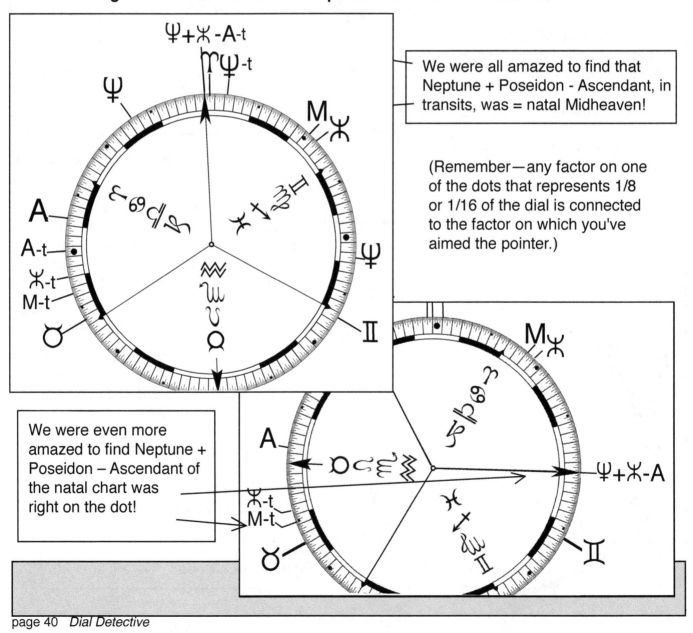

We were all amazed to find that Neptune + Poseidon - Ascendant, in transits, was = natal Midheaven!

(Remember—any factor on one of the dots that represents 1/8 or 1/16 of the dial is connected to the factor on which you've aimed the pointer.)

We were even more amazed to find Neptune + Poseidon – Ascendant of the natal chart was right on the dot!

CONTACT!

A favorite technique for astrologers to dig out all sorts of information about "what's happening" is to compare one chart with another. With the 90° dial the game is called Contact!

Two or more charts are entered on the same dial. Of course this procedure is much less confusing if you use a different color pen for each chart. Spin the dial for an instant look at inter-aspects between the two charts. You'll find it is especially revealing to investigate the planets of one chart in aspect to the midpoints of another. All kinds of chart combinations can be used in Contact!

We have already played, in fact, in our comparison of natal charts with solar arc directions and transits. We could also compare natal charts with secondary progressed charts, or natal charts with solar or lunar returns. People can be compared with businesses, with events, or of course, with other people. Our first Contact! case investigates the favorite topic of personal relationships.

A DEADLY RELATIONSHIP

Here are the charts of a married couple. We should expect that the contacts between their two charts will show appropriate "pictures" for marriage, and indeed they do.

Husband (-h)
April 8, 1948
3:10 AM PDT
Los Angeles, CA

Wife (-w)
May 13, 1949
6:00 PM PST
Los Angeles, CA

The charts are taken from the "A" section of Lois Rodden's **American Book of Charts** (birth certificate data).

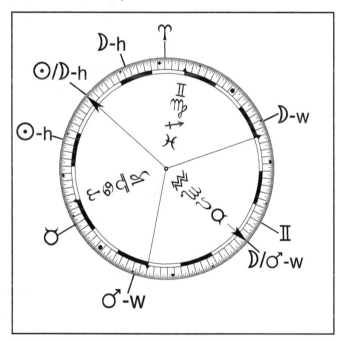

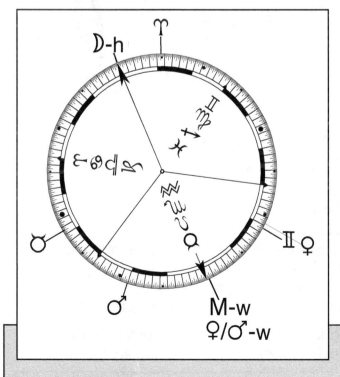

⊙/☽ (the husband and wife) =
☽/♂ (the wife)

♀/♂ = M (the establishment of a sex relationship/marriage)
♀/♂ = ☽ (entering into marriage)

That the relationship is far from blissful is easily seen by the other planets contained within the marriage "pictures." Look again at the illustration with the pointer on the Sun/Moon axis and add some of the other planets. Any one of these configurations included with a string of "happy" combinations could be disregarded or given a more "positive" interpretation. But here we see a heavy preponderance of "problem" configurations. (The delineations given below that do not include Uranian planets are from *CSI*.)

⊙/☽ = Ψ Ψ (inner discontent, upset, torment, illusions, deceptions, undermining associations)

☊/♅ = Ψ Ψ (deception, undermining assoc.)

☽/♂ = Ψ Ψ (negative attitude, weak will, worry, grief, misdirected energy and emotions)

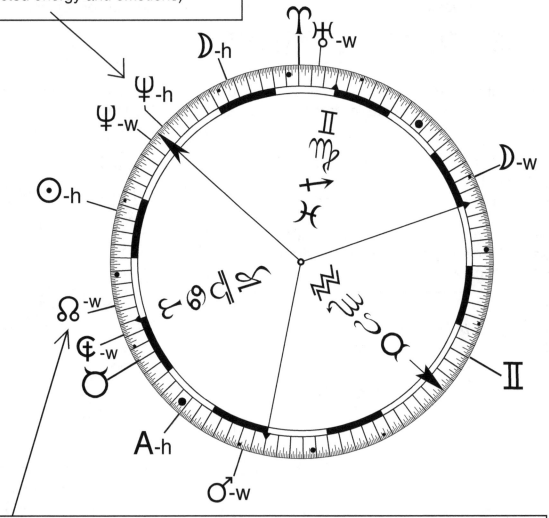

Add in just one Uranian planet, Hades, with delineations from *Rules*—and the plot thickens...
 ♂/⚷=Ψ (cheated, unusual death, murder through treachery)
  =A (vulgar and evil acts of others, danger of being murdered)
   (A is 22°30' from Ψ-h and Ψ-w; ♂ and ⚷ are equal arcs from A)

On the opposite page, at top left, the illustration again shows the pointer turned to the Moon axis. More planets have been added, with interpretations of the planetary pictures.

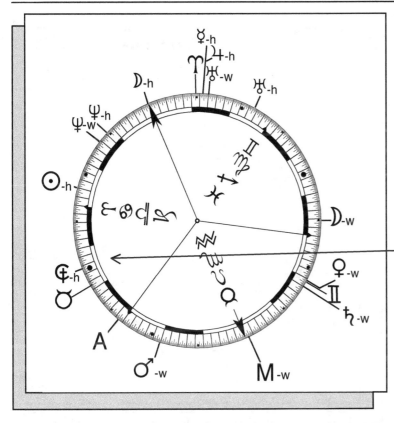

☉/☽ =☽-h (deceived or deceptive woman) =M-w (imagination, lies, self-deception)

(♃/♆ =☽)-h =M-w (speculator, squanderer)

♅/♆ =M-w (unconscious, lacks stamina, nervous) =☽-h (highly impressionable)

☉/♅=☽-h (emotional, impulsive, rash)=M-w (emotional upheaval, restless, excitable)

♂/♄=M-w (mourning, death) =☽ (illness, separation, death of females)

And again, let's add Hades, ♅, which at the 22°30' dot from ☽-h and M-w, is in aspect to all of the same midpoints:

☿/♆-h=♅-w (to plot dirty tricks)

♃/♆-h=♅-w (rough awakening from bliss)

☉/♅-h=♅-w (loss through misdeeds, participants in murder)

♀/♂=♅-w (illicit sex, misfortune through intimate relatives)

♂/♄=♅-w (unusual death)

The Event Transits . . .

In Lois Rodden's **American Book of Charts**, "Husband" is listed under "Homicide" and "Wife" as "Homicide Victim." The husband, a drug dealer, philanderer, and wife beater, shot and killed his wife on March 10, 1976, at 7:39 PM in Encino, California.

For a final glimpse at this sad tale, here is a "picture" from a three-way contact that shows strong transits to the personal points of the husband (♂/♄-t=☉/☽ and A), to the ♆ of both husband and wife, and to the wife's ☽/♂.

Transiting M, A and ☽ cross the natal Neptunes, with transiting ♂/♄ and ♆ also in the picture.

I'll admit this is not a very romantic way to introduce the subject of contact charts...but it is definitely dramatic!

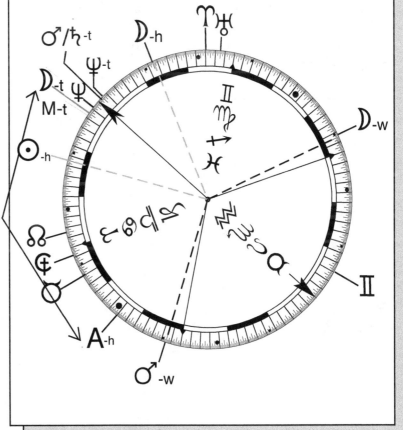

Here, in contact, are the charts of a couple who were married for sixty years, during which they were always devoted to each other.

Egon
May 3, 1906
8:45 MEZ
Berlin, Germany
52N30 13E23

Gerda
July 16, 1904
1:04 GMT
Heidemühle, Kr. Rosenberg,
Germany 53N43 19E20

(Positions on the dials for each of them are shown with the first name initial.)

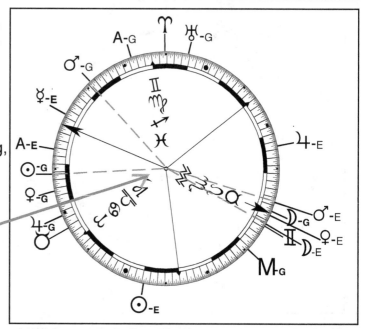

Her (G) ☉/♂ (husband)= his (E) ☽/♂ (wife)
☉/♂-G =♀-E (urge to beget children, intense love expression)
♃/A-G =♀-E (a happy love union)
♀/♂-E =☽-G (entering into marriage, motherhood)

She has ♅ on her ☉/☽ midpoint which could be upsetting. One of the upsets this couple survived was a bomb attack during WWII.

His ☉ and A on her ♃/M is certainly fortunate and harmonious. Her ♅ in his ☿/♃ configuration indicates that she has been quite stimulating to his very considerable intellectual creativity.

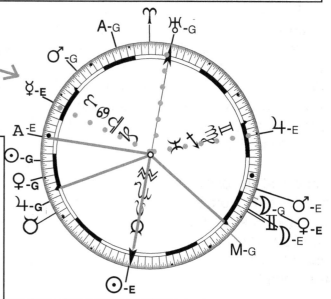

Note Egon's M is 22°30' the axis of symmetry.

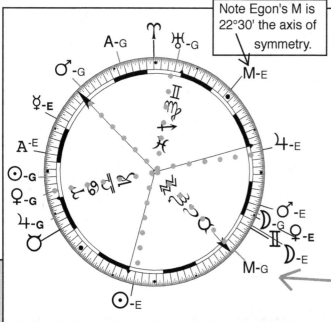

What more romance than this!
♀/♅ =♂-G (great excitability in love)
   =M-G =M-E (sudden adventurous love)
☉/♃-E =♂-G (successful activity, the happy husband)
   =M-G =M-E (happy, harmonious, wealthy, good luck in enterprises)

THE MIDPOINT COMPOSITE CHART

Transits to a contact chart work very well, as was demonstrated in the case of The Deady Relationship. Even more dramatic, in the case of an event that involves a couple, are the transits and directions to the Composite Chart.

A composite chart is formed by midpoints between the same factors in the charts of each individual. For example, the composite Sun is the midpoint between the Sun of each individual. You add the degrees of the Sun in each chart and then divide by two to get the composite Sun. The Midheaven of the composite chart is found the same way, by adding each person's Midheaven and then dividing by two.[3] You can calculate a midpoint Ascendant, but you should also find an Ascendant and house cusps for the location where the couple reside. You do that by looking in a table of houses for the composite Midheaven and then using the corresponding Ascendant and house cusps for the latitude of the city of residence. The composite chart is interpreted as the chart of the relationship, itself, not either individual alone. It is possible to do a composite chart of the relationship of more than two individuals. You could do a multiple composite of an entire family or of a committee, for example. Just add up all the Suns and divide by the total number of individuals, and so on for each factor in the chart.

Can you work with a midpoint composite chart on the 90° dial? Is it valid to look at midpoints of midpoints? Of course! Why not? It works.

Here are the planets and points within the composite chart of our "golden" couple that demonstrate the legal marriage. Nearly all of the personal points are in aspect to ♃/⚴!

⊙/A is on ♈ and M is 22°30' from ♈, on the same axis as ♃ and ⚴ on the opposite 22°30' dot. Not every composite of a married couple will work quite so dramatically as this special couple.

I have found, though, at least one planetary picture for legal marriage, tying ♃ (marriage) and ⚴(legal authority) to the personal points, in every "married composite" I've ever studied.

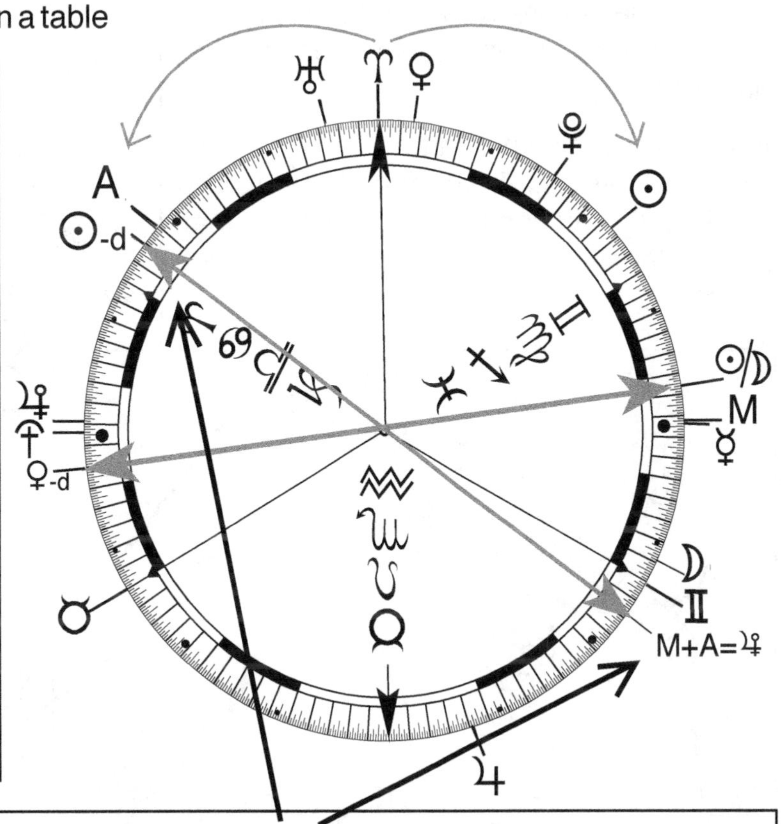

Note that the sensitive point for a marriage formula, M + A = ♃ is less than a degree off the axis of the composite Ascendant. The composite solar arc directed ⊙ (-d) came exactly to that position for the wedding. Also, directed ♀ came to ⊙/☽. You can do solar arcs by simply adding the solar arc of each person in the composite and divide by the number of people, in this case, 2. The composite solar arc for the September 17,1932, wedding is 25°30'.

The formula for Meridian of the Day (DM) is directed M + transiting ☉ - natal ☉.

As the top illustration shows, dial the pointer to the midpoint of M-d/☉-t. Look for the natal Sun and mark **DM** at an equal arc on the other side of the pointer.

Now look at the second illustration. DM, you see, is exactly on the midpoint ☽/♃ and 22°30' from Sun. ☽/♃ is "the bride" and ☽ + ♃ -☉ shows optimism and "the wife who is happy with her husband."

Note, also, that ♀ is at the midpoint of M-d/☉-t

The **Meridian of the Day** is a good way to pinpoint the nature of a particular day, for surely it will "hit" an appropriately descriptive planet or midpoint.

Test it on your own chart. It will help you anticipate events. If you find that it works consistently you can be quite confident that your Midheaven is accurate and your chart is rectified.

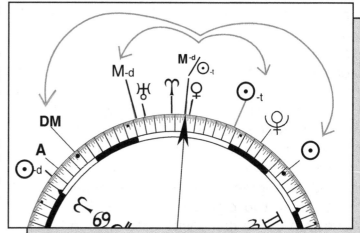

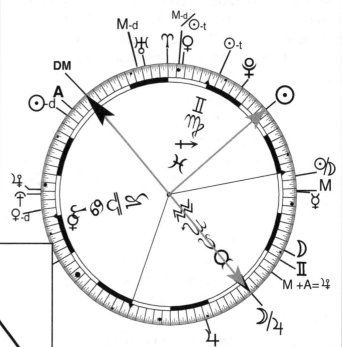

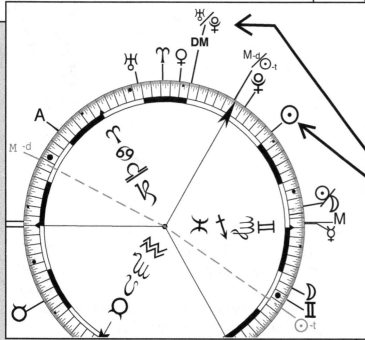

Let's practice the DM one more time. The World War II bomb attack that the "golden couple" survived was on November 21, 1944. Transiting ☉ is 29° ♏.

With pointer on M-d/☉-t, find ☉ and mark DM at an equal arc on the other side of the pointer. DM is on the midpoint ♅/♀ (explosion).

The married couple from our "deadly re-lationship" are no exception to the "rule" that composites of married couples show the legal marriage.

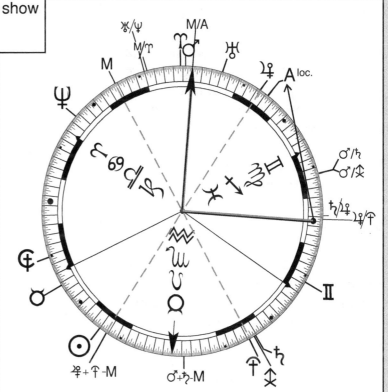

Here the location Ascendant (the composite Ascendant that is derived from the Midheaven in the table of houses–see page 27) is used. Pointer on M/A shows a very tight 22°30' aspect to ♃/♈. Unfortunately for the long-term survival of this marriage, ♄/♃ (separation of marriage) is also found at the same position.

It is not really necessary to turn the dial to see that the sensitive point for the legal marriage formula ♃+♈–M will fall in the same degree as the ☉. (Note the equal arcs shown by the gray dotted lines.)

The potential for the unusually tragic end to this marriage is also shown in the composite chart.

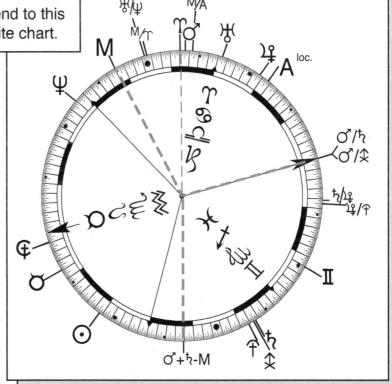

The connection of ♂/♄, ♂/♇, ♅/♆ and ⚷ with the personal points clearly shows the potential for death, and more specifically, a death with fire arms (♂/♇).

The ♈ axis is important for showing how the native (or in this case, the cou-ple) is known to the world in general. With the pointer on ♂/♄, find M and mark the equal arc to the opposite side of the pointer. The gray dotted line from that points straight up to ♈ demonstrates that the death formula ♂+♄ -M falls right on the Aries axis.

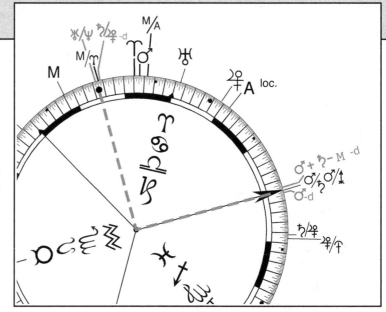

These final three illustrations show a few of the transit and direction contacts for the date and time of the murder.

If you have set up your practice chart according to the birth data given, you can turn the pointer on your dial to the positions shown and see how these symmetrical pictures are found.

Both directions and transits are shown here. The directions are identified with **-d** and transits with **-t.** The composite solar arc for this event is 26°29'.

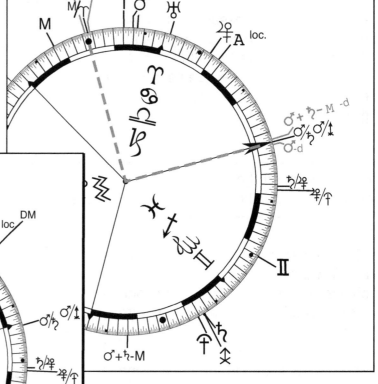

It is easy to see the repetition of the theme of ♂/♄ (in this case death—♂/♄ and the other formulas used here can, of course, mean other less dramatic things in less dramatic circumstances*), ♂/♇ (murder), ⚷ (the gun), and ♄/♃ (the separation of the marriage).

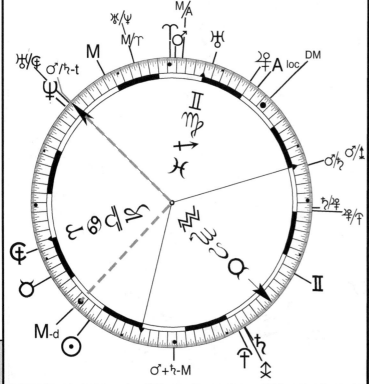

* Please be sure you read Chapter 4, "A Few Words of Caution..." and also read Appendix III, which suggests alternative delineations for the more grim and drastic formulas.

MULTIPLE CONTACT CHARTS

The number of charts you can enter on the same dial is limited only by the degree of confusion you can tolerate, and the number of different colored markers you have available.

Have you ever questioned whether in an event involving a number of people, all charts would show similar configurations? The following case involves five charts: the time of an accident and the natal charts of four teenagers who died in...

A SENSELESS TRAGEDY

Four teenage boys cruised the country roads in a pick-up truck, enjoying the warm, fall evening —and a few cold beers. The town cops spotted the boys in the back of the truck, beer cans in hand, and tried to pull them over.

Maybe the driver panicked—all of the boys were too young for the beer. Maybe it all started out as a lark. All the whys may never be known. The truck took off in a burst of speed, with the police in hot pursuit. Witnesses estimated the chase, over dark, curved and hilly country roads, at 80+ mph.

For weeks afterwards the newspapers raged at the police for chasing at such high speeds. Had they watched too many "cops and robbers" T.V. shows? Sadly, it was too late to ask. The four boys were dead. They had crashed into a tree.

The first illustration shows the crash, which was:

September 10, 1982
9:55 PM EDT
Newtown, CT
41N24, 73W17.

One interpretation of ☽ = ♂/♄ is a death of interest to the public.

♃ = ♂/♄ can be either an escape from death, or a quick death. This one was tragic, but very quick. All were dead at the scene.

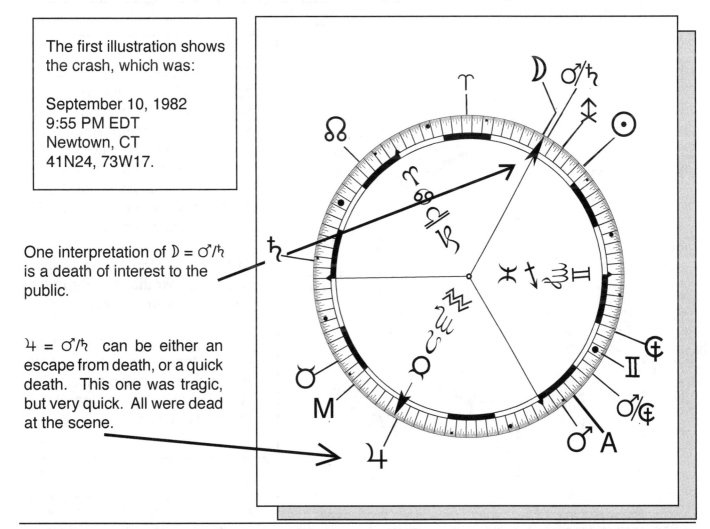

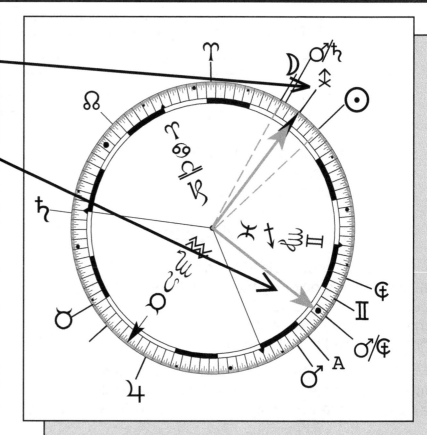

♂/♀ = ♇ is "death by auto." This configuration falls at the midpoint ☉/☽ for "the day and the hour."

It would be interesting for you to look at all four charts in contact with the transit chart. It can be helpful to use a different color marker for each chart.

Obviously, I do not have four colors to use here in this book, but let's try just one example of all five charts together.

As shown below, the event chart is black, and chart positons of all four boys are smaller and are numbered

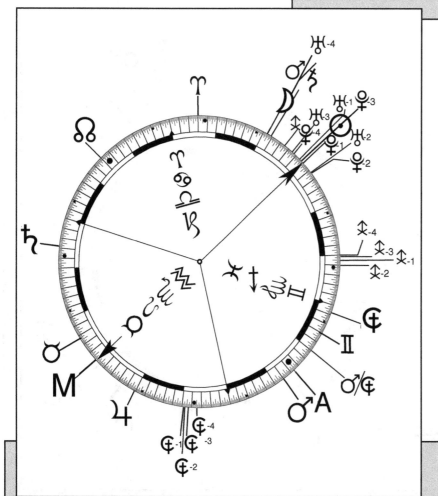

All the boys were near the same age, so outer planets from each chart cluster on the contact dial. Note that ♅ and ♀ from each chart cluster around the accident ☉. On that same axis are accident M, A and ☊. Each of the boys' positions for ♀ and ♇ cluster in midpoint relationship to the axis.

Of course, all teenagers of that same age would have similar outer planet positions.

In order to link just these four specific teens to this event chart we must find contacts from the event transits to the personal points of each boy.

Since we do not have timed charts for each of the boys, so M, A and ☽ cannot be used. Let's see, though, what we can find in the event transits that will contact ☉ in the chart of each boy. We will use both the natal Sun and the solar arc directed Sun positions.

A common link of these four teenagers to such a tragic accident is the fact that all four have ♂/♄ in some contact with ☉. Three of the boys have ♂/♄ = ☉ (hard aspect configuration) within the natal chart. The fourth has ♂/♄ only in "soft" (trine or sextile–found on a small triangle from the pointer) aspect to the ☉, but his solar arc directed ♂/♄ is right on his natal ☉ axis.

Now let's look at the specific planetary picture for death in an automobile accident (from **Key to Planetary Pictures**).

The planetary picture for death by auto is ♂ + ⚷ - ⚴.

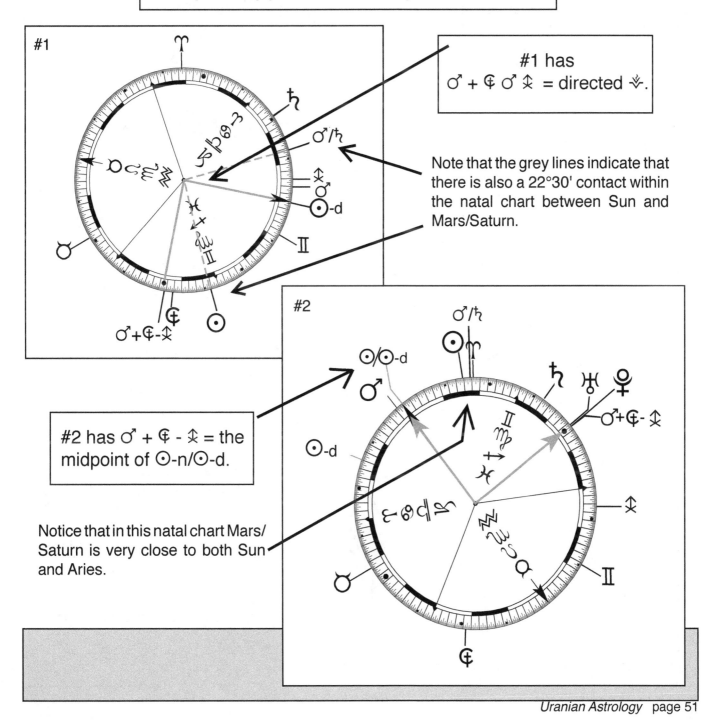

#1 has
♂ + ⚷ ♂ ⚴ = directed ⚥.

Note that the grey lines indicate that there is also a 22°30' contact within the natal chart between Sun and Mars/Saturn.

#2 has ♂ + ⚷ - ⚴ = the midpoint of ☉-n/☉-d.

Notice that in this natal chart Mars/Saturn is very close to both Sun and Aries.

#3 has ♂ + ⚷ - ⚵ = ♅, and also ☉ by the rather wide orb of 2°.

Notice that this boy's natal Sun is very near the midpoint of his natal Mars/Saturn—only 1/2° from exact. The gray dotted lines show the close connection of transiting Midheaven, Sun and Ascendant to his natal Sun at the time that the car crash occured.

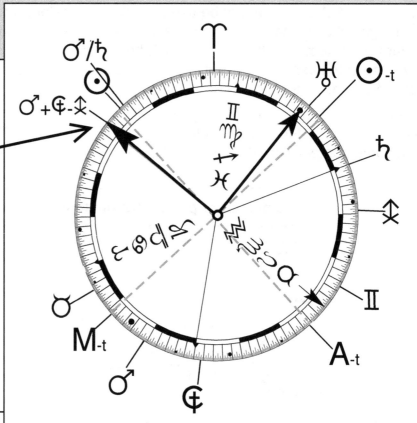

#4

#4 has ♂ + ⚷ - ⚵ = ☉, ♆ and ♅ and directed ♂/♄

If you have read the lists of planetary positions for this case in Appendix I, you will have noted that this boy's Pisces Sun is less than 1° opposite the event Sun.

That means, of course, that this illustrated planetary picture is also quite close in orb to the M, A and Sun axis in the event chart. If we rotated the pointer to Mars, we'd be just about "right on."

1/16 dot

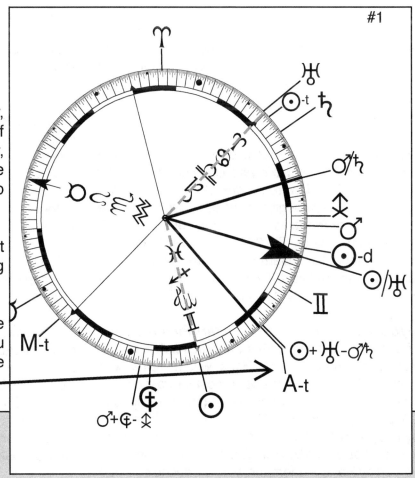

To return to the chart of boy #2, we need only rotate the arrow slightly to again pick up the event chart's Sun, M and A axis.

The only boy of the four, then, to not have a personal Sun connection with the personal points of the event chart is #1.

Well, there is another sensitive point for a planetary picture that "works" for his chart. At the risk of being accused—as Uranian astrologers frequently are—of being able to show anything if we look at enough factors, I will show you. In any case, this particular sensitive point gives me the opportunity to demonstrate a planetary picture formula that includes a midpoint.

> ⊙+♅ -♂/♄ means
> "sudden death through
> accident"

To find this sensitive point visually, you must first enter the position of the midpoint that is the third factor, in this case ♂/♄. Then move the pointer to the midpoint of the first two factors (⊙/♅).

Now you can enter the sensitive point ⊙ + ♅ -♂/♄ at the exact reflecting point (or equal arc) from ♂/♄.

Note how close ⊙+ ♅- ♂/♄ is to the transiting Ascendant, which as you see, is only a few minutes from the planetary picture for the event.

Now, you may ask, if all this means that I think such an accident is "fated"–that no alternative possibility existed for these boys. I must honestly answer that I do not know for sure.

What I believe through my experience is this: It is fairly easy to "prove" an event with astrology **after** it has happened.

Predicting the event in advance is quite another matter– and touchy to handle, even when you may feel quite sure that you are "right."

When we attempt to predict, alternative possibilities can always be found. Perhaps an accident seems to be the strongest of those alternative possibilities for a given future time period.

Suppose we see such a possibility in our own chart—or in someone else's–and we tell them. Take care!

Are you sure that you, or the other person, can handle that information positively and make the choice to manifest one of those alternatives–or might your prediction set up an emotional state that will create a self-fulfilling prophecy? More on "fate and free-will" in the next two chapters, which deviate from the "picture-book" format into mostly just text.

Please read them thoughtfully. They contain some of the most important things that I want to tell you before you start "doing" Uranian astrology for yourself or for others.

Notes:

1 The list of Vohryzek translated Ebertin anatomical correspondences was published in **NCGR Journal**, Winter 1985, "Medical Astrology" theme issue. The list currently (Autumn, 2001) appears on the NCGR web site **www.geocosmic.org** in the section with other articles from past publications.

2 **Lexikon für Planetenbilder** (Dictionary for Planetary Pictures) by Ilse Schnitzler and Herman Lefeldt. © 1957 by Ludwig Rudolph (Witte-Verlag), Olenland 24, D-2000 Hamburg 62, Federal Republic of Germany. This book is in German and, so far as I know, is out-of-print.

Egon also sometimes read to us from **Ergänzungen zur Methodik der astrologischen Häuser und zum Regelwerk für Planetenbilder** (Supplement to the method of the astrological houses and to the **Rules for Planetary Pictures**) by Herman Lefeldt. © 1977 by Herman Lefeldt, D-2351 Bornhöved/ Holstein, Federal Republic of Germany. Collected by Institut für Astrologie, Bertoldstr. 27, D-7800 Freiburg, Federal Republic of Germany. 179 pages, out-of-print.

My old and tattered **Key to Planetary Pictures** is one of a pilot edition copyrighted and self-published by Hans Niggemann in 1969. Hans, whom I remember from NCGR conferences as a most interesting and charming man, is now deceased. (More on Hans in Chapter 4.) He produced 2500 copies of the book by mimeograph. In 1978 a revised (and much improved) version was edited by Gary Christen and again copyrighted by Hans Niggemann, who produced 400-500

copies by xerox. The galley proofs were destroyed. A couple of my students were lucky enough to get a copy of that edition, after they went personally to meet Hans at his New York apartment. (Hans, it seems, was not willing to put his book into the hands of just anyone!) To my knowledge, any attempts, thus far, to get any reasonable permission from the executors of his estate to reprint the book have been unsuccessful. The **Lexikon** is in public domain, but the English translation, Niggemann's **Key**, is still bound by copyright laws.

3 It is also possible to make a composite chart of more than two people. Just add the Sun positions of everyone involved, then divide by the number of people. Say you want to have a chart that describes the dynamics of your entire family or, for example, a committee of five people. Add all five Suns and divide the result by 5; then, add all five Moons and divide the result by 5, and so on. The Midheaven will be the result of all 5 Midheavens divided by 5, and the Ascendant will be either all 5 Ascendants divided by 5, or the Ascendant that corresponds to the composite Midheaven for the location where the group lives.

If the above confuses you or seems unduly tiresome, then contact Astro Computing Services by phone, email or postal mail to place your order for charts, reports or books. The ofice phone is 603-734-4300 Monday-Friday 10am-4pm EST. Our 24-hour toll-free order line is 866-953-8458 to place orders for a huge variety of chart formats, books or interpreted reports. charts, books. To place online orders visit

www.astrocom.com

My very first Uranian charts looked something like this:

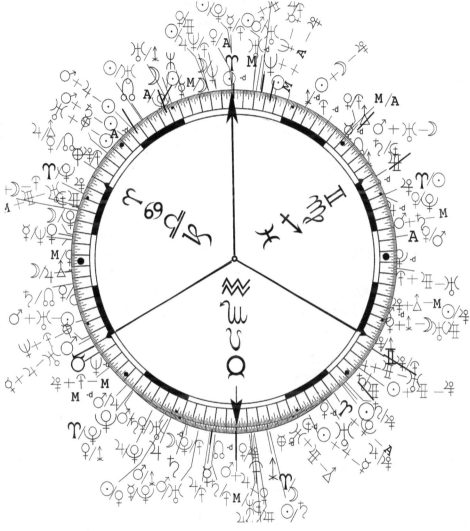

It was almost enough to make me give up Uranian in despair. The more you put in the less you can see.

Ever since then I have been determined to simplify. Most of the illustrations in this book show only the most pertinent factors and not whole charts. I advise that when you investigate known events, try to first put in only those factors that you expect should be active. Then see how they work, before you add in others. Try to keep your work clean and uncluttered.

Working from the broad to the particular is even more important when you are trying to investigate a chart for a known event. In this case, to immediately use complex planetary formula involving the Uranian planets can be dangerously misleading/.

If you project into the chart your unsubstantiated guess about what is there, you are almost sure to find confirming evidence, no matter how flimsey — and you might miss contradictory indicators that are as "broad as a barn." For the investigation of unknown events you have to muster up all the objectivity that you can and look first for the broad overview—such as major natal configurations, major directions and outer planet cycles—before you start honing in on sensitive points and Uranian planets for details and confirmation of what the major trends suggest. Uranian astrology is very potent stuff, so do use especially extreme caution when you work with your own chart, or the chart of someone emotionally close to you. Be calm. Don't scare yourself by looking for chart factors to confirm something you don't want to be there, but you're afraid might be. Remember—if something is really important, it will show dramatically. There is no question that you can learn a great deal by studying your own chart, so I encourage you to do so. Motivation is high, and who knows you better than you—right? Well, not always—especially when you're worried about something that might happen and you do not want it to happen. Ask another astrologer before you lose sleep over something that you think you see. Also, don't put planetary pictures, especially one that includes the Uranian planets in your chart and then decide that just because it contacts a personal point, it is going to happen. Remember, any important theme in a chart will be repeated over and over. Many astrologers will give the "rule of thumb" opinion that if it is important, it will show in at least three different ways—and if it does not show in three ways, it is probably nothing to be concerned about.

The amazing thing about the investigation of events with Uranian astrology is the precision and detail with which planetary pictures can be found to describe an event after it happens. It never fails! Once you know what you are looking for, you can surely find it.

Your problems come when you try to apply that same technique to the future, i.e. you decide what you are looking for and then you examine every detail of that chart until you find it! Sorry, it doesn't work that way–unless you are determined to make a self-fulfilling prophecy.

Before you attempt to forecast anything you should first reason whether or not the natal chart really suggests the potential for the situation you have in mind. In doing that you should consider not just the chart but also the background, the general environment and the current attitude of the person to whom the chart belongs. Then you should first look at the broad picture.

What do major planet-to-planet directions indicate? Then, what is suggested by the major transit cycles? Now–what is currently going on in the person's life? What does he/she want to happen–or fear might happen? What is his/her level of personal awareness?

If all of these things together suggest, repetitively, the same possible course of events, then try the appropriate planetary pictures and the Uranian planets to see if they add confirming evidence... and even then, keep in mind that the future is most likely subject to plenty of alternation through the exercise of free will and change of attitude—and anyway, you could be wrong! So

your counsel to both yourself (if it is your chart) as well as to others (if you are telling them about their charts) must accent freedom of choice, the use of astrology as a tool for more enlightened choices, and the more positive ways that one's energies, suggested by the themes of futue directions and transits, might be utilized.

That little "caution lecture" is given in the attempt to spare beginners one of my early experiences with Uranian, in which I nearly frightened myself into giving it up.

I had only been studying astrology for one month when a letter came from my friend Mark, who had first suggested to me that I should study astrology. He had also mentioned Uranian astrology, without any explanation of just what that was. Since Mark was in New York and I was in San Francisco, and our contact with each other was infrequent, I set out on my own to visit Bay area bookshops to see what the "Uranian" term meant. All I could find was a little booklet introduction to the Hamburg School, which was very small [1]—and a $30 copy of **Key to Planetary Pictures**.[2]

These were my struggling free-lance artist days, understand, so I bought the little booklet. But I became so intrigued in reading it, that I went back to the store a few days later and really splurged by buying the "**Key**." (I had no idea at the time how rare but important that book would become!) Of course I did not have anything to tell me how to use the "**Key**," so I called every bookshop in the San Francisco Bay area attempting to find more Uranian books, but found nothing. In frustration I wrote to Hans Niggemann in New York City, whose address was in the book that I had, to ask why there were no other Uranian books in the Bay area and if he would please send me a book list.[1]

On January 31, 1974, I received a very breezy letter from Hans, in which he said that he had a box of his books ready to send to Australia but he had sent them to me instead. I was, of course, very glad to receive this letter and waited with great anticipation for the arrival of the boooks. Within a few days both the books and the bill had arrived—ALL of Hans Niggemans' books, along with some cardboard dials. The bill was for $31, a large amount for me at that time, but I decided that somehow I was just "meant " to have these books. So, I sent Hans his money, along with my thanks, and proceeded to try to read and understand these new Uranian instructional books.

Anyone farmiliar with the Hans Niggemann books knows that this was not exactly easy. For one who had only studied astrology for a few months, it was probably impossible, however I had no one around to tell me that. Also, I was in that newly-obsessed-with-astrology state that I am sure many of you understand, and I was very determined. I was so intense that I saw Uranian formulae in my dreams— and that then helped me to understand what I had nearly given up on the day before.

I was, of course, working primarily on personal charts, mine and those of my family. In the procces of this study, I became convinced that a member of my family was going to die in an auto accident in about three months. It seemed to show in everyone's chart, and once I got the idea, I could find all kinds of formulas to add to my anxiety. Finally, after days of morbid oppression, pouring over the charts, I had the presence of mind to set up the charts of a friend who had accidentally lost a family member in an automobile accident.

When I saw how much more dramatically and also obviously the formulas worked for that family than for mine, I was finally able to relax. I put all of the Uranian books in a drawer and decided I'd best go back and try to learn something a little more basic, so I bought the Ebertin books. I worked with the vastly simplified Cosmobiology method for a year, until my move east and my reintroduction to Uranian astrology when I took classes from Charles Emerson in New York City.

In later years, with a more balanced perspective and more experience, I have used Uranian very effectively, to help myself and family members through some difficult decisions, while at the same time with firm focus on positive attitudes for all.

But, I have also experienced and observed what people are capable of doing to themselves! Many times I've seen people (even those who are good at counseling others) work themselves into a huge emotional upset over something they've seen in their own charts. I remember a friend who once called me because she was seriously considering cancelling a vacation she had been much looking forward to because she had a Mars-Uranus combination by transit. She had figured the sensitve point for a Uranian formula for air accidents and found it was hitting some personal point in her chart by solar arc direction. I looked at her chart and didn't think it looked that strong. There were other factors that looked quite positive—certainly alternative possibilities!

"So," I asked, "If you really want to be morbid, then study your husband's and your children's charts. Do they look like a great impending tragedy at that time? "

"No, I guess not," she replied.

"Remember, Mars-Uranus could just mean excitement...when you figure all the possible aspects to personal points that are possible on the dial, do you really think it is that significant? The configuration is latent, too—no personal point completes it." She went on the trip and had a marvelous time. Mars-Uranus meant excitement!

Fate and Free Will and Forecasting

Are some things fated or do we have total free will? That question has been debated a million times and probably will be debated a million more. I dealt with that issue and called it a paradox in my first book, *Twelve Wings of the Eagle*, so if you're interested in my philosophical opinion, read that.[2] Here we deal with more practical matters.

The way I see it, it really doesn't make much difference whether we have freedom of choice or if some–or all–events are destiny. We still must behave as though our choices matter. Because no matter how skillful we get at astrological forecasting, and even if we are psychic, too, there is no way we can be absolutely sure we are right. We must, then, make decisions. Even the decision to remain passive and do nothing is a decision.

must, then, matter how skillful we get at astrological forecasting, and even if we are psychic, too, there is no way we can be absolutely sure we are right. We must, then, make decisions. Even the decision to remain passive and do nothing is a decision. Decision implies choice. No matter how much you think you have tomorrow figured out, you can't experience tomorrow until you get there. You live in today–in the Now. So what are you going to do with Now?

Your alleged foreknowledge of the future is part of the Now. You can muck up the Now with a lot of worry, negative thinking and misuse of energy, and who knows? You may even succeed in creating the problem you were worried about. It's the old "that which I have feared has come upon me" syndrome. If what I have said just is the way you are going to use your astrology, then forget it. This system is **not** for you.

Astrological forecasting is only worthwhile if you maintain the attitude that working through various potential options will help you make choices that will positively contribute to your growth and well-being. **You must understand and believe that whatever the planetary aspects in your chart may seem to be saying, you have the power of choice!**

About the Guidebooks

A few more words of caution must be added about the two guidebooks that I have recommended.

You must keep in mind that both **Combination of Stellar Influences** (**CSI**) and the interpretive book for Uranian Astrology, **Key to Planetary Pictures** were written in Germany during the times of the World Wars. Most likely at least in part due to that environment, many of their delineations are understandably grim. You just can't apply some of these, as written, to the chart of your average, middle-class person of today.

Also, some of the delineations may sound far too patriarchal and out-of-date to apply to liberated women of today. Use the books as a guideline but don't throw out your own common sense.

Learn the basic meanings of the planets and then redefine the combinations, taking into consideration the person to whom the chart belongs. Astrology does not exist in a vacuum. No matter how true its correspondences may be, It remains only one of several methods of exploring the vast complexity of a human being...or an event. A chart must be seen in conjunction with other factors, such as background, environment, attitudes, beliefs, and perhaps, as well, all of that within the context of other people or entities who are significantly involved. If you ignore the context, the likelihood is high that you could misinterpret the astrology.

Especially if you are interpreting a chart for someone else, caution is essential. Ask questions, listen well. Suggest possible alternatives, not absolutes!

Notes

[1] Hans Niggemann, who died Sept. 1, 1985, was largely reponsible for bringing the techniques of Witte's Hamburg School of Astrology to the USA, and it was he who dubbed the system "Uranian Astrology." He translated a number of books into English. He lived in New York and was highly influential in making it a center for the study of this system. Uranian teachers are few and far between in most areas, but in New York I couldn't begin to give you a count of the number of people who are familiar with the system, and use it at least eclectically, along with other methods. I would think it fair to say that most Uranian teachers outside of New York originally came from that area and were taught by former students of Hans, if not by Hans himself.The introductory booklet that I bought at first is **The Hamburg School of Astrology: An Explanation of its Methods**, by Udo Rudolph, copyright 1973. It was published by the Astrological Association, England. English translation by Kurt Knupfer, A.F.A.

[2] **Twelve Wings of the Eagle** was published by ACS in 1988. It correlates precessional ages with history, myth and scripture and philosophizes on how collective concepts of God change with ages.

America is on the move and relocation astrology is an increasingly popular subject. No one in my files has lived in more cities than I have, so I will use my own chart as an example of how dial techniques can add detailed information to the question, "How will it be if I move to...?" (I'm not going to tell you all my secrets, but I will show you how the axis of M, A or M/A points out a significant aspect in each of several of my relocations.)

A Relocation Chart is simply the natal birth date and time calculated for the longitude and latitude of the new location. All planetary positions are exactly the same; only the Midheaven, Ascendant and house cusps will change.

In my case the move from the small town in Illinois, where I grew up, to the Chicago area, where I held my first teaching position. I also had my first art exhibitions as a professional artist In Chicago, my Midheaven changed from 28♍05 to 00♎04, which could be interpreted as a strengthening of my connection with the general public.

My own birth data is:

November 18, 1940
8:01 am CST
Princeton, Illinois
41N22'05"   89W27'53"

This means I have AA data, based on birth certificate. time. My dial chart is shown to the right on this page.

Obviously if you move clear across the country the Midheaven and Ascendant will change many degrees, perhaps even a whole sign or more.

Some difference can be seen in the midpoint axis of Midheaven and Ascendant when one moves from one city to another in the same state or area. For short distance moves, though, it may be just a matter of tighter orbs for the same aspects.

Still, however, even a small difference in the position of Midheaven or Ascendant could be significant in some cases, as my "choose your solar return example," showing a change from Tucson to Phoenix will demonstrate.

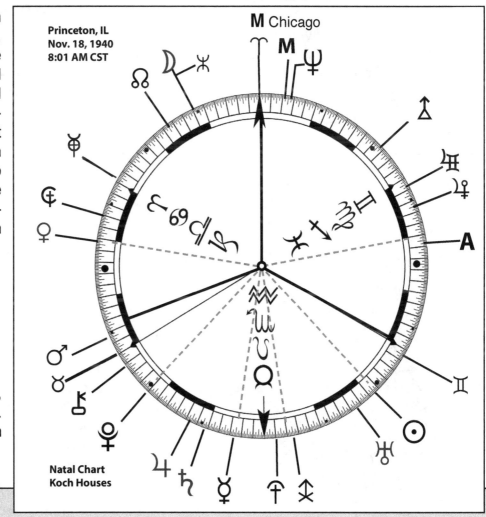

Princeton, IL
Nov. 18, 1940
8:01 AM CST

M Chicago

Natal Chart
Koch Houses

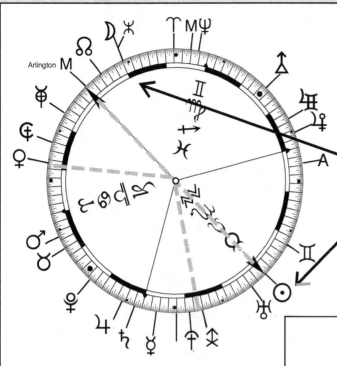

At the age of 25 I moved to Arlington, Virginia, where my first husband was stationed with the army.

We had been wanting a baby for quite some time and it was in Arlington that the wish was finally fulfilled. M is right on the axis of my ☉, which is 22°30' ♀/♆ with ☽ on a 1/16 dot.

♀ + ♆ - ☉   "generative ability"
♀ + ♆ - ☽   "pregnacy"

After Arlington we were living in Omaha for just a year and a half. My second daughter was born there.

M/A = ♀/♀ = ♃
"desired family increase"

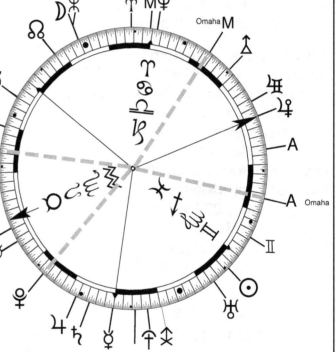

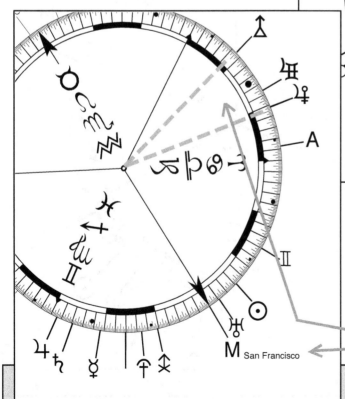

During the five years that we lived in San Francisco I enjoyed my peak years as an exhibiting artist. I sold a great many paintings through three galleries, and I also did a number of commercial art assignments.

♃ /♆ = **M**
"to be an outstanding artist."

In the summer of 1973, my husband was to be singing for the Central City Opera Festival (in Colorado) as Bartolo in *The Barber of Seville*, and the girls and I went along. It was there that I met Mark Howard, who sang the role of "Figaro." It was he who introduced me to astrology and suggested that I study it.

After we moved east in late 1974, it was Mark who sent me to Charles Emerson, who became my Uranian teacher and who also "recruited" me for NCGR. This example suggests that relocation charts "work" even when one merely visits a place.

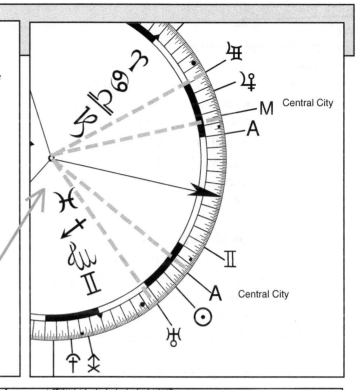

Central City

Central City

⛢ + ♅ - M "to be an astrologer"
⛢/♅ "revolutionary knowledge, new science, astrology"

From the mid-1970s into the mid-80s I lived in three different towns in southwestern Connecticut. All of them were too close together to make a significant difference in the axes of M or A.

In New Milford (M—15 ♎ 31) I started a metaphysical bookshop and an arts and crafts gallery on a proverbial "shoestring." Mystic Arts became a center for astrology and other related activities. To be more accurate, it was not a "corporation," just a sole proprietorship, but stil, the configurations (as shown below) seem to fit.

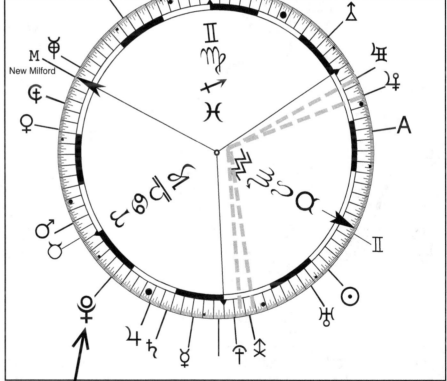

New Milford

M

A

♃/⚶ = M "founder of a corporation"   ♃/⚶ = ☿ "difficult beginning of a young firm"
♇/♅ = M "to be an authority" and "to gain great experience"
♇/♅ = ☿ means "specialist; authority for few in a small circle, dealing with special products"

A few years after that, in Newtown (M = 15 ♎ 40), I was involved in helping my husband, who is a chemical engineer and inventor, to start a new corporation so he could produce custom-designed metal brazing pastes. Again, the configurations were appropriate.

In July 1986, we divorced, and after that I was able to make an independent choice of where I would move—and you can bet that I looked at the relocation charts for myself and for the two daughters who would move with me. When I accepted a job in Lakeland, Florida, I moved with confidence that we were going to a place that would be good for all of us.

My chart had M on the ☽ axis, with M/A = ♈. My location Ascendant was on the axis of ♃ and the midpoints ☿/♀, ♂/⚷ and ☉/♀, which with ♃ is interpreted to mean "a fortunate and happy change of conditions, successful creation, and the joy of love."

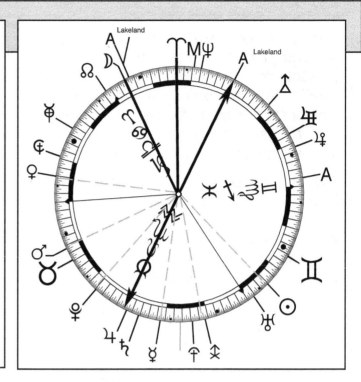

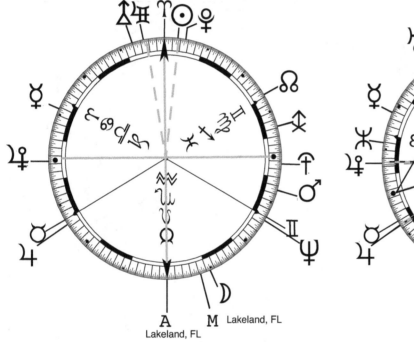

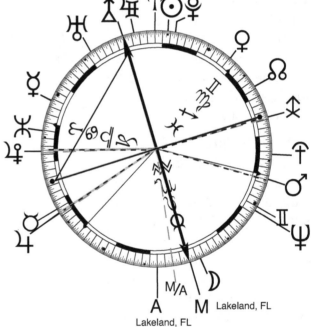

I was particularly optimistic about the relocation chart for my daughter Molly. The move would be between her junior and senior years of high school, so not an easy thing to ask of a teen-ager), but her relocation angles suggested outstanding successes in art (whic was her major career interest). A is on the axis of ♈ which = ☉/♅ and ♃ (to be known as an artist). M is on ⚷ (power), and by 22°30' ♃/♅ (good fortune with art) and ⚷ (creativity). M/A (see equal arcs formed by dotted lines on illustration at right) = ♂/♃ (successful work) and ♃/♅ (art creation). Even though I stayed in Florida for only 1 year, moving west right after she graduated, she remained there, having won the award for the outstanding artist in her Lakeland senior class, and a portfolio scholarship to Ringling School of Art and Design.

The "joy of love" that was shown in my Florida chart became Neil Michelsen, whom I married in October of 1987, a few months after I had moved to San Diego to become Art Director for his business, ACS Publications. On no more appropriate axis could M/A possibly be ("I" in this place, my social and professional relations) than in San Diego where I had ♅ (astrology, computers, technology) and ☊ (unions and connections).

(I tend to be partial to my "average" Node, because it is right on the Uranus axis, It is also my pre-natal eclipse point, and it seems that interesting things have also coincided with transits to 8° cardinal. Here, I have also added the "true" Node because it is exactly on M/A of my chart when relocated to San Diego.)

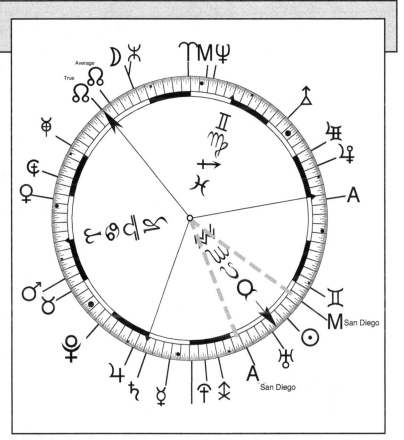

Choose Your Solar Return!

Once I would have scoffed at the idea that I should deliberately go somewhere other than where I lived for my birthday in order to get a "better" solar return. Now I'm not so sure!

For four successive birthdays (three times by chance, not by plan) I have been away from my residence on my birthday. In retrospect, there's no doubt in my mind that the solar return for the location where I actually was more appropriately reflected the coming year than the solar returns for either my place of residence or my birth location. So, to conclude this saga of "Have Dial, Will Travel," I'll tell you about one time when I deliberately chose to travel to have a more desirable solar return. A month or so before my 1986 birthday I did my solar return for Lakeland and was less

than pleased to see that it had Saturn right on the Midheaven and Mars rising. (At that time the romance with Neil was developing, but not to the point of decisions.)

During a telephone conversation with Neil I mentioned that I did not like my upcoming solar return. He suggested that he might run an **Astrolocality Map** for my solar return so I could search for a location where my solar return was more favorable. Without much conviction I said, "Why not?"

The **Astrolocality Map** (a map of the U.S. that graphs paths where transiting planets are on the angles of one's chart, in this case, my solar return chart) showed Venus conjunct the Midheaven line coming down right over Tucson, Arizona. My eldest daughter, Shannon, was a student at the

University of Arizona, and I had not seen her since July. I decided to give myself the birthday present of a trip to Arizona and began making my plans for the trip.

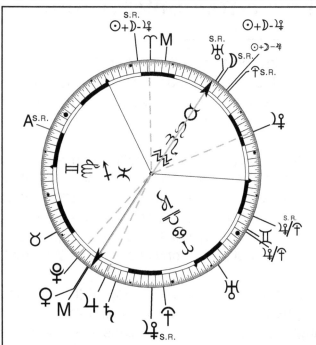

As it turned out, I wasn't in Tucson for my planned solar return after all. At the exact moment that the Sun returned to its natal position, I was in Phoenix. So it was not until later that I was able to have a detailed 90° dial look at that solar return recalculated for Phoenix.

Now, there is not much difference between the M and the A for Phoenix or Tucson–a little over 1° for M and about 2° for A. But one of the most fascinating things about Uranian astrology is how the appropriate planetary pictures will be visually "right on"–without orb–when the chart is accurate.

Solar return A for Tucson was on M/♃, which is a nice enough aspect, but only vaguely descriptive of the year to come. Phoenix A was right on ♈/♀ and ♃/♄, both of which mean "change of residence." It was also on ♇/♈ and the midpoint of natal M/solar return M (the 2nd M is location M which with ♇/♈ is a configuration of legal marriage. Of course, Neil found time to visit me in Arizona, and it was during this solar return year (Nov. '86 to Nov. '87) that I moved to San Diego where Neil and I were married.

The axis of solar return M is not quite so specific, but it certainly does indicate pleasant and successful developments (♃/♀) in a relationship (♀,♃) that could happen suddenly or with surprise (♅).

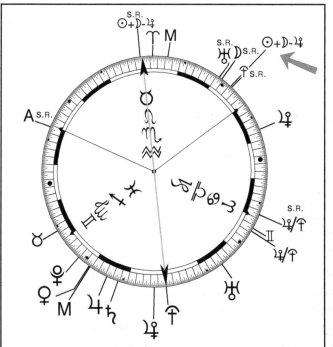

☉ + ☽ - ♃ = ♈ is a formula for legal marriage. Here you can see that the natal formula for ☉ + ☽ - ♃ is completed by solar return ♈, and the solar return ☉ + ☽ - ♃ is completed by natal ♈.

NOVEL PREDICTIONS—
OR IS FICTION FACT?

The exercises in this chapter and the next are based on two groups of charts that were collected during the years that I had my Uranian workshop in Connecticut. Don't expect to find many practical details for daily life in these case studies–in fact, they could almost be called "flights of fancy." I offer them to you because they will give you extra practice in looking at some of the more complex planetary pictures, because they are thought-provoking, and most of all, because they are fun! I call the first group of charts "Novel Predictions."

My Uranian class had been playing "Mystery Chart" for several weeks. So far each person had presented an exactly timed event chart and the challenge was for others in the group to guess what happened. Some people had offered events from their personal lives while others found events from newspaper stories. Sometimes Egon tested us with challenges that had been printed in a cosmobiology book from Germany. We had become pretty good at figuring out at least the general character of event charts (or event charts as transits to natal charts), and sometimes we were even able to pinpoint "what happened" quite specifically.

One evening Patti suggested an interesting idea. "I've been reading a novel" she told us, "in which an event is given exactly timed to the second. Do you suppose a chart of that time would show anything that fits the event? Let's try it. I won't tell you what book I'm reading or anything about it until you've tried to guess."

After we ran a computer chart on the data Patti gave us, everyone set up the chart on the 90° dial. As was our usual practice, we worked in silence for about a half hour or so and then the comments and guessing began.

Before I show you the chart and tell you about the comments that were made, you should know some of the factors that my group found most valuable in the investigation of mundane charts. Most of these could be found by looking through **Rules**, but to my knowledge they are not published anywhere as a separate group relating specifically to mundane interpretations. We might not have thought to use them had we not had the benefit of Egon's long experience looking at mundane charts and his contacts with the original German tradition.

Understand that these factors are "read" with these special meanings when you are looking at event charts.

M = the moment
A = the place
$\odot/\mathbb{D}$ = the day and the hour
$\odot + \mathbb{D} - A$ = the day and the hour in this place
M/Υ = how this moment connects with the
        world in general
$\Upsilon/\odot$ = the body on earth, or many on this day
Υ/A = this place in connection with the world
$\Upsilon/\rlap{\raise0.3ex\hbox{$-$}}\phi$ = the general thinking

In a slightly modified way the above factors are useful in the study of mundane charts such as ingresses, eclipses and lunations. For example, in an Aries Ingress chart set for Washington, D.C. you might read $\Upsilon/\rlap{\raise0.3ex\hbox{$-$}}\phi$ as an important issue on the minds of the general public during the spring quarter. $\Upsilon/\odot$ might identify an issue affecting the environment or the general health of the people. M/Υ relates to an issue involving "I" (the U.S.) in relation to the rest of the world (Υ). Other important issues are likely to be found on the axes of the other listed factors. Always remember–that which is important will connect to the personal points.

The class conversation began:

"Without even turning the dial you can see problems. Right on the ♈ axis there's ☽/⚷ for 'hours of anguish.' ♃/⚷ has to do with politics.

With ♂/⚷ and ♄/⚷ there could be obstacles or restrictions in work, damage to machines, or maybe fire.

♆/⚷ is poison, or a change in substance. Then ☋/⚷ on ♈ suggests death or mourning."[1]

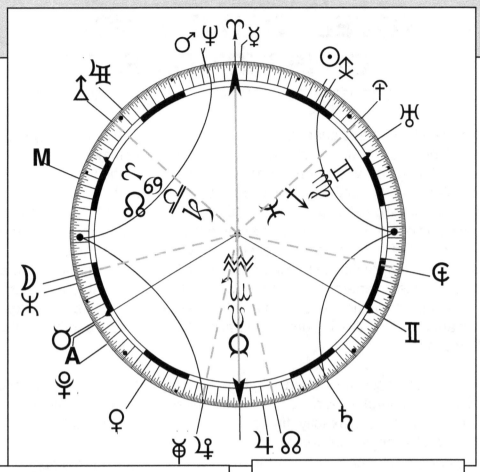

The curved lines show that ♆/⚷ and ♄/⚷ each have equal arcs to the 22°30' dots. So without turning the dial you can see that they, too, are in contact with ♈.

"M/♈ and ☉/☽ are on the same axis as ♅/♀. Was there an explosion or a mutation?"

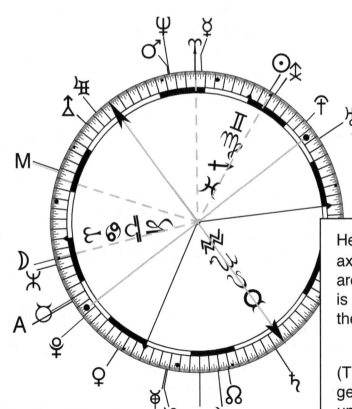

Here the pointer is on the common midpoint axis of M/♈, ☉/☽ and ♅/♀. Uranus and Pluto are less than 1° off the 22°30' dots and Saturn is 1° off the central axis. So one can read the following:

$$M/♈ = ☉/☽ = ♄ = ♅ = ♀$$

(This moment connects with the world in general in a manner that is serious, quite unexpected and explosively transforming.)

"Look at the Ascendant axis! This was a very grave event. Something happened very suddenly that involved death."

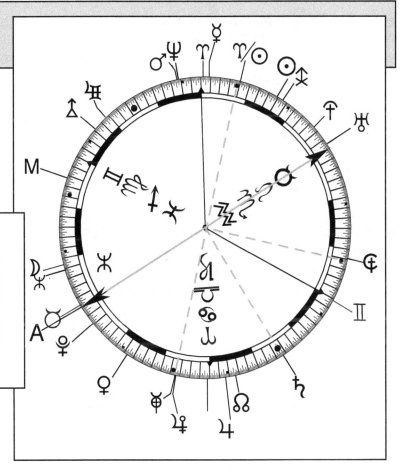

The illustration shows the pointer on the axis of A and ♅. The dotted lines show other factors that fall on dots. If you look up various combinations of all these you will see why the above comment was made. (See **Rules** and Appendices II and III.)

"☉ + ☽ - A is on ♈. That repeats a possible political connection. There's unusual death, murder or serious sickness on that axis, too (♂/♇). ☽/♇ is 'dying populace.' ♆/♇ could be 'damage through error.' With ♅ it means 'chemical science.' "

"Well?" Patti was then asked. "Did something blow up or break and cause a lot of deaths–and did it involve chemicals or poison?"

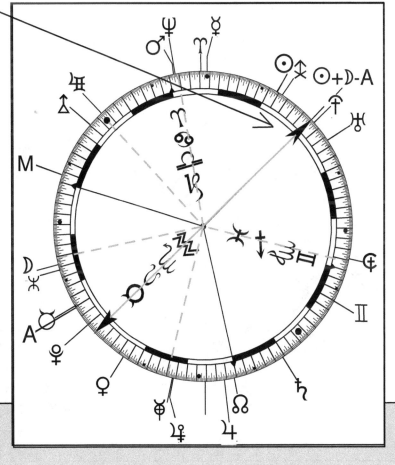

"Pretty close!" she answered. "The novel is **The Stand** by Stephen King. An accident in a secret government installation for the development of chemical warfare caused a virus to escape. Most of the population of the United States died. The rest of the story is about the survivors."[2]

We were all fascinated by how well this fictional event worked. "Why? How?" we asked each other. Did King have a special reason for picking that time? Probably not. More likely it was a random choice. Would anything happen at that time and place that would remotely resemble the event in the novel?

It was August, 1982 on the evening of that particular class. The event in the novel was set for 1985. As we all know, nothing remotely like **The Stand** happened in '85–at least not anything that got national news attention. Why, then, do appropriate planetary pictures show so well that we could guess an event close to that which was depicted in the book? What does that say about astrological prediction? Would other fictional events work, too?

One possibility was suggested for the next meeting of our workshop. Three of us had recently read a novel called **The Virgin** by James Patterson. It was a story about a new virgin birth and the second coming. The new messiah's birth data was given as October 13, 1987, 3:04 PM, in Rome.[3]

Rejected by the Vatican because she was a girl, Noel was raised in obscurity. Her career began at the age of 19 when she came upon a fatal automobile accident and performed her first miracle by bringing the victims back to life.

We decided to do Noel's chart to see if appropriate Uranian formulas would work. We were delighted to find that the natal chart worked — and even more exciting, so did the solar arc directions!

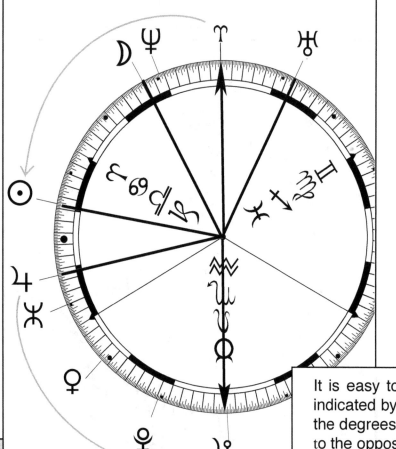

The Virgin

The axis of ♈ (the native's connection to the world in general) is very strong.

♈ contacts ♅ (spiritual), ♃ (community), ♀ (love, peace), ♆ (illusion, spirituality), ♀ (transformation), ☽/♅ (awake, tension), and ☉/♃ (success).

At the solar arc of 19-1/2°, ♈ comes to the ☉ and ♃ to ♈.

It is easy to count the solar arc. As it is indicated by the gray curved arrows, count the degrees from ♈ to ☉ and then from ♃ to the opposite end of the ♈ axis.

In order to be truly significant, remember, Uranian formulas must contact a personal point (M, ♈, ☉, A, ☽, or ☊).

☉/♅, key midpoint for a spiritual leader, aspects ☽ for her womanhood, and ♃ for authority, and ♈/♂ for her work in the world. (See the small dots.)

At the solar arc of 19-1/2°, ☉/♅ comes to V/M for "the emergence of the I" and ♂/♅ for the accident. (Count degrees as indicated by the gray curved arrow.)

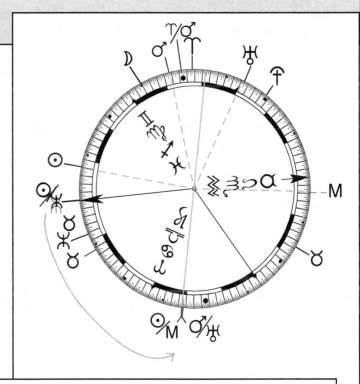

The directed ☉ at 19-1/2° is conjunct, and semi-square ♀, appropriate for both the accident and her own transformation. To be precise:

$$☉d=♅/⚷=♀.$$

From **Rules for Planetary Pictures**:

"Production suddenly jumps sky high through development of internal or external forces. Development of volition".

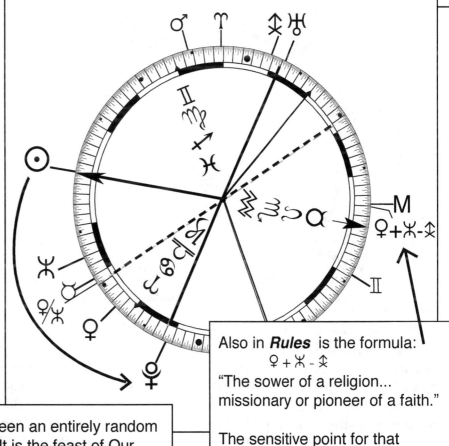

Also in **Rules** is the formula:
$$♀ + ♅ - ⚷$$
"The sower of a religion... missionary or pioneer of a faith."

The sensitive point for that formula is on Noel's Midheaven!

October 13 might not have been an entirely random choice for this fictional birth. It is the feast of Our Lady of Fatima. But why should this date and time in 1987 fit so well with this novelist's idea?

Having no more fictional events to try and no conclusive answers to our questions, we filed these charts and went back to "reality". Months later another novel was brought to our attention. Again it was presented as a mystery challenge, and again it involved events that were projected by the novelist to happen at a time that was then still in the future. Only one person in the group knew the name or the plot of the novel.

Three timed events were given: August 4, 1985, at "0400" and at noon in Devon, England, and August 20, 1985, at 11:29 AM in Birmingham, England.

Well, I will concede that maybe the "0400" hinted military, and that this was a group that had studied charts of Hiroshima–but It took very little working time before someone said, "This has got to be one of those future nuclear war novels!"

It was very easy to find Uranian formulas for war. The novel was **The Third World War– August 1985** by General Sir John Hackett. According to the General's story, at 0400 on August 4, a very massive air attack began, which was announced on the radio at noon. The 11:29 am time that was given for August 20 was the red alert for a nuclear attack.[4]

THE THIRD WORLD WAR – AUGUST 1985

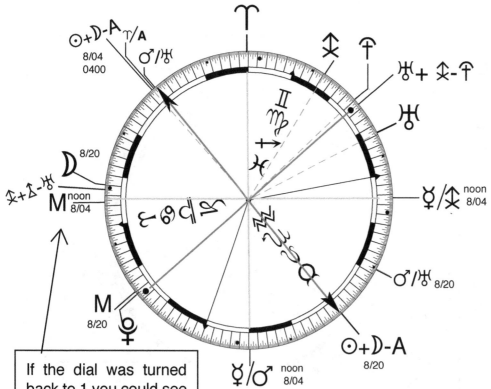

The pointer arrow and dark gray lines show how important factors from both the initial attack chart (0400) and the nuclear attack chart (Aug. 20) connect with ♀ and with ⛢ + ⚷ - ♇ (war). The August 20 positions of ♂/⛢, ☽ and ⚷ + ⚸ - ⛢ (explosion, great force, atomic energy) are on small dots.

If the dial was turned back to 1 you could see that the noon M is in an exact 22°30' aspect with ♈, with ☿/♂ and ♀/⚷ also on the axis–the timing is just as "the world in general" got the news on the radio!

Uranian planets move very slowly so there is little difference in their positions between 8/4 and 8/20. However, the dotted lines show that ☉+☽ - A (the day and the hour in this place) for 8/4 would line up perfectly with the ⚷, ♇ and ⛢ positions for 8/4. The sensitive point ⛢ + ⚷ -♇ is based on 8/20 positions, and it is in a perfect visual lineup with ☉ + ☽ - A for 8/20.

That was the total of our "novel" events–but later that year we couldn't resist a look at the chart for another nuclear blast. This time it was on the widely viewed T.V. movie, **The Day After**. The date was November 20, 1983, and the ficticious bomb hit Kansas City at 8:12 PM CST. We calculated the chart for the explosion site and relocated the angles for Lawrence, Kansas, (the setting for the movie), for Washington, DC, and for Moscow.

THE DAY AFTER

Notice that the atomic energy formula, ♇ + ⚷ - ♅ is on a small dot and therefore also in contact with Midheaven.

♇ + ⚷ - ♅

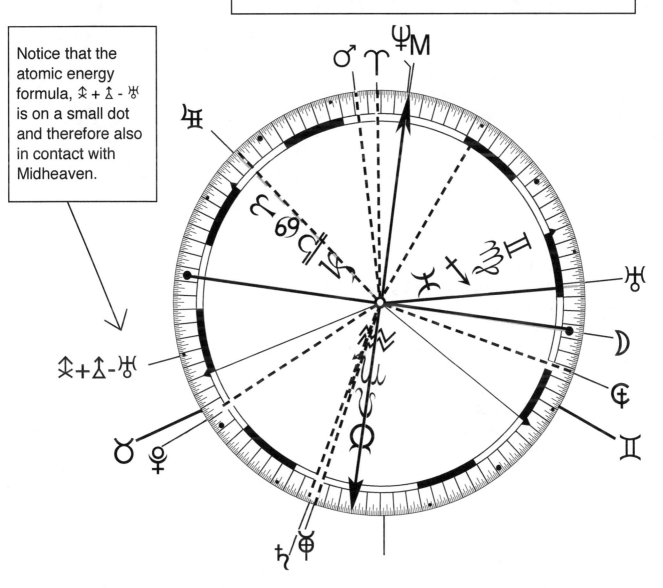

Here is the axis of the Kansas City Midheaven. Rules' delineations for this planetary picture say "murder, death, defenseless against attack, grave end, widespread dying."

$$☽ = ♀/♃$$

From **Rules**: "Test cases (precedent). First time event in public. Events to which later reference is made." This certainly fits the extensive public discussion before and after this particular T.V. show.

Relocated angles for Washington DC show M/A = ♅.

And how might the other side fare in this event? Moscow's M/A is found on the axis of ♃ and ♈ (lucky, successful manager)!

Just for fun we tried the Uranian formula for television. (Remember "The Prize Winning Mystery" on page 22?)

$$Ψ + ♅ - A = M$$

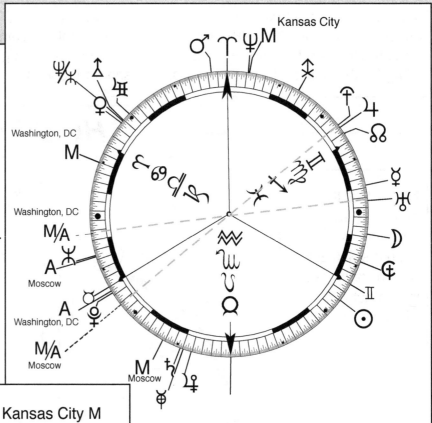

Ψ + ♅ - Lawrence A = Kansas City M
Ψ + ♅ - Washington A = Washington M
Ψ + ♅ - Moscow A = Kansas City M

Here's a little review on finding four part formulas. In the illustration below left, the arrow points to the midpoint of the first two factors, Ψ and ♅. The Lawrence A is found to the left of the arrow. Count exactly the same arc to the right of the arrow and enter the sensitive point: Ψ + ♅ - A. Now rotate the pointer to the sensitive point (illustrated at right, below). You will find the Kansas City M on a small dot. It is therefore in contact with the sensitive point, and completes the formula: Ψ + ♅ - A = M.

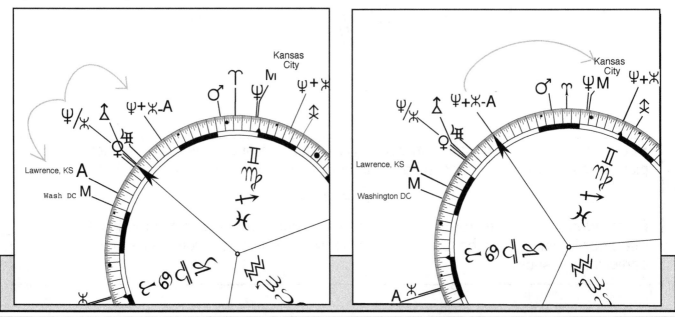

In the illustration to the right the pointer is on the first three factors in the sensitive point for television, using the Washington, DC Ascendant.

The formula is completed by the M for Moscow, which is within one degree of the other end of the pointer arrow. M for Washington, DC is also not far off. It is about one degree from the 22°30' dot

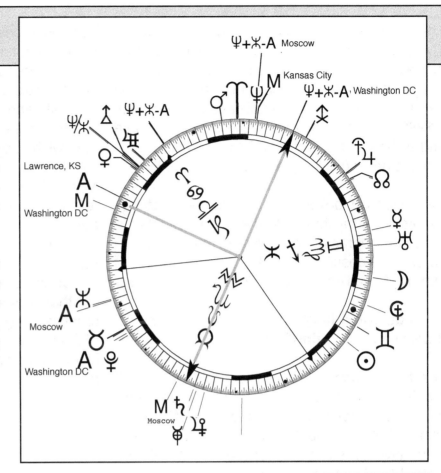

At the right we again look at the midpoint ♃/♄. Notice that this is also the midpoint of A for Moscow and M for Kansas City. This means that

Ψ + ♅ - A (Moscow) = M (Kansas City).

And the formula works again!

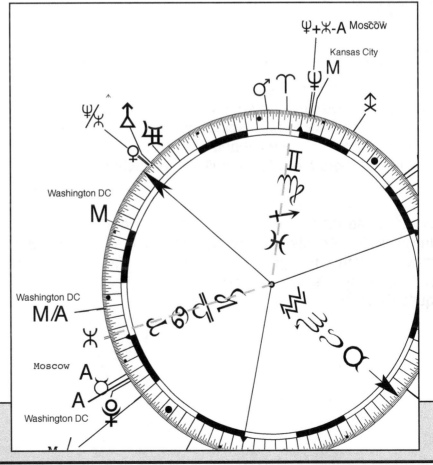

The dates in all of the novels have now passed. The year 1985 went by with nothing in the news that was nearly so drastic as the fiction authors imagined. The fears of nuclear threat from Moscow had (by the time of first publication of this book in1989) turned to optimism for continued peace and a thaw in the "cold war" through the Soviet Union's new policy of glasnost.

Still, when we looked at charts for these fictional events in our mystery chart game we were able to guess the character or potential of the events. Apparently the possibility existed in these moments of authors' fantasies for their plots to become reality.

What do you think? Have we proved—or disproved—anything?

The first person to whom I told this story said, "You've proved that astrological prediction is so much garbage–can't be done." I don't agree with that at all. In each moment and place many alternative possibilities exist. We know that with a chart (and some knowledge of the background circumstances) we can often make a prognosis about the future and be right. We have also seen how changes in attitude can change the outcome, and so, if we are wise, we limit our suggestions to alternative possibilities and leave it to those whose charts we are reading to decide what outcome they wish to project.

Many different things can happen to many different people in the same moment in the same general location. Some things happen only in the mind. There is much we do not know about the human mind. Perhaps at one moment in time— a moment of creativity—the mind can travel to another moment that perfectly expresses the creative thought. Consciously the novelist's choice of time for an event may be random. On another level of consciousness, though, exactly the "right" moment is chosen.

Notes: ————————————————

[1] Keep in mind that this conversation is among people who have studied many charts of mundane events such as accidents, explosions, etc. They know that this is an event that is significant to a novel, and therefore it is most likely somewhat dramatic.

So, of course, they are guessing the more drastic of the possible delineations for the planetary pictures they see. If they thought they were "reading" the natal chart of a person, the delineations could be quite different.

See Appendix III.

[2] Stephen King, **The Stand**, A Signet Book, New American Library, 1980

[3] James Patterson, **The Virgin,** Bantam Books, 1981.

[4] General Sir John Hackett, The Third World War—August 1985, Macmillan, New York, 1978

Dial a Past Life

8

After taking such a flying leap away from hard material facts with charts from novels, we may as well digress to an even more esoteric plane.

IS SHE HER OWN GRANDPA?

Grandma was startled by things that little Betsy told her. Betsy was not quite three years old. She never knew her grandfather. He passed away three years before Betsy was born.

Grandma had never told anyone the special secrets she and Grandpa shared. Yet Betsy knew! How could that be?

My friend, who was Betsy's uncle, was curious. He asked, "If there's a chance that Betsy could be her grandfather's reincarnation, do you suppose anything about it would show in their charts?"

Looking for past lives in charts is definitely not my forte. In fact, I'd never tried it before. But, my friend's story had intriguing possibilities.

Although the grandfather's birth time was unknown, striking results can often be found even with a Sun chart, if one uses a 90° dial and solar arc directions. I reasoned that a chart doesn't just vanish with the physical death of the native. If I directed the grandfather's chart beyond the point of death, might I find birth configurations?

It was easy! Grandpa's solar arc at death was 62°39'. Beyond the time of death, at the 65°32' solar arc for Betsy's birth, Grandpa's chart does indeed show typical, expected planetary pictures that denote birth.

For this investigation I gave myself a strict limitation of using only the Sun, Pluto (symbolizing rebirth) and specific birth configurations that did not rely on M, A or Moon. (There is no birth time and therefore no M or A and no reliable Moon position.) I used noon planetary positions right out of the ephemeris. I was intrigued that the Moon positions for Grandpa's and Betsy's birthdays were opposite within just a few minutes of arc, so I did enter Grandpa's noon Moon on the dial–but with no intention of depending on it. Illustrated below is my set-up. Birth would have to show with just these factors, I reasoned, or I would not be impressed. (The whole idea was weird enough to begin with, without putting in the whole chart and being tempted to rationalize the idea with most anything that "hits.")

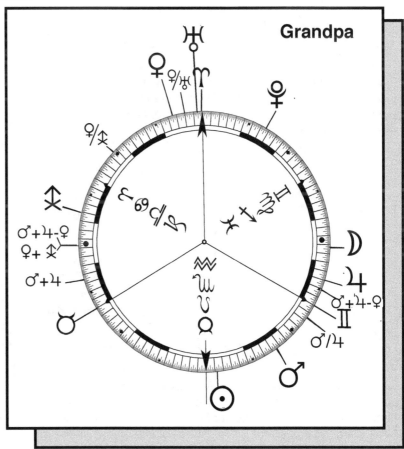

Grandpa

Key midpoints for birth are ♂/♃, ♀/♅ and ♀/♇. The first two combinations are used in both Cosmobiology and Uranian systems. Zeus, of course, is Uranian. A Uranian astrologer would use both the sums and the half-sums.

Sums and Half-sums: New Terminology!

Surely you will want to expand your new "Dial Detecting" techniques through attending lectures by Uranian astrologers whenever you get the opportunity. A Uranian astrologer is likely to refer to a midpoint as a half-sum. It means the same thing.

A sum is the value of one factor plus another one, for example ♂ + ♃. You can find the sum mathematically by simply adding the longitude of the two factors, in the same manner as was demonstrated with sensitive points on page 14.

But sums can also be easily found with the dial. You don't have to do the math.

The illustration below shows, step-by-step, how to find ♂ + ♃ in Grandpa's chart, and also ♂/♃ + ♀, which is given in **Rules** to mean the "birth of a girl."

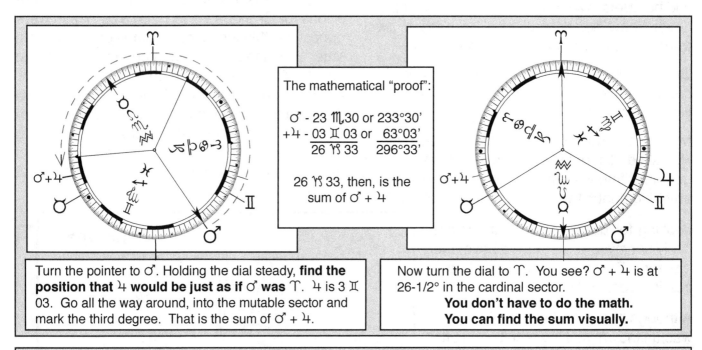

The mathematical "proof":

♂ - 23 ♏ 30 or 233°30'
+♃ - 03 ♊ 03 or   63°03'
        26 ♑ 33   296°33'

26 ♑ 33, then, is the sum of ♂ + ♃

Turn the pointer to ♂. Holding the dial steady, **find the position that ♃ would be just as if ♂ was ♈**. ♃ is 3 ♊ 03. Go all the way around, into the mutable sector and mark the third degree. That is the sum of ♂ + ♃.

Now turn the dial to ♈. You see? ♂ + ♃ is at 26-1/2° in the cardinal sector. **You don't have to do the math. You can find the sum visually.**

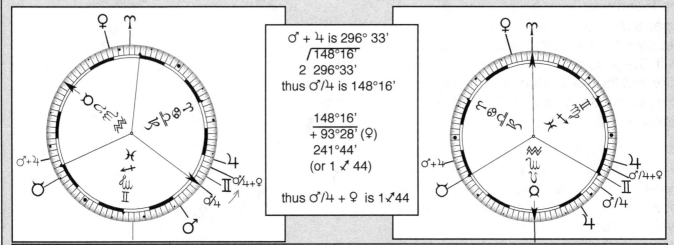

♂ + ♃ is 296° 33'
√148°16'
2 296°33'
thus ♂/♃ is 148°16'

148°16'
+ 93°28' (♀)
241°44'
(or 1 ♐ 44)

thus ♂/♃ + ♀ is 1 ♐ 44

One more time: Find ♂/♃ + ♀. Pointer on ♂/♃. ♀ is 3 ♋ 28. Mark 3°28' counter-clockwise from ♂/♃. (Remember, ♂/♃ is "♈" so ♀, in the cardinal sector, would be just 3°28' away.) Now turn the dial back to ♈. ♂/♃ + ♀ is now seen to be at about 1-3/4° mutable, or as shown in the math above, 1 ♐ 44. You don't have to do the math!

This chart also offers a good opportunity to show you one more technique that you are likely to encounter when you attend dial lectures, that of marking the dial for solar arc.

When I have limited factors on the dial, I usually prefer to draw in the solar arc positions in a different color. For me, that method makes it easier to see a total picture of both directed midpoints in contact with natal factors and natal midpoints in contact with directed factors.

Another method of working, especially helpful when you are trying to look at a great many factors at once, is to mark solar arc right on the dial. I will demonstrate this for you with the next three illustrations of Grandpa's chart. When you attend conference lecturers on the dial, you'll find many teachers use the dial marking method. It offers a quick way of seeing all possible contacts between natal and directed factors.

As is shown below, you should count off the solar arc both ways from the pointer and mark the dial. It is helpful to include an arrow to remind you of the direction in which you are counting. (On a laminated dial, the type of marking pen that is used for transparencies or white boards is ideal because it will mark on the slick surface and rub off easily.)

Now count off and mark the solar arc from the opposite end of the pointer axis, too. When you turn the dial to point at any factor you will now instantly see any other factor that would be in contact by that solar arc.

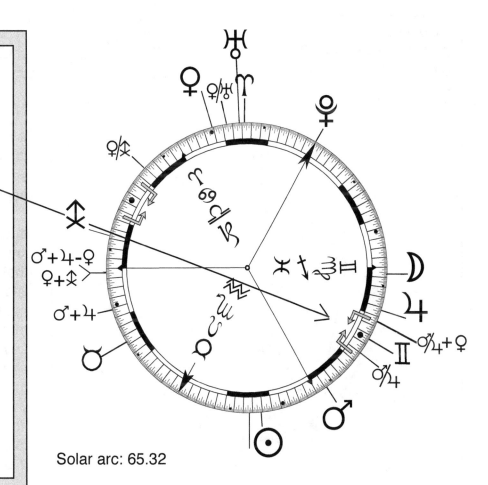

Here you can see that directed ♀ will come to ♂/♃ in another 1/2° (or about 6 months in time). But ♀'s contact with ♂/♃ + ♀ (as seen by the marker with the arrow that is going the other way) is "right on."

"But..." (you may now be asking) "How does that work? Which factor is directed, which is natal? How can you mark the solar arc four different ways?"

Solar arc: 65.32

Turn the page for your answer...

Turn the pointer to ♂/♃ + ♀. Count off the solar arc of 65°32' in the normal counter-clockwise direction, just as the gray dotted lines with arrows show. The directed position of ♂/♃ + ♀ is then entered as shown.

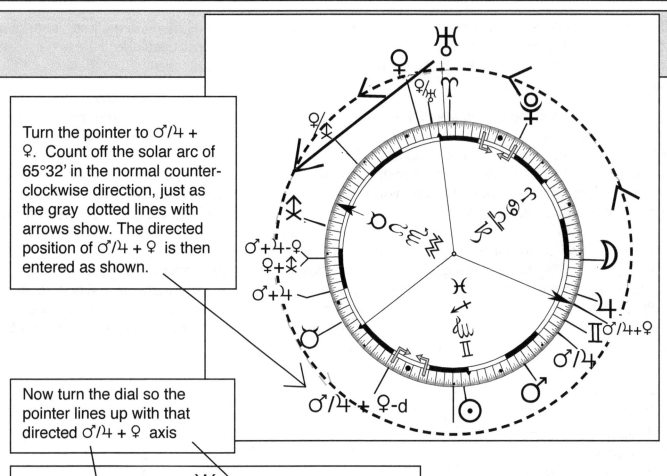

Now turn the dial so the pointer lines up with that directed ♂/♃ + ♀ axis

It is now obvious that directed ♂/♃ +♀ makes either a semi-square or a sesquiquadrate aspect to natal ♀.

It isn't particularly important to know this. It is enough to know that a visually exact contact exists between the directed and natal factors–and you can tell that by putting the pointer on any factor and then looking to see if any of the four solar arc markers, that you've drawn on your dial, "hit" another factor. I demonstrate it in this way only to show you "why" marking the dial works.

With that little digression into technical details out of the way, we can now return to the question of whether Grandpa could indeed have been born again!

Here is one more look at Grandpa's chart.

The axis of ☉ and ♅ shows combinations of ♃-d/♂ and ♂-d/♃.

(I've been asked in classes if one can combine natal and directed factors that way. Some practitioners do, some don't. I don't know what is "orthodox." So far, in the case studies presented in this book, I haven't used such combinations. With the strictly limited factors considered in this case, it does seem striking that such a "picture" would form. A few similar examples will be shown as I continue.)

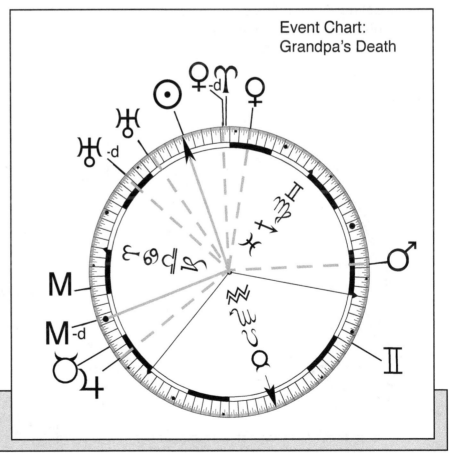

Grandpa's natal chart

The exact time of Grandpa's death was known (December 26, 1969 at 7 in the morning—see Appendix I for full data). I decided to see if that chart would also show the birth. Here I would expect that M (for the moment), must contact appropriate planetary pictures for birth.

The illustration shows M-d in exact 22°30' aspect with ☉ and ♂/♃ and also natal and directed combinations of ♀/♅.

Event Chart:
Grandpa's Death

Continuing with Grandpa's death chart:
A four-part Uranian formula for birth of a girl is
M + ♅ - ♀ = ⚴.

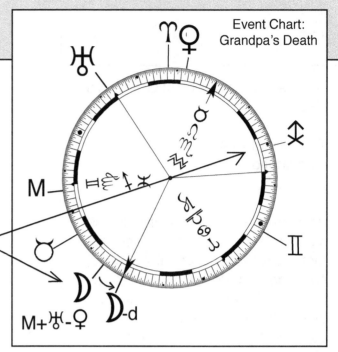

Event Chart:
Grandpa's Death

The sensitive point for M + ♅ - ♀ is found on the
☽ axis. At the solar arc for the grand-daughter's
birth, ☽ directed (carrying the sensitive point
with it) has moved into contact with ⚴ (small
dot), completing the formula.

The Meridian of the Day for the time of birth
(directed M + transiting ☉ - natal ☉) is on the
midpoint of ☽-n/☽-d, and the midpoint M-d/☉-t
is on ♀. Both can be "read" as reflections of
the feminine birth.

So it seems that Grandpa really could have
been born again!

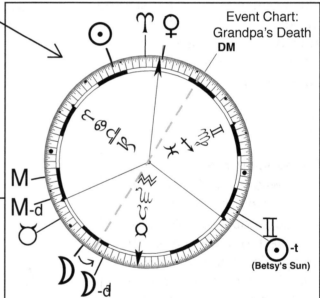

Event Chart:
Grandpa's Death
DM

(Betsy's Sun)

What of Betsy? Could anything be done with
her chart? I knew her birthdate, but not the
time. I looked at the planets for her birthday–
and laughed at the very obvious and
appropriate configuration.

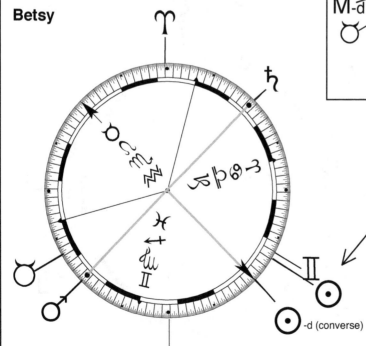

Betsy

The ☉ is 3° past the midpoint ♂/♄.
Therefore, if we "back up" (let's say
"regress") the ☉ to a point three
years before Betsy's birth, we have
♂/♄, which can mean death of the
physical body, or more specifically,
death of a male!

I thought no more about my little "reincarnation technique" until I was asked to speak at a conference that had "Karma, Fate and Free Will" as its theme. At first. at a bit of a loss to find a topic for my dial techniques that would fit in with that theme, I remembered the charts of Grandpa and Betsy. If I was to construct a lecture along those lines I'd need more than one case study. This was during the time that I had a metaphysical book-shop in Connecticut. There were a lot of books on Edgar Cayce in the shop, and in looking through one of them I came across the information that Cayce had said in a trance reading that his most recent previous life was as a man named John Bainbridge who was born in 1742. He died by drowning after saving the life of a child who fell from a raft in a raging river. Would Cayce's chart show birth if it was "regressed" **before** the time of his birth to 1742? I decided to try.

Now, my old lecture handouts indicate that I used transits for November 1742 as well as Cayce's "regressions." I honestly can't remember if the book said Bainbridge was born on November 4, or if I just decided to try that for the fun of it since it was the derived date if I counted backwards in the ephemeris to find the solar arc (I suspect the latter).

I sold the book and I don't remember the exact title. It was one of the numerous Cayce paper-backs that are on the market. But, again, just for fun–and for dial practice–let's fantasize a chart for Bainbridge for November 4, 1742. (Some people will probably criticize me for showing you all these "fantasy charts" instead of using the space for additional "practical every-day life" case studies. I do have an ulterior motive for this, which I will tell you in time.)

November 4, 1742 is 134 years, 4 months and 14 days before Cayce's birth, March 18,1877. Count 134 days backwards in any ephemeris from

March 18. I used 1974, which gave a derived date of November 4, 1973. The difference between the Sun positions yields a solar arc of 135° 35', which would represent Cayce's birthday solar arc for 1743. To get to our target date, we continue backwards 20' for the 4 months, and then 2' for the 14 days, and arrive at a solar arc of 135° 56' for Cayce for November 4, 1742. Obviously that will go all the way around the dial and then some, so let's just subtract "one whole dial" or 90° and use the remainder: 45°56'.

I had an Astro "regressed" chart computed for Cayce for November 4, 1742 (which caused some interesting conversations among the staff on the proper instructions to give the computer), so now we have three charts to consider: Cayce's natal chart with solar arc directions, Cayce's second-ary progressed (actually regressed) positions (day-for-a-year) that correspond to November 4, 1742, and a hypothetical chart for John Bainbridge for November 4,1742 at noon (since we don't have the foggiest notion of what time he might have been born). As for place of birth, we don't know that either, so why not let's just use Virginia Beach? Using the same strict limitation of birth factors as we did for Grandpa, let's try it and see what we get.

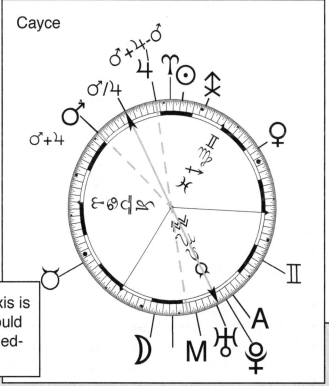

Cayce

Here is Cayce's natal chart only. The ♂/♃ axis is seen to be just about 1° from Pluto, which would mean that directed ♂/♃ = ♀ (a visually rounded-off 46° backwards from ♂/♃).

If you'll **look again at the illustration on page 81** you can see that the dotted line across the dial from ♃ shows a 46° difference between ♃ and M. Jupiter is also the position of ♂+♃-♂ which is one of three formulas listed in **Key to Planetary Pictures** as meaning "birth of a boy."

This is one of the Uranian formulas that I really fail to understand, unless it is **intended** for use only with **mixed** factors (natal-solar arc, natal-transit). Obviously, if you use all natal factors, it will **always** wind up on Jupiter, so why bother? It is then more than a bit sexist, because the im-

plication is that a Jupiter direction or transit to a personal point at the time of a birth would always mean "boy." In any case, there it is, ♃ directed to the Midheaven.

Below is a dial chart for Cayce in which I have removed everything that does not apply to the specific configurations shown. Hopefully you will not be confused with an all black-and-white illustration that includes natal factors (-n), progressed factors (-p) and the "regressed" factors for the John Bainbridge chart, with its transits (-t) for November 4, 1742.

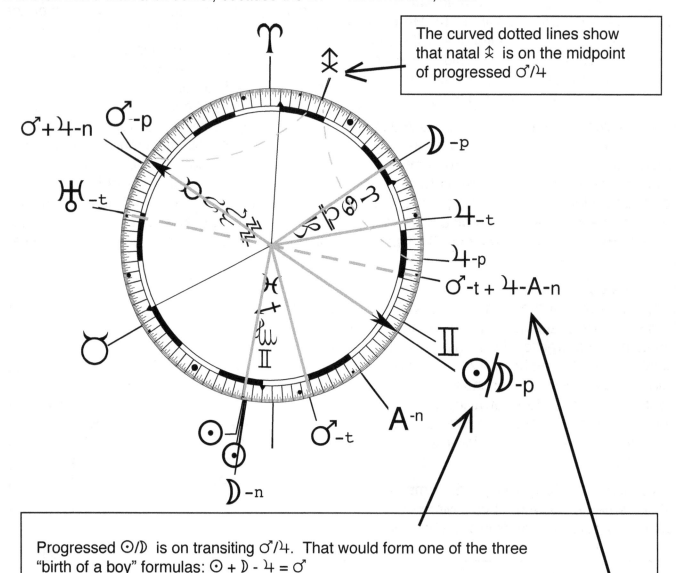

The curved dotted lines show that natal ♅ is on the midpoint of progressed ♂/♃

Progressed ☉/☽ is on transiting ♂/♃. That would form one of the three "birth of a boy" formulas: ☉ + ☽ - ♃ = ♂

Just above that you'll see the third "birth of a boy" formula: ♂ + ♃ - A = ☉, made up of the transiting ♂/♃ minus the natal A in 22°30' aspect with progressed and transiting ☉. Natal ☽ is also there, just for good measure. Isn't this fun? All three "work!"

Let's take Cayce's chart a little further and see if the **death** of John Bainbridge shows. **The Key** and **Rules** give three Uranian formulas for death by drowning:

$$\Psi + \text{♆} - A \qquad \Psi + \text{♆} - ♂/♄ \qquad \Psi + \text{♆} - ☉$$

Personal death of the native is shown by this: ♂ + ♄ - M. We know that Edgar Cayce did not drown. Yet death by drowning "works" as a natal potential. In the illustration we see the positions of **all three** of the formulas linked with M/♈ and with ♂ + ♄ - M. I remember that Charles Emerson

once said, in a lecture on "Karmic Astrology," that the axis of the M/♈ midpoint was very important in investigating a chart for past lives.

Cayce's reading did not give the age of John Bainbridge at the time of his death. It could have been at about 34. Look at the directed M which was found by "regressing" the chart **backwards**. If we now move it **forward** 34° (please bear with me and keep your sense of speculative fantasy alive!) M-d will come to the "death by drowning," axis within 1° of a second formula of the three cited, and the third is on M/♈.

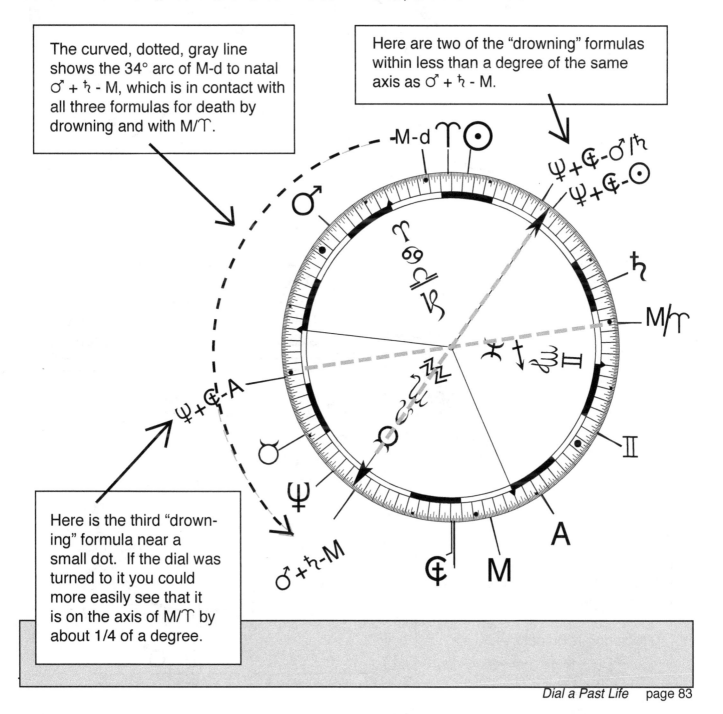

The curved, dotted, gray line shows the 34° arc of M-d to natal ♂ + ♄ - M, which is in contact with all three formulas for death by drowning and with M/♈.

Here are two of the "drowning" formulas within less than a degree of the same axis as ♂ + ♄ - M.

Here is the third "drowning" formula near a small dot. If the dial was turned to it you could more easily see that it is on the axis of M/♈ by about 1/4 of a degree.

Having already gone far "out on a limb" we may as well include a look at the hypothetical chart for John Bainbridge. Indeed, he could have died by drowning at about the age of 34, and he could have been born again on Cayce's birthday!

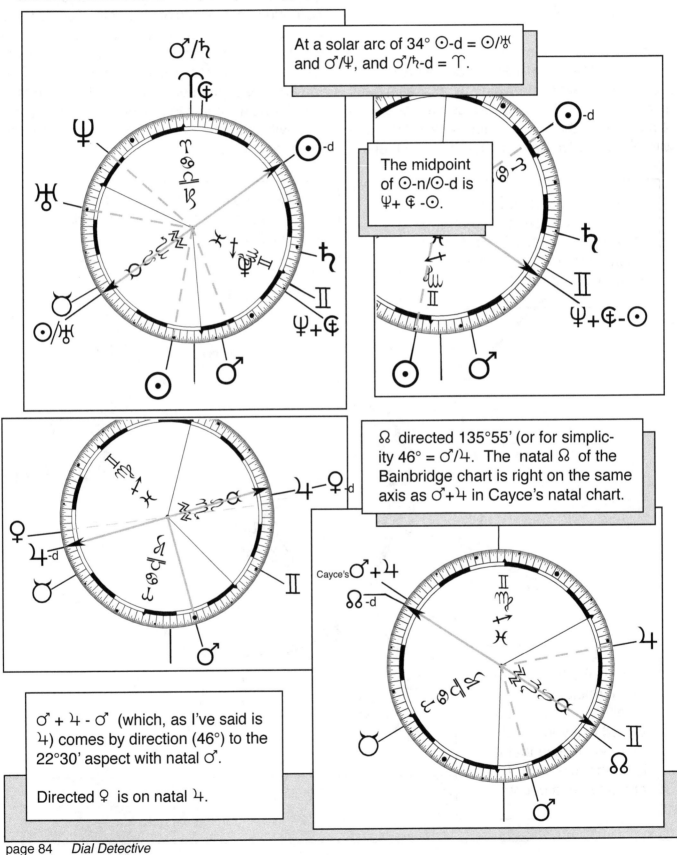

At a solar arc of 34° ☉-d = ☉/♅ and ♂/♆, and ♂/♄-d = ♈.

The midpoint of ☉-n/☉-d is ♆+ ☊ -☉.

☊ directed 135°55' (or for simplicity 46° = ♂/♃. The natal ☊ of the Bainbridge chart is right on the same axis as ♂+♃ in Cayce's natal chart.

♂ + ♃ - ♂ (which, as I've said is ♃) comes by direction (46°) to the 22°30' aspect with natal ♂.

Directed ♀ is on natal ♃.

To have one more case study to round out that lecture, I asked a psychically gifted friend for permission to use his chart.

I remembered an interesting story he had told me of his childhood experiences that had led him not only to feel sure of the nature of his previous life, but to understand a possible reason for his homosexuality. Although his public persona is not obviously gay, Colin (not his real name) has always felt he was a woman inside a male body. He has worked hard, he says, to cultivate masculine characteristics in order to protect his career.

Born on a farm in a very rural area, Colin, as a toddler, had little or no exposure to world events. World War II had begun, for the United States, by the time this child learned to talk, but in 1941 there was no daily T.V. news to invade his mind. Yet, Colin's very earliest memories are of waking in the night terrified from the same recurrent dream.

From the time he began to talk he told his parents about the nightmares. He was racing across a field with his family–only he was not himself. He was in the body of a girl, that he thinks was about

eight years old. They were being chased by sol-ders, whom he now realizes wore Nazi uniforms. At last they were caught, and Colin watched in horror as his mother's throat was slit. Then Colin (as the little girl) was killed, too, and he woke up screaming. Always the dream was the same.

Colin now believes that he actually was the little girl in his dream. He thinks that he feels like a woman inside because his life as a female was cut off too abruptly, and his reincarnation as a boy came too fast for the soul to adjust.

There are a striking number of murderous configurations in contact with personal points in Colin's chart, but there's nothing in his personal life so far to account for their presence.

Especially interesting is the fact that so many of these Uranian formulas fall just one degree or less behind the personal point, or behind a fourth factor that completes a four-part planetary formula.

A violent death within a year before Colin's birth fits with his dreams. Some of the formulas and their delineations will be shown later. First the birth.

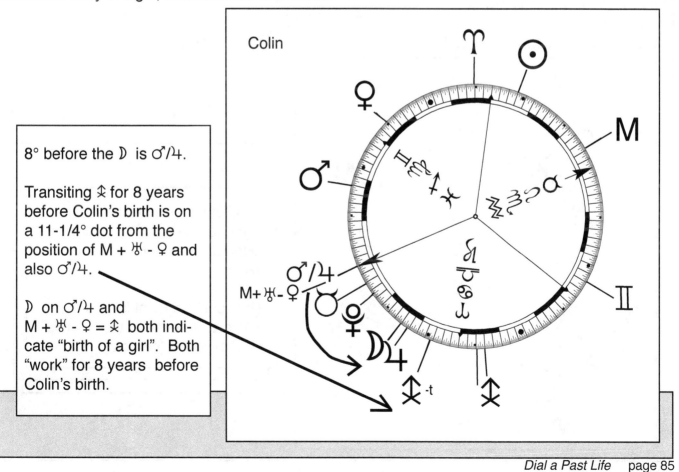

8° before the ☽ is ♂/♃.

Transiting ♇ for 8 years before Colin's birth is on a 11-1/4° dot from the position of M + ♅ - ♀ and also ♂/♃.

☽ on ♂/♃ and M + ♅ - ♀ = ♇ both indicate "birth of a girl". Both "work" for 8 years before Colin's birth.

Colin

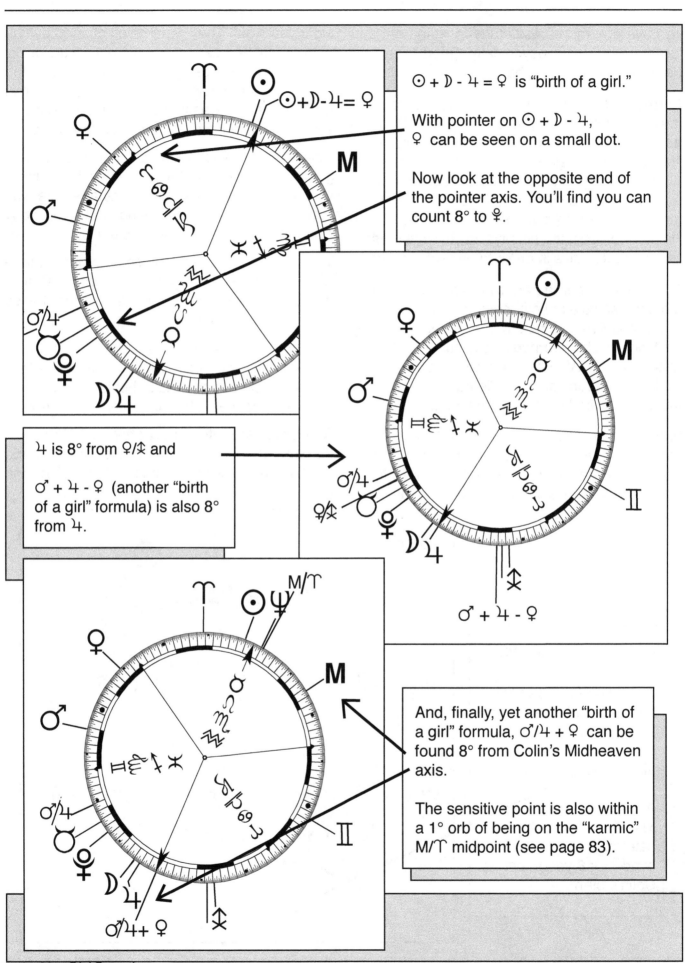

☉ + ☽ - ♃ = ♀ is "birth of a girl."

With pointer on ☉ + ☽ - ♃, ♀ can be seen on a small dot.

Now look at the opposite end of the pointer axis. You'll find you can count 8° to ♀.

♃ is 8° from ♀/♎ and

♂ + ♃ - ♀ (another "birth of a girl" formula) is also 8° from ♃.

And, finally, yet another "birth of a girl" formula, ♂/♃ + ♀ can be found 8° from Colin's Midheaven axis.

The sensitive point is also within a 1° orb of being on the "karmic" M/♈ midpoint (see page 83).

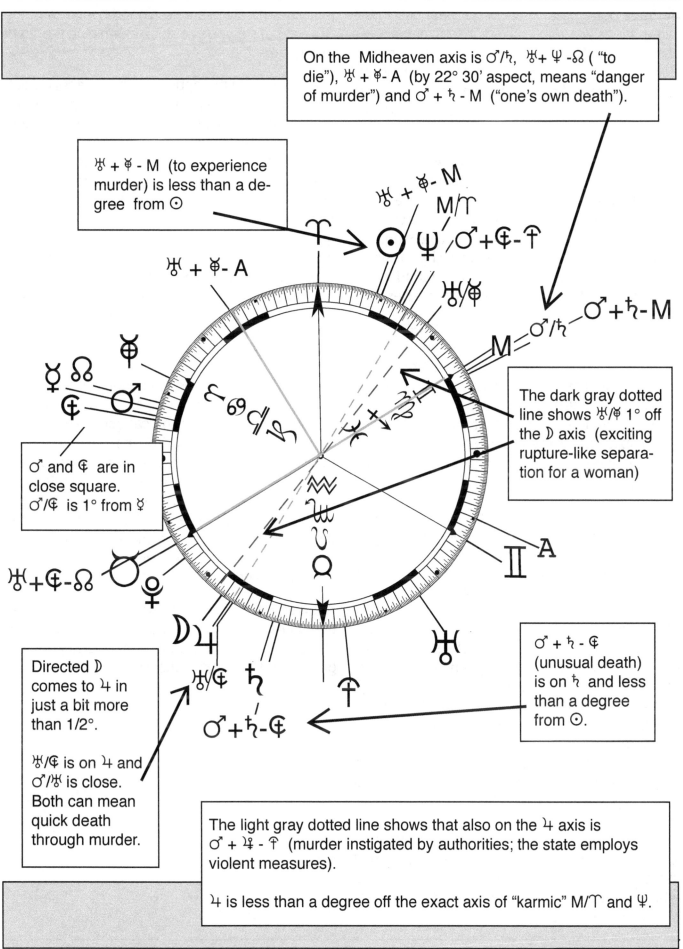

On the Midheaven axis is ♂/♄, ♅+ Ψ -☊ ("to die"), ♅ + ♇- A (by 22° 30' aspect, means "danger of murder") and ♂ + ♄ - M ("one's own death").

♅ + ♇ - M (to experience murder) is less than a degree from ☉

♅ + ♇- A

♂ and ♀ are in close square. ♂/♀ is 1° from ☿

The dark gray dotted line shows ♅/♇ 1° off the ☾ axis (exciting rupture-like separation for a woman)

♅+♀-☊

Directed ☾ comes to ♃ in just a bit more than 1/2°.

♅/♀ is on ♃ and ♂/♅ is close. Both can mean quick death through murder.

♂ + ♄ - ♀ (unusual death) is on ♄ and less than a degree from ☉.

The light gray dotted line shows that also on the ♃ axis is ♂ + ♃ - ♈ (murder instigated by authorities; the state employs violent measures).

♃ is less than a degree off the exact axis of "karmic" M/♈ and Ψ.

Perhaps our charts do show our past and future incarnations. Certainly the solar arcs for the three cases presented here support the memories of Betsy, Edgar Cayce, and Colin. Does this "prove" reincarnation? Of course not! Three case studies on any subject, no matter how fascinating, are insufficient to consider as proof.

A very good comment was made by a person in the audience as I finished my presentation of this material at a Houston conference: "At least this is an interesting way to explain how dire Uranian formulas can 'work' in our charts, yet have nothing to do with our lives so far. I think now I won't worry about some of the awful ones I've found in my chart–obviously they are only from another life!"

So there you have it–my "ulterior motive" I promised to tell you about later. Part of the reason to include the "novel predictions" and the "reincarnation" case studies is just because they are fun–and you might as well have fun while you're practicing a new technique. But the other important reason is to help assure that you strike a healthy balance in considering your own charts and what you find in them.

Think about it... have I perhaps demonstrated that, even with very limited factors, I was still able to find what I wanted to find in these charts? Or could anybody have found them because they are valid and true? What is truth?

At least realize that if you get hold of an idea and project it into your chart, you'll quite probably find a way to "prove" it. Objectivity is never easy–especially when you have a stake in the outcome. This ability to find what you want is not unique to Uranian astrology. I've heard plenty of "traditional" astrologers build elaborate astrological justifications, too! And scientists have been known to play interesting games with statistics to find what it was important to them to find.

Don't take it all too seriously! "Dial Detecting" is fun–you can learn a lot, and often make good use of what you learn. Just remember to always retain a healthy skepticism in regard to your ob-jectivity, and always take a good overview of the "forest" before you get stuck examining the "bark on one tree."

I've provided in the appendix an alphabetical listing of the planetary pictures used in this book and others that I've found to work in chart rectification. (Uranian astrology is a good way to test a chart rectification. I insist that M or A must contact an appropriate planetary picture for each of at least six events before I consider a chart "right.") Rectification will be introduced in the Chapter 9. I mention it only because I want to echo my "caution words" from Chapter 4, and to suggest that you use the dire formulas of death and destruction only to investigate events that have already happened. They will work–but to apply them in attempts to forecast will, all too often, only feed your fears and result in unproductive negative thinking.

Astrology may well be analogous to a map or blueprint for our lives, but I strongly believe that our spirits always have the capacity to transcend astrological indicators. You can find gloom in your chart–and in your life–if that's what you are looking for. Or, when you see those challenging aspects coming up, you can look for and find "the silver lining." Alternative possibilities will always be there, and the chart and its cycles—and life—are never static. For every ending there is always a new beginning.

Astrology is a useful tool only if you believe that every challenge comes with an opportunity for a choice you can make which will lead to personal growth and eventual success.

An Introduction to Use of the Dial for
Rectification of Unknown Birth Time

9

Some of the case studies in this book were chosen for stark contrasts and dramatic effect rather than for practical day-to-day life situations. The techniques presented, however, demonstrate what you need to know in order to use the 90° dial as a favorite astrological tool.

This final chapter on the 90° dial expands upon the technique of marking the dial, as shown on page 77 and introduces you to the ways in which dial technique can assist you in chart rectification.

Rectification is a complex process testing everything you know about astrology and, perhaps most of all, your ability to be objective about it. I feel that subjective opinions or prejudices on the meanings of, or outward appearance of, signs or even angular planets are particularly fraught with potential error, especially if you rely on them too much. Subjective analysis, in my opinion, may be valid (many of us are intuitive), but subjectivity is at least equally likely to result in what could be termed "wrecktification." This is especially true when, as I have sometimes seen, a recorded birthtime is rectified because an astrologer, using primarily subjective criteria, just doesn't think the chart based on recorded time "fits."

A far more objective approach is the mathematical proof of the activation of a natal chart by current patterns. This means exact timing of solar arc, progressed and/or transiting aspects involving the natal Moon, Midheaven and Ascendant. Positions of these three personal points are the most variable, depending upon exact time of birth. Obviously, if their positions are accurate, they should be activated at important life events.

In the case of Uranian Astrology, there are specific formulas for specific events that have been observed over time to "work." If you stick to an objective system of proving charts through timing, I can't guarantee you that you will discover the "right" chart—can it indeed be completely determined

precisely when a soul is "born?" I can speak to you, though, from my experience that if your rectified chart works consistently for significant past events, it will work for future events, as well.

I am not going to offer a full rectification study here. That would take many more pages than I wish to add to this book. I will introduce you to the basic procedures for using the dial to rectify an unknown or speculative birthtime.

In this chapter, techniques will be introduced or reviewed that can also be used for looking ahead in your life or lives of others whose charts you read, in the attempt to determine or confirm what you think might "happen." Always keep in mind the inherent dangers of looking ahead, especially in cases where your objectivity may be compromised. There are wide variances in how planetary combinations might manifest. (

See Appendix III, "Grim Planetary Pictures Changed to 'Good'...or at Least, 'Better!'") Of one thing you can be certain in astrology, it is much easier to be "right" when you know what you are looking for...and, hindsight is always exceptionally brilliant!

Let's Rectify Mom's Chart

Your first attempt at rectification is likely to involve an older relative whose birth time was unrecorded, and memory is uncertain or no longer available to you. In that light, I will use my own Mother's chart as an example exercise. Years ago I attempted a rectificaton for her which worked fairly well, but in hindsight I realize I was less than objective and was seeing her chart more through my own impressions and feelings rather than focusing on **her** own separate individuality. Later, in using only the strictly objective criteria, as demonstrated here, I found a chart that works better for events, and "fits" her much better, too.

Determine Dates for Significant Events

To attempt a recification you should have six (or more) significant life passage or emotionally dramatic events. This includes such things as deaths of either parent or other members of the immediate family, marriage, divorce, births of children, accidents, surgeries...the more you can list, the better.

Emotional impact of events is important, for we will first try to determine the degree of the Moon before we proceed to even consider what the M or A might be. Why? Because of all the planets, the Moon is the only one that moves significantly more than a degree each day. You can count on the other planets to be within a degree or less whether you calculate the birthdate for 00 hour or 23:59, but the Moon may be in a range of 12 to 16 degrees, a completely unacceptable gulf for 90° dial work!

Pin down the degree of the Moon, and then you will logically have a much shorter range of possibilities for where Ascendant and Midheaven might be. This eliminates the all too often potentially prejudicial opinion of guessing what the Rising Sign "ought" to be, based on known personality or appearance.

Mark Event Solar Arcs on the Dial

As shown on the illustrations on the next page, enter solar arc for each event directly on the dial with an erasable marker. Of course you can work with one event at a time, but the method shown allows a way of scanning all events at once, which can save time. To avoid confusion, I like to use a code initial for each event, and this is shown in the illustration Event Key.

Note that each solar arc is entered both ways from each end of the pointer. This will show all major hard aspect hits of one factor to another: conjunction, square, opposition, semi-square or sesquiquadrate Shown at right is my Mother's chart with no M or A. Note that a full 24-hour range of the Moon is indicated for her birthday. This is

how you begin to investigate. We know that none of the other factors shown will vary more than one degree; most of them much less than that. The Moon is the only variable factor. Scanning for what position within its range "hits" other appropriate factors for the solar arcs will help us determine Moon's most likely degree.

First, Scan for Likely Moon Degrees

Scan the entire range of the Moon for the birthday, (or portion of it, if you can be sure the birth time was somewhere within). In my example Moon has to be somewhere between 2 ♌ 42 and 14 ♌ 54. Look for degrees that make multiple contacts by solar arc.

Next, Tally the Best Potential Moon Degrees

Check exact positions for Moon that visually appear to most often "work" by solar arc, especially in the case of "hits" to factors specific to an event, or involving other personal points. The illustration at lower right, page 91, shows four degrees where multiple contacts occurred. Moon #1 proved to have decidedly more contacts than the others. I calculated what an exact Moon would be for each contact and averaged them. Here is just one example of how "exact" Moon for a contact is found:

> 327.08 ☉ at 27♒ 08
> +20.50 Solar arc for Marriage-M
> 347.58
> - 45.00 (to get to other side of axis)
> 302.58

The result, 2 ♒ 58, a fixed degree, would
    be equivalent to a possible Moon position for ☉-d = ☽. Since Moon on the birthday must be in Leo, 2♌ 58 would be an exact "hit" of ☉-d.

The math involved is easy; figuring out where you are can be confusing. Take your time, and use common sense in noting which way you are going on the dial. It will be much easier to see this if you set up a rotating dial on paper.

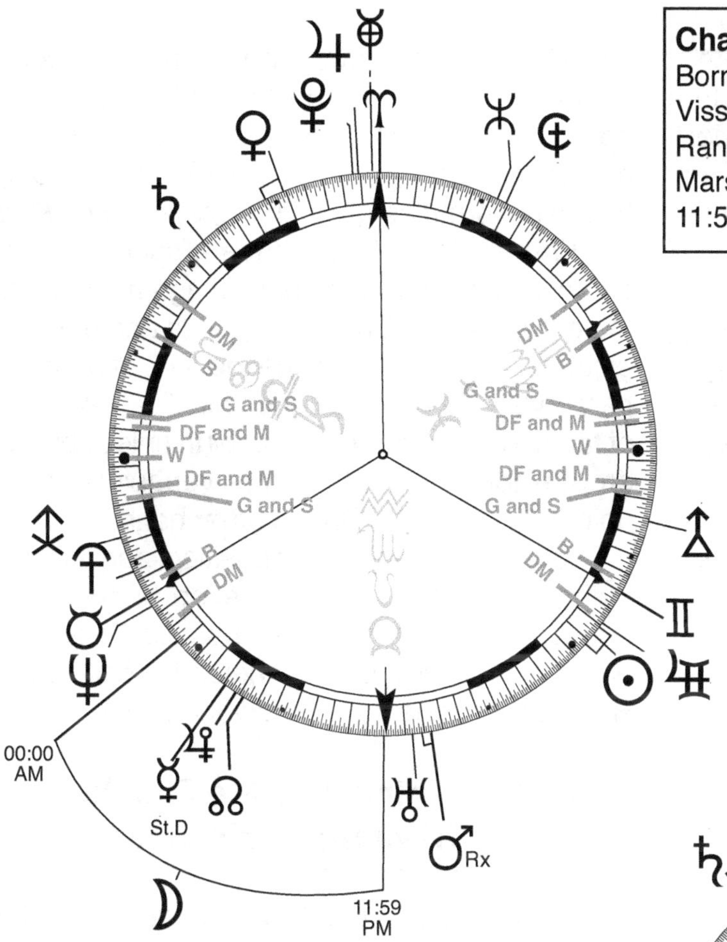

Chart for Anna Simms
Born February 17, 1916
Vissenbjerg, Denmark
Range of Moon (and Sun, Venus and Mars) shown from 00:00 CET to 23:59, or 11:59 PM CET. Mercury was stationary.

Event Key with Solar Arcs
M—Marriage: 10/31/36, SA 20.50
DF—Death of Father: 11/27/36, SA 20.55
G—Birth of Girl: 11/18/40, 24.50
B—Birth of Boy: 8/26/45, 29.35
DM—Death of Mother: 10/24/47, 31.43
W—Widowed: 2/24/84, 67.23
S—Major surgery: 11/16/85, 69.33

Moon #1 worked the best of those scanned. Here is a list of corresponding "exact" Moon positions to the solar arc aspects shown.

Average ☽: 2 ♌ 59

If it is not immediately clear how to "see" these aspects visually, set up a rotating dial turn it to find which way the solar arc comes to the natal planet. On some you will need to think of the 45° aspect. Though visually it is only necessary to note that a contact **is** made, you must understand **how** it is made in order to check your math .

☽-d = ♄	for W	☽ 2 ♌ 26
☽-d = ☉	for G	☽ 2 ♌ 18
☽-d = ☉	for S	☽ 2 ♌ 34
☉-d = ☽	for DF	☽ 3 ♌ 03
☉-d = ☽	for M	☽ 2 ♌ 58
♅-d = ☽	for DM	☽ 3 ♌ 08
♃-d = ☽	for DM	☽ 2 ♌ 48
♇-d = ☽	for DM	☽ 3 ♌ 11
☽ -d = ♂ + ♅ - ☿	for S	☽ 2 ♌ 53
☉ + ☽ - ⯙-d = ⯕	for M	☽ 2 ♌ 29

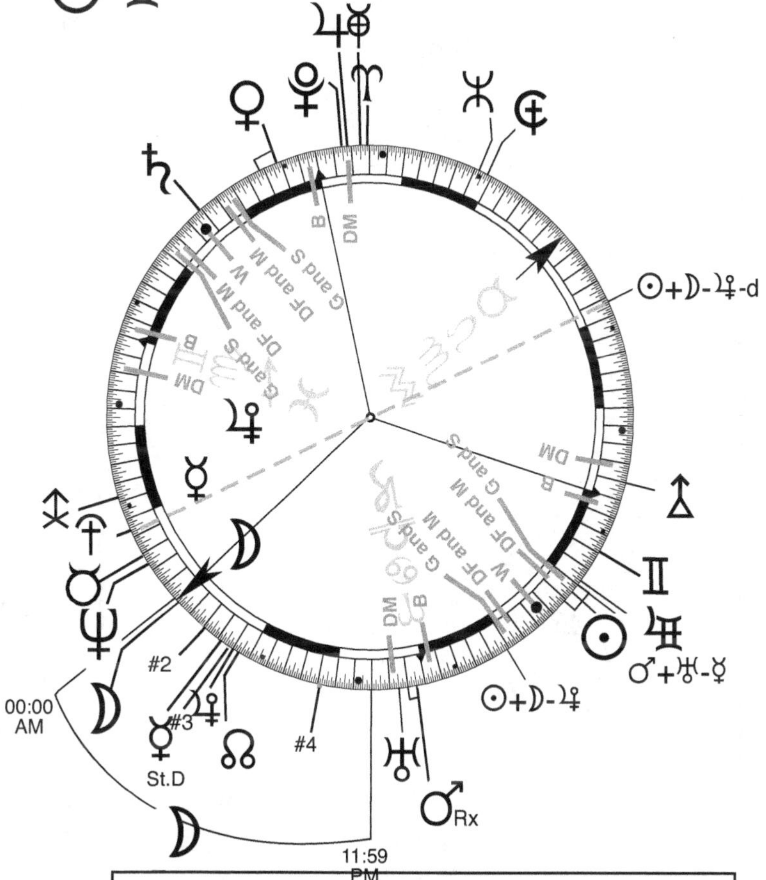

To see how this formula works, you must turn the dial to point to it. Then it will be seen that a gray M marker contacts ⯕.

☉ + ☽ - ⯙ -d, found 20.50 forward on the dial, is directly opposite (45°) from ⯕, as is shown by the gray dotted line, thus completing the formula for legal marriage: ☉ + ☽ - ⯙-d = ⯕.

After average Moon is determined, calculate a chart using the corresponding time. Solar Fire has a rectification assist that makes this easier.

Enter M and A on Your Dial Chart

Include the range of possible M and A degrees for your Moon range. Don't count on the average Moon as being the exact birth time. In my case, the lowest degree Moons of my "exact hits" would be before midnight and therefore not on my birthday. My full range of Moon hits from midnight to the topmost 3 ♌ 11 give a possible M of 18♌ to 3♍ and A from 3 to 13 ♏. Multiple solar arc hits occur for any event. Some will become exact a bit before it, some after. You will now be looking for the most likely M and A that will work with your approximate Moon degee, in the same manner as you did before to find the Moon. Use direct hits, plus formulas given in Appendix II or ***Rules for Planetary Pictures*** that are specific to your events. Test the Moon position again for any formula that uses it. Check midpoints and planetary pictures on those that refine the time of birth. Non personal point formulas such as ♂ + ♃ - ⯡ (death of father) do not prove time of birth unless by solar arc the formula contacts the variable personal points: ☽, M and A. On the other hand, ☉ + ☽ - ♃ = ♀ serves to test the Moon position, and therefore birth time. As you begin to refine M and A, test and average your finds, as before. Check your ephemeris for transits to angles for each event. Run event charts if you know the times.

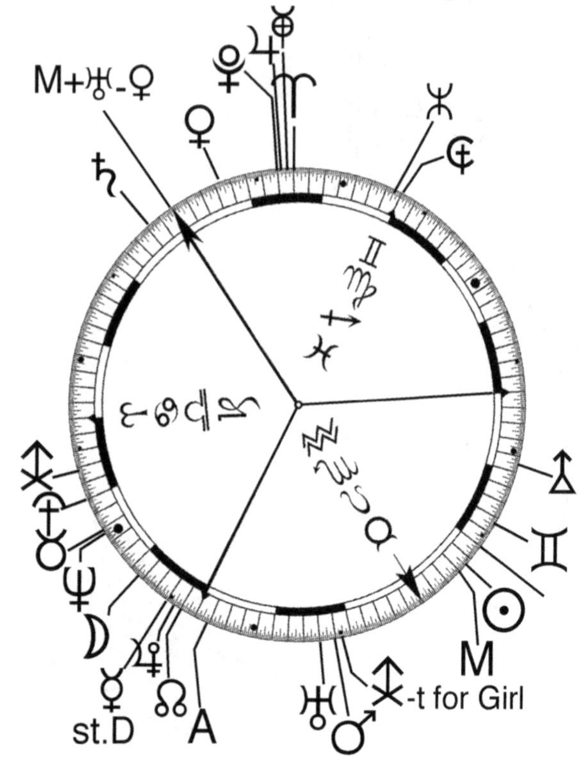

A personal point formula that is completed by a transit can also prove birth time because of the presence of the fast moving personal point. For example, if my mother's chart has M at about 25 ♌ 45, M + ♅ - ♀ is completed by ⯦-t for birth of a girl (me), and the formula also contacts her Moon by solar arc.

When You Think You Are Finished... Do You Have the Right Chart?

My opinion at this point? Mom was most likely born at about 29 to 31 minutes after midnight, CET. M is 25-26° ♌, A is 8-9°♏, ☽ 2° ♌ 57-59°. Since she came to America as a toddler and lived most of her life in or near Princeton, Illinois, I also checked a relocation chart. It has M at 21° ♉ and A at 27° ♌. The charts fit her. She has a reclusive and very private side, shown more by her natal chart, but also a more outgoing side, indicated by the relocated Leo Ascendant. She is highly creative and very fixed in temperament.

Am I absolutely sure of my results? No. Though M and A continued to work well on other events in Mom's life I am not completely satisfied that I am "right." Continuing to follow a rectified chart into the future is the ultimate test. If it continues to work, it may mean you have the "right" chart or perhaps, just the only one that "works!" The process of rectification is a research project in which objectivity must be maintained, tested and retested. But it can be fun, too and it is both an interesting test of astrology and an advanced challenge of your skill in "Dial Detecting!"

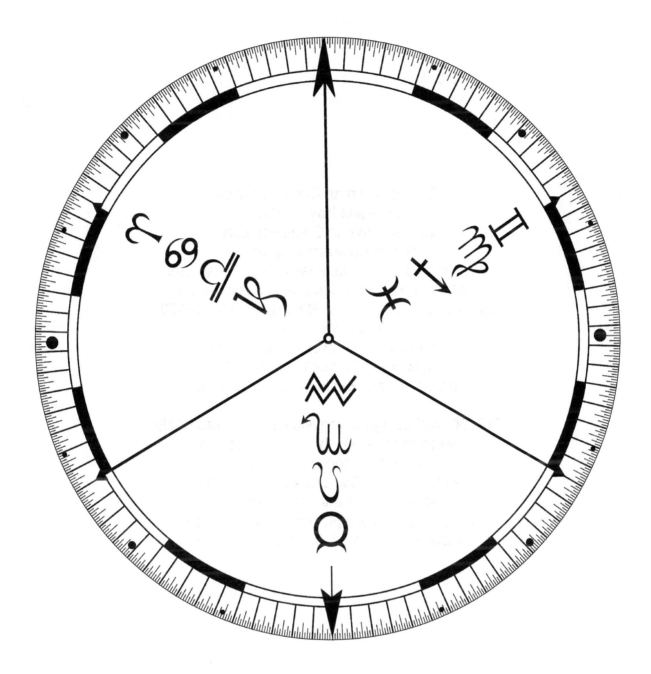

This 90° Dial is intended for you to cut out and use for practice as you follow the case studies in *Dial Detective*. It is exactly the same style and size as the **90° Uranian Laminated Dial** that is offered by **Astro Computing Services** when you order the **MKS Dial** (see Bibliography and Resources). Before you cut this one out, you could have several copies made at your local copy shop, and there you can likely have laminations made, as well. (Yes, you have my permission to photocopy this dial—not the book, mind you, but the dial, yes.) Then, if you don't strengthen the paper by laminating it, at least reinforce the center with a piece of transparent tape before you punch the tack hole. Take great care to punch the hole right in the center. See instructions for setting up a dial chart on page 2.

This 90° Uranian Dial was drawn
by Maria Kay Simms
on a Macintosh Computer with
Adobe Illustrator software.
Clear reproductions, laminated, if you wish, are
available from Astro Computing Services, Inc.
68-A Fogg Road, Epping, New Hampshire 92123
1-800-888-9983
Order MKS 90° Uranian Laminated Dial.
Dials are also availabe from ACS
in 360° format and in other harmonics.

This 90° dial design is very similar to a more finely
calibrated one which was produced by
Gary Christen of Astrolabe,
350 Underpass Rd., Brewster, MA 02631,
and is redrawn with his permission.
Gary's dial, in hard plastic version, may be
available from Astrolabe. 1-508-896-5081

Appendix I
Data for Charts, in Order of Appearance

page 3
Sir Arthur Conan Doyle
May 22, 1859, 4:55 AM LMT
Edinburgh, Scotland

M	10	♒	36
A	23	♊	13
☉	00	♊	33
☽	00	♒	46
☿	05	♉	25
♀	27	♈	07
♂	18	♊	29
♃	25	♊	49
♄	07	♌	10
♅	03	♊	21
♆	26	♓	45
♇	07	♉	35
☊	23	♒	57
Cupido	19	♉	31
Hades	26	♑	58
Zeus	26	11	♊
Kronos	20	♓	23
Apollon	22	♋	02
Admetos	25	♒	25
Vulkanus	04	♉	08
Poseidon	25	♌	09

page 31
Lee Harvey Oswald
Oct. 18, 1939, 9:55 PM
CST, New Orleans, LA

M	25	♓	00
A	08	♋	54
☉	24	♎	52
☽	13	♑	52
☿	11	♏	59
♀	06	♏	18
♂	11	♒	27
♃	01	♈	04rx
♄	28	♈	02rx
♅	20	♉	07rx
♆	24	♍	13
♇	10	♌	51
☊	17	♎	18rx
Cupido	10	♍	53
Hades	17	♈	30rx
Zeus	17	♌	00
Kronos	16	♉	07rx
Apollon	13	♍	28
Admetos	14	♈	24rx
Vulkanus	18	♊	08rx
Poseidon	05	♎	03

page 32
John F. Kennedy
May 29, 1917, 3:00 PM EST
Brookline, MA

M	23	♋	46
A	19	♎	59
☉	07	♊	51
☽	17	♍	13
☿	20	♉	36
♀	16	♊	45
♂	18	♉	26
♃	23	♉	03
♄	27	♋	10
♅	23	♒	43 rx
♆	02	♌	40
♇	03	♋	16
☊	11	♑	15
Cupido	07	♌	53
Hades	26	♓	01
Zeus	27	♋	24
Kronos	00	♉	41
Apollon	28	♌	07
Admetos	02	♈	13
Vulkanus	05	♊	23
Poseidon	23	♍	16rx

page 32
Kennedy Assassination
Nov. 22, 1963, 12:30 PM
CST, Dallas, TX

M	03	♐	43
A	19	♒	19
☉	29	♏	44
☽	11	♒	14
☿	09	♐	45
♀	21	♐	27
♂	20	♐	31
♃	09	♈	49rx
♄	17	♒	19
♅	09	♍	49
♆	15	♏	55
♇	14	♍	04
☊	11	♋	56
Cupido	14	♎	02
Hades	11	♉	45
Zeus	06	♍	23
Kronos	02	♊	42
Apollon	28	♍	41
Admetos	28	♈	12
Vulkanus	28	♋	12
Poseidon	16	♎	58

page 35
Shannon
Dec. 14, 1967, 6:45 PM EST
Washington, DC

M	02	♈	22
A	19	♋	36
☉	22	♐	18
☽	00	♊	14
☿	14	♐	33
♀	08	♏	47
♂	10	♒	11
♃	05	♍	45
♄	05	♈	40
♅	29	♍	01
♆	25	♍	06
♇	22	♍	50
☊	26	♈	38
Cupido	19	♎	51
Hades	15	♉	33 rx
Zeus	09	♍	37 rx
Kronos	05	♊	15 rx
Apollon	01	♎	19
Admetos	00	♉	22 rx
Vulkanus	03	♋	00 rx
Poseidon	19	♎	05

page 38
Egon
May 3, 1906. 08:45 AM
MEZ. Berlin, Germany

M	19	♌	02
A	19	♋	59
☉	11	♉	58
☽	00	♍	24
☿	15	♈	20
♀	01	♊	27
♂	03	♊	12
♃	10	♊	06
♄	12	♓	43
♅	08	♑	20
♆	08	♋	09
♇	21	♊	18
☊	16	♌	49
Cupido	10	♍	53
Hades	14	♓	40
Zeus	18	♋	23
Kronos	22	♌	41
Apollon	21	♌	21
Admetos	25	♓	36rx
Vulkanus	29	♉	07
Poseidon	29	♍	02rx

page 38
Prize
June 4, 1983, 4:00 PM EDT
Danbury, CT

M	27	♋	10
A	22	♎	59
☉	13	♊	38
☽	24	♓	20
☿	20	♉	19
♀	28	♋	33
♂	13	♊	16
♃	05	♐	04rx
♄	28	♎	18rx
♅	06	♐	50rx
♆	28	♐	15rx
♇	27	♎	00rx
☊	25	♊	10
Cupido	09	♍	07rx
Hades	02	♊	08
Zeus	20	♍	07
Kronos	16	♊	17
Apollon	09	♎	26rx
Admetos	10	♉	28
Vulkanus	10	♋	56
Poseidon	25	♎	24

page 41 Husband
April 8, 1948, 3:10 AM PDT
Los Angeles, CA

M	23	♏	13
A	04	♒	59
☉	18	♈	29
☽	05	♈	30
☿	28	♓	52
♀	04	♊	01
♂	18	♌	41
♃	28	♐	52
♄	15	♌	37rx
♅	22	♊	46
♆	11	♎	26rx
♇	12	♌	37rx
☊	14	♉	11
Cupido	20	♍	55rx
Hades	26	♈	06
Zeus	22	♌	06rx
Kronos	21	♉	15
Apollon	17	♍	48rx
Admetos	19	♈	29
Vulkanus	21	♊	29
Poseidon	08	♎	48rx

page 41 Wife
May 13, 1949
6:00 PM PST
Los Angeles, CA

M	20	♌	50
A	14	♏	24
☉	22	♉	57
☽	13	♐	46
☿	13	♊	58
♀	00	♊	13
♂	10	♉	25
♃	02	♒	06
♄	29	♌	27
♅	28	♊	29
♆	12	♎	49rx
♇	14	♌	13
☊	25	♈	27
Cupido	21	♍	50rx
Hades	27	♈	50
Zeus	22	♌	48
Kronos	22	♉	57
Apollon	18	♍	09rx
Admetos	20	♈	34
Vulkanus	22	♊	23
Poseidon	08	♎	57rx

page 43
Homicide
March 10, 1976
7:39 PM PST, Encino, CA

M	13	♋	59
A	12	♎	46
☉	20	♓	42
☽	13	♋	59
☿	02	♓	38
♀	25	♒	12
♂	26	♊	52
♃	26	♈	35
♄	26	♋	17
♅	06	♏	46rx
♆	13	♐	58
♇	10	♎	53rx
☊	14	♏	03
Cupido	00	♏	52rx
Hades	23	♉	34
Zeus	15	♍	12rx
Kronos	10	♊	24
Apollon	05	♎	53rx
Admetos	05	♉	15
Vulkanus	06	♋	38rx
Poseidon	22	♎	49

page 44 Gerda
July 16, 1904, 1:04am GMT
Heidemühle, Kr.
Rosenberg, Germany

M	26	♒	33
A	04	♋	27
☉	22	♋	57
☽	23	♍	03
☿	13	♌	58
♀	25	♋	13
♂	10	♋	11
♃	28	♈	15
♄	19	♍	28rx
♅	26	♐	56rx
♆	06	♋	19
♇	20	♊	27
☊	19	♍	58
Cupido	21	♋	27
Hades	12	♓	45rx
Zeus	17	♋	55
Kronos	22	♈	02
Apollon	20	♌	30
Admetos	24	♓	41rx
Vulkanus	28	♉	58
Poseidon	17	♍	09

page 45
A Composite Chart
for Egon and Gerda

M	07	♓	47
A	12	♋	13
☉	17	♊	30
☽	01	♍	12
☿	07	♊	42
♀	28	♊	19
♂	19	♉	11
♃	19	♉	11
♄	01	♓	06
♅	02	♑	38
♆	07	♋	14
♇	21	♊	08
☊	03	♍	24
Cupido	22	♋	00
Hades	13	♓	42
Zeus	18	♋	09
Kronos	22	♈	22
Apollon	20	♌	51
Admetos	25	♓	08
Vulkanus	29	♉	02
Poseidon	17	♍	35

page 47
Composite Chart
of Deadly Relationship
Encino, CA

M	07	♎	02
A	20	♐	29
☉	05	♉	43
☽	09	♒	38
☿	06	♉	25
♀	02	♊	03
♂	29	♊	33
♃	15	♑	29
♄	22	♌	38
♅	25	♊	56
♆	12	♎	08
♇	13	♌	25
☊	04	♉	49
Cupido	21	♍	23
Hades	26	♈	58
Zeus	22	♌	27
Kronos	21	♉	53
Apollon	17	♍	59
Admetos	20	♈	02
Vulkanus	21	♊	56
Poseidon	08	♎	52

page 49 Number 1
"Senseless Tragedy"
Accident, Sept. 10, 1982
9:55 PM EDT, Newtown, CT

M	02	♒	57
A	25	♉	21
☉	18	♍	01
☽	22	♊	43
☿	14	♎	19
♀	03	♍	56
♂	23	♏	57
♃	07	♏	50
♄	20	♎	44
♅	01	♐	02
♆	24	♐	17
♇	25	♎	22
☊	10	♋	55
Cupido	07	♏	50
Hades	02	♊	16rx
Zeus	20	♍	28
Kronos	16	♊	42
Apollon	09	♎	26
Admetos	10	♉	13rx
Vulkanus	11	♋	35
Poseidon	25	♎	09

page 51, Number. 1
Feb. 7, 1966,
Noon EST,
Danbury, CT

M	16	♒	26
A	11	♊	29
☉	18	♒	29
☽	17	♍	39
☿	19	♒	40
♀	29	♑	35rx
♂	06	♓	38
♃	23	♊	21rx
♄	21	♓	20
♅	18	♍	47
♆	22	♏	07
♇	17	♍	53rx
☊	01	♊	09
Cupido	17	♎	16rx
Hades	13	♉	14
Zeus	07	♍	31rx
Kronos	03	♊	22rx
Apollon	29	♍	54rx
Admetos	29	♈	10
Vulkanus	01	♋	19rx
Poseidon	18	♎	10

Page 51, Number 2
Noon PST,
Fullerton, CA

M	02	♈	07
A	16	♋	37
☉	01	♈	45
☽	08	♈	48
☿	29	♓	21rx
♀	16	♒	18
♂	10	♈	16
♃	23	♊	15
♄	21	♓	20
♅	6	♍	59rx
♆	21	♏	58rx
♇	16	♍	47rx
☊	26	♉	37
Cupido	16	♎	37rx
Hades	13	♉	42
Zeus	06	♍	53rx
Kronos	03	♊	31
Apollon	29	♍	24rx
Admetos	29	♈	36
Vulkanus	01	♋	11
Poseidon	17	♎	48

page 52 No. 3
Jan. 1, 1966
Noon EST
Bridgeport, CT

M........ 11 ♑ 41
A........ 21 ♈ 53
☉...... 10 ♑ 51
☽........ 29 ♈ 36
☿....... 21 ♐ 24
♀....... 13 ♒ 24
♂....... 07 ♒ 26
♃...... 24 ♊ 21rx
♄...... 12 ♓ 29
♅........19 ♍ 36rx
♆...... 21 ♏ 27
♇....... 18 ♍ 26rx
☊...... 04 ♊ 05
⚷...... 17 ♎ 19
⚳...... 13 ♉ 18rx
⚴...... 07 ♍ 55rx
⚵...... 03 ♊ 37rx
⚶...... 00 ♎ 06rx
⚸...... 29 ♈ 06rx
⚹...... 01 ♋ 41rx
⚺...... 18 ♎ 06rx
⚻......... 01 ♋ 44rx
⚼.........18 ♎ 26rx

page 52 No. 4
March 8, 1957, Noon EST
Bridgeport, CT

M........ 16 ♓ 25
A.........08 ♋ 43
☉....... 17 ♓ 26
☽........ 20 ♒ 02
☿....... 08 ♓ 40rx
♀........ 15 ♈ 43
♂....... 03 ♏ 12
♃...... 24 ♋ 41rx
♄...... 00 ♈ 35
♅........22 ♍ 36rx
♆...... 00 ♏ 13rx
♇.........18 ♍ 26rx
☊.........08 ♉ 13
⚷........18 ♎ 17rx
⚳........14 ♉ 18
⚴........ 07 ♍ 54rx
⚵.........14 ♊ 18
⚶........ 04 ♊ 07
⚸........00 ♎ 13rx
⚹.........00 ♉ 00

page 59
Maria
Nov. 18, 1940
8:01 AM CST
Princeton, IL

M........ 28 ♍ 05
A........ 09 ♐ 14
☉...... 26 ♏ 06
☽........ 05 ♋ 54
☿........ 12 ♏ 41rx
♀........ 20 ♎ 19
♂........28 ♎ 36
♃........ 08 ♉ 34rx
♄. ....10 ♉ 08rx
♅........ 24 ♉ 03rx
♆........ 27 ♍ 13
♇........ 04 ♌ 18rx
☊........ 08 ♎ 30
⚷........ 12 ♍ 43
⚳........ 18 ♈ 04rx
⚴........ 17 ♌ 56rx
⚵........ 16 ♉ 26rx
⚶........ 14 ♍ 22
⚸........ 14 ♈ 41rx
⚹........ 18 ♊ 25rx
⚺.........05 ♎ 52

Relocations
Chicago
M ....00 ♎ 04
A........ 10 ♐ 25

Arlingon, VA
M........ 11 ♎ 31
A........ 21 ♐ 12

Omaha, NE
M........ 20 ♍ 57
A........ 04 ♐ 02

San Francisco, CA
M........ 22 ♌ 57
A........ 14 ♏ 42

Central City,CO
M........ 10 ♍ 42
A........ 27 ♏ 16

Lakeland, FL
M........06 ♎ 16
A........ 23 ♐ 08

San Diego, CA
M........28 ♌ 24
A........ 20 ♏ 57

page 62 Molly
Dec. 20, 1969
2:59 AM CST, Omaha, NE

M........ 05 ♌ 13
A........ 29 ♎ 32
☉...... 28 ♐ 19
☽........ 20 ♉ 15rx
☿........ 16 ♑ 12
♀........ 19 ♐ 50
♂........ 03 ♓ 34
♃........ 00 ♏ 36
♄........ 02 ♉ 15rx
♅........ 08 ♎ 31
♆........ 29 ♏ 31
♇........ 27 ♍ 22
☊........ 15 ♓ 34
⚷........ 22 ♎ 39
⚳........ 17 ♉ 31
⚴........ 11 ♍ 13
⚵........ 06 ♊ 37
⚶........ 02 ♎ 35
⚸........ 01 ♉ 32
⚹........ 04 ♋ 03
⚺........ 20 ♎ 03

Relocated, Lakeland, FL
M........19 ♌ 09
A........ 15 ♏ 03

page 64 Maria's Solar Return Phoenix, AZ

M........ 06 ♏ 10
A........ 16 ♑ 38
☉...... 26 ♏ 06
☽........ 20 ♊ 40
☿...... 14 ♏ 21
♀........ 06 ♏ 01
♂........25 ♒ 04
♃........ 13 ♓ 09
♄........ 10 ♐ 20
♅........ 21 ♐ 01
♆........ 04 ♑ 08
♇........ 08 ♏ 02
☊........ 20 ♈ 25
⚷........ 15 ♏ 06
⚳........ 05 ♊ 32
⚴........24 ♍ 45
⚵........ 19 ♊ 08
⚶........12 ♎ 53
⚸........11 ♉ 52
⚹........ 13 ♋ 43
⚺........ 27 ♎ 55

Maria's 1986 Solar Return
Relocated to Tucson
M........ 07 ♏ 15
A........ 18 ♑ 30

and to Lakeland, FL
M........ 05 ♐ 51
A........ 24 ♒ 22

page 66 *The Stand*
June 13, 1985
2:37:16 AM EDT
37 N 54 117 W 01

M........ 17 ♑ 29
A........ 00 ♉ 11
☉...... 22 ♊ 19
☽........ 25 ♈ 47
☿........ 29 ♊ 25
♀........ 06 ♉ 34
♂........02 ♋ 38
♃........ 16 ♒ 51
♄........ 22 ♏ 50
♅........ 15 ♐ 43
♆........ 02 ♑ 31
♇........ 02 ♏ 09
☊........ 17 ♉ 50
⚷........ 11 ♏ 47
⚳........ 04 ♊ 19
⚴........ 21 ♍ 44
⚵........ 17 ♊ 49
⚶........ 10 ♎ 40
⚸........ 11 ♉ 50
⚹........ 12 ♋ 08
⚺........ 26 ♎ 20

Exact coordinates for this chart are a "best guess." since the location is in a fictional story...somewhere in the California desert.

page 68
The Virgin "Noel"
Oct. 13, 1987, 3:04 PM
ST, Rome, Italy
M........06 ♐ 55
A........ 18 ♒ 26
☉........19 ♎ 42
☽........ 06 ♋ 51
☿......... 12 ♏ 39
♀........ 03 ♏ 23
♂........03 ♎ 04
♃........25 ♈ 21rx
♄........ 16 ♐ 53
♅.........23 ♐ 27
♆........ 05 ♑ 25
♇........ 09 ♏ 06
☊........ 02 ♈ 13
⯠........ 15 ♏ 19
⯡........ 07 ♊ 10rx
⯢ .... 24 ♍ 59
⯣........ 20 ♊ 09rx
⯤........ 13 ♎ 00
⯥ ....12 ♉ 52rx
⯦ .... 14 ♋ 24
⯧....... 27 ♎ 57

page 70
World War III—Attack
Aug. 4, 1985, 0400 GDT
Devon, England
M........23 ♓ 14
A........ 21♋ 18
☉....... 11 ♌ 41
☽........ 20 ♓ 22
☿........ 23 ♌ 12rx
♀........ 01 ♋ 59
♂....... 06 ♌ 25
♃....... 12 ♒ 05rx
♄........ 21 ♏ 32
♅ ....14 ♐ 07rx
♆.........01 ♑ 14rx
♇........ 02 ♐ 04
☊........ 13 ♉ 42
⯠........ 11 ♏ 29
⯡....... 05 ♊ 10
⯢ .... 22 ♍ 11
⯣........ 18 ♊ 34
⯤.........10 ♎ 50
⯥ .... 12 ♉ 42
⯦ .... 12 ♋ 50
⯧....... 26 ♎ 18

page 70
Radio Announcement
Aug. 4, 1985,Noon GDT
Devon, England
M........22 ♋ 20
A........ 17 ♎ 09
☉...... 12 ♌ 00
☽........ 24 ♓ 30
☿.........23 ♌ 01rx
♀........ 02 ♋ 22
♂........06 ♌ 38
♃....... 12 ♒ 02rx
♄........ 21 ♏ 33
♅........14 ♐ 06rx
♆....... 01 ♑ 14rx
♇....... 02 ♏ 05
☊........ 13 ♉ 39
⯠........ 11 ♏ 29
⯡........05 ♊ 10
⯢ .... 22 ♍ 12
⯣........ 18 ♊ 34
⯤........ 10 ♎ 50
⯥....... 12 ♉ 39
⯦ ....12 ♋ 50
⯧....... 26 ♎ 18

page 70
Nuclear Attack
Aug. 20, 1985 11:29 AM
GDT
Birmingham, England
M........ 01 ♌ 52
A........ 23 ♎ 42
☉....... 27 ♌ 21
☽........ 20 ♎ 49
☿........ 13 ♌ 14rx
♀....... 20 ♋ 54
♂........16 ♌ 52
♃........10 ♒ 01rx
♄....... 22 ♏ 00
♅ ....13 ♐ 58rx
♆....... 00 ♑ 59rx
♇....... 02 ♏ 21
☊....... 12 ♉ 07
⯠....... 11 ♏ 36
⯡........ 05 ♊ 17
⯢ .... 22 ♍ 27
⯣....... 18 ♊ 42
⯤........ 11 ♎ 00
⯥....... 12 ♉ 05rx
⯦ .... 13 ♋ 01
⯧....... 26 ♎ 24

page 71
The Day After
TV Nuclear Attack
Nov. 20, 1983
8:12 PM CST
Kansas City, KS
M........27 ♓ 42
A........ 16 ♋ 10
☉........ 28 ♏11
☽....... 05 ♊ 20
☿........ 10 ♐ 17
♀........ 12 ♎ 26
♂........01 ♎ 34
♃........16 ♐ 41
♄........ 09 ♏43
♅........ 08 ♐ 41
♆....... 27 ♐ 51
♇....... 00 ♏35
☊........ 15 ♊ 55
⯠........ 10 ♏58
⯡........ 02 ♊ 28rx
⯢ .... 22 ♍ 20
⯣.........16 ♊ 56rx
⯤........ 11 ♎ 04
⯥........ 10 ♉ 03rx
⯦ .... 12 ♋ 03rx
⯧....... 26 ♎ 32

The Day After nuclear attack relocated:

Lawrence, KS
M........ 27 ♓ 02
A........ 15 ♋ 34
Washington, DC 48
M........ 16 ♈ 00
A........ 00 ♌ 25
Moscow
M........ 07 ♌ 41
A........ 26 ♎ 36

page 75 Grandpa
Planetary Positions for
August 9, 1905 at Noon
M....... 16 ♌ 12
A....... 06 ♐ 43
☉........12 ♍ 05
☽........ 03 ♍ 28
☿........ 23 ♍ 30
♀........ 03 ♋ 28
♂........23 ♏ 30
♃....... 03 ♊ 03
♄...... 00 ♓ 33rx
♅........00 ♑ 38rx
♆........ 09 ♋ 17
♇........ 22 ♊ 23
☊ ....00 ♍ 18rx
⯠........23 ♋ 25rx
⯡........ 13 ♓ 29rx
⯢....... 19 ♋ 06rx
⯣ .... 29 ♈ 40
⯤........ 22 ♈ 43rx
⯥........ 21 ♌ 28
⯦........ 25 ♓ 06rx
⯧ .... 29 ♉ 40
⯨....... 17 ♍ 52

page 79
Grandpa's Death
Dec. 26, 1969 7:00 AM
CST Blue Island, IL
M........ 23 ♎ 57
A........ 29 ♐ 31
☉....... 04 ♑ 36
☽........ 05 ♌ 15
☿........ 24 ♑ 12
♀....... 27 ♐ 35

Grandpa's Death cont
♂........08 ♓ 10
♃........01 ♏ 33
♄........ 02 ♉ 07rx
♅ ....08 ♎ 08
♆....... 29 ♏ 43
♇....... 27 ♍ 23
☊....... 14 ♓ 14
⯡........22 ♎ 44
⯢........ 17 ♉ 28rx
⯣ .... 11 ♍ 11rx
⯤........ 06 ♊ 31rx
⯥........ 02 ♎ 36
⯦........ 01 ♉ 29rx
⯧ .... 03 ♋ 58rx
⯨....... 20 ♎ 07

page 80 Betsy
Planetary at noon for
Nov. 21, 1972
☉....... 29 ♏ 17
☽....... 06 ♐ 58
☿....... 09 ♐ 46rx
♀........ 26 ♎ 14
♂........03 ♏ 41
♃........08 ♑ 50
♄.........18 ♊ 30
♅....... 21 ♎ 07
♆....... 04 ♐ 46
♇....... 03 ♎ 50
☊....... 17 ♑ 47rx
⯡........26 ♎ 09
⯢....... 21 ♉ 03
⯣ ....13 ♍ 34
⯤........ 09 ♎ 06rx
⯥.........04 ♊ 16
⯦....... 03 ♉ 03rx
⯧ .... 06 ♋ 00rx
⯨......... 21 ♎ 16

page 81
Edgar Cayce
March 18, 1877
3:06 PM CST
Hopkinsville, KY

Cayce Natal Chart
M..........18 ♉ 49
A...........23 ♌ 49
☉..........28 ♓ 24
☽.......... 12 ♉ 21
☿...........11 ♓ 43
♀............5 ♓ 44
♂..........11 ♑ 14
♃..........02 ♑ 03
♄.........12 ♓ 49
♅ .... 21 ♌ 16rx
♆...........03 ♉ 39
♇...........22 ♉ 56
☊..........10 ♓ 31
⯡..........12 ♊ 30
⯢.......... 14 ♒ 56
⯣ .... 24 ♊ 58
⯤..........01 ♈ 58
⯥..........03 ♌ 08rx
⯦...........08 ♓ 17
⯧ ....12 ♉ 58
⯨...........04 ♍ 13rx

Page 83 Cayce Chart
"Regressed"
to November 4, 1742
M........ 02 ♑ 04*
A........ 03 ♈ 38
☉....... 12 ♏ 24
☽........ 15 ♊ 38
☿........ 25 ♎ 41
♀........ 00 ♎ 26
♂........13 ♎ 51
♃........06 ♐ 12
♄........ 01 ♓ 23
♅ .... 24 ♌ 26
♆....... 03 ♉ 39
♇....... 23 ♉ 48
☊....... 18 ♓ 25
⯡........ 14 ♊ 03rx
⯢........ 12 ♒ 40
⯣ .... 26 ♊ 17
⯤........ 01 ♈ 11rx
⯥........ 04 ♌ 23rx
⯦....... 07 ♓ 05rx
⯧ .... 13 ♉ 18rx
⯨....... 04 ♍ 58

page 84
John Bainbridge
November 4, 1742
Noon GMT positions
☉....... 11 ♏ 56
☽.........28 ♑ 41
☿.........04 ♐ 43
♀....... .24 ♎ 00
♂........18 ♌ 30
♃.........09 ♍ 44
♄.........04 ♍ 06
♅ ....19 ♑ 34
♆....... 13 ♋ 58rx
♇....... .13 ♏ 51
☊....... .28 ♉ 07
⯡.........08 ♐ 24
⯢........ 28 ♍ 36
⯣ .... 07 ♓ 18rx
⯤........ 27 ♐ 24
⯥........ 09 ♉ 49rx
⯦........ 19 ♐ 49
⯧........ 29 ♒ 49rx
⯨....... 29 ♊ 57rx

page 85 Colin
June 15, 1940
11:22 PM EST
EST Binghamton, NY
M........ 15 ♐ 09
A........ 01 ♓ 58
☉....... 24 ♐ 52
☽....... 05 ♏ 48
☿....... 18 ♋ 19
♀....... 11 ♋ 01rx
♂....... 19 ♋ 00
♃........06 ♉ 37
♄....... 10 ♉ 39
♅ .... 23 ♉ 55
♆....... 22 ♍ 46
♇....... 01 ♌ 26
☊....... 17 ♎ 49
⯡.........09 ♍ 27
⯢........ 19 ♈ 22
⯣ .... 15 ♌ 52
⯤....... 16 ♉ 49
⯥........ 12 ♍ 31
⯦....... 15 ♊ 41
⯧ ....18 ♊ 00
⯨....... 04 ♎ 49rx

About the chart data . . .

The data source for **Sir Arthur, and for the charts of the couple in the Deadly Relationship,** was Lois Rodden's *American Book of Charts*. Sir Arthur's data is also given in the database of the Astrological Association of Great Britain.

President Kennedy's birth information was published in the *AFA Bulletin*.

Lee Harvey Oswald's chart has been in my files for many years. I got it from a publication but I can't remember which one, and was not able to track it down.

Charles Emerson gave me the chart for **Cayce**.

Egon's and Gerda's charts are expertly rectified by Egon, and verified again and again by my class. They work perfectly.

The chart of the **accident** and the birthdays of **the four boys who died** in it are based on data published in the ***Danbury News Times***, Danbury, CT.

My chart, and the charts of my daughters, Shannon and Molly, are from birth certificate times.

The charts from ***Novel Predictions*** are based on data published in the referenced books.

The chart for ***The Day After*** is for the moment the bomb "hit" on the night of the first TV presentation.

Grandpa's, *Betsy's* and *Colin's data* are from personal friends. Grandpa's death and Colin's birth data are recorded times.

Alphabetical Listing of Planetary Pictures

Because there is no translation of the German *Lexikon* currently in print, and because alphabetical listings are so useful when you are trying to remember just what formula it was that had a particular meaning, I have compiled the following list. All of the formulas used in *Dial Detective* are included, alphabetically listed according to delineation. Many configurations will appear after more than one delineation. That is, of course, because it has more than one meaning and was probably used more than one way in different places within the text.

Delineations used in the text are given in the same wording as they were used in the text. They are a composite of delineations given in *CSI* and in *Rules*, along with some that I remember from classes or lectures, and some that are derived from the old trial and error method–combining logical factors to see if they work. Of course there are lots of other combinations that will mean just about the same thing in some cases, and many of the formulas given here have alternative meanings.

Use them in combination with the books that offer interpretative meanings for them. Obtain if you can, a copy of each of these books: **Combination of Stellar Influences by Reinhold Ebertin, Rules for Planetary Pictures** by Hans Niggeman and **Midpoints: Unleashing the Power of Your Planets** by Michael Munkasey. Use the books, but also exercise your own judgement.

I have also included a number of additional planetary pictures that were not used in the case studies in this book. Some were chosen because they apply to specific major life events that happen to most people sometime or other, and because they are combinations that I have found particularly useful in chart rectification. Others are included as more or less random choices– formulas that my classes have used in investigation of various mundane event charts, formulas that I found to indicate abilities or professions in individual charts that I've studied, etc.

Two part configurations are shown in midpoint format, such as ☉/☽. (Or, I could just as well have given the sum ☉+☽). Three and four part planetary pictures are given in the traditional format, such as ☉+☽-♃, or ☉+☽-♃=♈. It is important to understand that most any combination of the given factors could also have a similar interpretation. For example, ♃ might be on the midpoint of ☉ and ☽ (☉+☽= ♃), or ☉, ☽ and ♃ might all be involved in the same hard aspect configuration, such as ☽ □ ♃ and ⊡ ☉.

The delineations given include a number of events that are violent, or unpleasant, to say the least. Many of the book delineations were written in wartime Germany, so do not apply to the average current lifetime. No planet or configuration has only one meaning, and none of them are always negative or destructive. In many cases the time that a particular configuration forms in a chart will reflect quite different events, perhaps milder or even positive, instead of what you've found in this appendix...or there may be no physical event at all. Instead the configuration will reflect only inner psychological dynamics. Thoughts and emotions may exist, but no actual event will manifest.

For example, I have observed cases where the charts involved very strongly suggested divorce—all of the formulas were present, but the couple weathered through the period of challenging transits and directions and stayed together. Later, at time when their charts could have been read as a new romance, they had found renewed happiness in their relationship.

As a more personal example, take the miscarriage formula of ☉+☽-♃. During the 4th month of my third pregnancy I had a threatened miscarriage, and sure enough, that formula was in solar arc and transiting contact with a personal point in my chart. So, I was careful. I took three weeks off work and stayed in bed, like the doctor ordered. (I admit that it helped that I knew I had active birth configurations for the time the baby was expected.) The symptoms, the direction and the transit passed and I gave birth to a beautiful and healthy baby girl. Miscarriage was in my chart and thoughts during that fourth month, but it didn't happen. Did my positive mental attitude make a difference? I think it is more than likely that it did.

So, remember that you can't always tell. These planetary pictures will work just as expected when you study charts of known events. But be careful when you apply them to yourself or to other people, especially when speculating on the future. Be sure to look at the second list that follows this one—Appendix III, "Grim" Planetary Pictures Changed to "Good"—or at least "Better!" There I have listed in zodiacal sequence all of the formulas that are given grim or specific event-oriented delineations in Appendix II. The interpretations that given them in Appendix III suggest alternative ways that they could be interpreted that are reflective of inner dynamics, or of the personal choices that we can make so as to manifest the energies of the planets in a positive manner.

A

ability in magic, secret science Hades + Poseidon - Kronos
mental ☿ + Kronos - M
the own ability M/Cupido, M/Kronos
abortion, miscarriage ♂ + ♃ - Hades, ♂ + ♃ - ♆
accident ♂/♅, ☉/♅ ♂ + ♅ - ☉, ♂ + ♅ - ☽
airplane ♆ + Kronos - ♂
  automobile ♂ + Hades - Cupido
activity, mighty ♂/Vulkanus
anxiety, anguish ♄/Cupido, ☽/Hades
arrested, to be ♂ + Kronos - A, ☊ + Kronos - ♂
art creation Apollon/Cupido
artist, known as ☉ + Poseidon - Apollon, Apollon + Kronos - Poseidon,
  Apollon + Poseidon - ♈, Apollon + Poseidon - ☉, ☉ + Apollon - Poseidon
  outstanding Apollon + Vulkanus - M
  success in ♃/Apollon, ☉ + Poseidon - ♃, ♀ + ♅ - Vulkanus
artistic taste M/Apollon
assassination ♅ + ♆ - Hades = ♄
associations, undermining ☉ + ☽ - ♆,
  ☊ + ♅ - ♆
astrologer ♆ + Kronos - Admetos = ♄, Kronos + ♅ - M, M + Poseidon - ♅, ☿ + ♅ - M, ♅ + Poseidon - M, ♅ + Poseidon - ♂
  success as ♃ + Poseidon - ♅, ♅ + Poseidon - Vulkanus
atomic energy Cupido + Vulkanus - ♅
author ☉ + ♆ - ☿, ☿ + ♆ - ☉
success as ☉ + Poseidon - ☿
authorities, connections with ☊/Poseidon
authority, to be an Kronos + Poseidon - M
  for few in small circle Kronos + Poseidon - Admetos
authority figure ☉/Kronos, ☽/Kronos
awake ☽/♅

B

birth ♀/♅, ♂/♃
  of a boy ♂ + ♃ - ♂, ☉ + ☽ - ♃ = ♂,
  ♂ + ♃ - A = ☉
of a girl M + ♅ - ♀ = Cupido, ☉ + ☽ - ♃ = ♀,
  ♂ + ♃ - ☽
body on the earth ♈/☉
body, structural weak point of ♄/♆
boss ☉/Kronos, ☉ + Kronos - ☽
  to get a new one ♇ + Admetos - Kronos
bride ☽/♃
bridegroom ☉/Apollon

business
  agreement A + Poseidon - ☿
  difficult beginning of Apollon + Cupido - Admetos
  failures in Hades + Vulkanus - Poseidon, ♂ + Poseidon - ♆
  founder of Apollon + Cupido - M
  success in daily ☉ + ♃ - ♈
  happy, success in Kronos + Poseidon - ♃

C

change
  fortunate and happy ☿ + ♃ - ♇
  of residence ♃/♄, ♈ + ♇ - A,
  ♈ + A - ♇
  in substance ♆/Admetos
cheated ♂ + Hades - ♆
chemical science ♆/Poseidon, ♆ + Hades - Poseidon
children
  blessed with ♃ + Apollon - Cupido, ☉ + Apollon - Cupido
  urge for ☉ + ♂ - ♀
to be without ☉ + ☽ - Cupido = ♄
church, head of ☽ + Kronos - ♓, Kronos + ♓ - ☽
clairvoyance ♅ + ♆ - Kronos, ♅ + ♆ - ♀
commercial success ♂ + Poseidon - Vulkanus ♂ + Vulkanus - Poseidon
community minded M/Apollon
connections with scientific celebrities ☊ + Kronos - Poseidon
connections through death, mourning ˆ + ˙ - ¡
contemplation, inner ☽/Admetos
corporation, founder of Apollon + Cupido - M
corporation, difficult beginning of Apollon + Cupido - Admetos
corruption ☊ + Kronos - Hades, ♆ + Poseidon - ♈, Poseidon + Vulkanus - ♆
corruption, in goverment ♅ + Kronos - Hades
creative activity, success in ♃/Cupido
creativity, successful ♂ + Cupido - ♃
crisis ♅/♆
crowded ☽/Admetos

D

damage through error ♆/Hades
danger, great Hades/Vulkanus
danger, to avert Hades + Vulkanus - ♃
day and hour ☉/☽
day and hour in this place ☉ + ☽ - A
death ♅/♆, ♂ + ♄ - M, ♅ + ♆ - ☊
automobile accident ♂ + Hades - Cupido

- death, accident, continued
  - connections through ☊ + ⯤ - ♈
  - drowning ♆ + ⯠ - A, ♆ + ⯠ - ♂/♄, ♆ + ⯠ - ☉
  - female ♂ + ♄ - ☽
  - hour of ☽/⯤
  - in the family ♂ + ♄ - A, ♂ + ♄ - ⯟
  - interests the public ♂ + ♄ - ☽
  - male ♂ + ♄ - ☉
  - of the father ☉ + ♄ - ♂, ♂/♄ + ⯢, ♂ + ♄ - ⯢, ♂/♄ = ⯢
  - of the mother ☽/⯤, ☽ + ⯤, ♈ + ⯤ - ☽, ☉ + ⯤ - ☽
  - one's own ♂ + ♄ - M
  - of the physical body ♂ + ♄ - ☉
  - quick— or escape from ♂ + ♄ - ♃
  - unusual, murder, through treachery ♂ + ⯠ - ♆, ♂ + ♄ - ⯠
- **deception**
  - in marriage/ associations ☉ + ☽ - ♆
  - by others ☿ + ♆ - A
  - of self ☿ + ♆ - M
- desired family increase ♀ + ♇ - ⯟
- destiny, fate ⯤/⯥, ⯤ + ⯥ - ♇
- diabetes ♄ + ♆ - ♀
- dignity ⯥/⯦, ⯥ + ⯦ - ♂
- diplomat ⯡ + f - ›
- director, of company or association ♈ + ⯢ - ☉, ♈ + ⯢ - ☽
- disappointment, mighty ♆/⯥
- discontent ☉ + ☽ - ♆
- divorce ♄/⯟, ☉ + ☽ - ♄, ☉ + ☽ - ♆, ♄/♇, ♄ + ♇ - ⯟, ♄ + ⯟ - ♇, ♂ + ♄ - ⯟
- drowning ♆ + ⯠ - A, ♆ + ⯠ - ♂/♄, ♆ + ⯠ - ☉
- dying populace ☽/⯤
- dynamo, dynamic ♅/⯡

E

- earthquake ♅/⯤, ♅ + ⯤ - ☉, ♈ + ⯡ - ⯤, ♅ + ⯡ - ⯠, ♅ + ⯡ - ⯤
- economy, dying ♆ + ⯣ - ⯤
  - rise in ♃ + ⯢ - ⯣
  - sinking ⯠ + ⯤ - ♈
  - success in ♀ + ⯣ - ⯥
- education, educational methods ♄/⯣, ⯤/⯦
- educator, successful ☿ + ♇ - ♃, ♄ + ⯦ - ☉
- **elected** for office ☊ +⯡ - M, ♀ + ⯡- ⯢, ☊ + ⯡ -♃
  - to become President ☉ + ⯢, ☉ + ⯢ - ⯡
- electric energy ♅/⯥
- emergence of the "I" M/☉
- emotional ☉ + ♅ - ☽
- emotional upheaval ☉+ ♅ - M
- employee A/⯢
- **employment**, changes in A + ⯢ - ♇
  - to lose job A + ⯢- ♄
  - to quit job A + ⯢ - ♆
- enlightenment, flash of ♅/⯦
- error, damage through ♆/⯠
- eruption of volcano ♅ + ⯡ - ⯠, ⯡ + ⯤ - ⯥
- ethics, moral behavior ♂/⯦
- evidence ⯡/⯦
- excitable ☉ + ♅ - ☽
- exclusion of the public ☽/⯤
- experience, to gain great ⯢ + ⯣ - M
- explosion ♅/♇, ♅/⯥, ⯡ + ⯥ - ♅

F

- **failure**, of banks ♃ + ⯟ - ♆
  - in business ⯠ + ⯥ - ⯣
  - in speculation ♃ + ♆ - ♄, ♃ + ⯣ - ⯠
- faith, sower or pioneer of ♀ + ⯦ - ⯡
- famine ♄/⯠
- father ☉/⯢
- finance scandal ⯠ + ⯢ - ♃
- financial power ♃/⯥, ♃/⯢, ♈ + ♃ - ⯥
- fire, flames ♂/⯡
- fire, sudden ♅/⯡
- firearms ♂/⯡
- fugitive ♄/⯠
- future, science of the ♆/⯣
- future, to deduce scientifically, from study of past events ⯠ + ⯣ - ♆

G

- garbage ⯠/⯣
- generative ability ♀ + ⯡ - ☉
- God, one who is near to ⯢/⯦
- government ♈/⯢
- guard, on guard, guarded ♄/⯥

H

- happy ☉ + ♃ - M
- hate ⯠ + ⯡ - M
- heart attack ☉/♅, ☉ + ♅ - ⯤
- heathy ☉/♃, ♃ + ⯥ - ☉, ☉ + ♃ - ⯥

honors, esteem from many ⯛+ ⯜ - ⯙
hours of anguish ☽/⯖
hindrances in activity ♄/⯗
hindrances, mighty ♄/⯛
history, knowledge of ⯖/⯙
husband ☉/♂
husband, happy ☉ + ♃ - ♂
husband and wife ☉/☽

I

ideas, ideals ☿/⯜
illusions ☉ + ☽ - ♆
imagination ☿/♆, ☿ + ♆ - ☉ or ☽ or M
  in love ☿ + ♆ - ♀
  purposeful ☿ + ♆ - ♂
  rich powers of ☿ + ♆ - ♃
  pessimistic ☿ + ♆ - ♄
  inventive ☿ + ♆ - ♅
impulsive ☉ + ♅ - ☽
impressionable ♅ + ♆ - ☽
inheritance ♃ + ♅ - ♆, ♅ + ♆ - ♃
injury ♂/♅, ☉/♅, ♂ + ♅- ☉, ♂ + ♅ - ☽
  good luck in ♂ + ♅ - ♃
intuitive M/♆, ♅ +♆- ☽, M + ☿ - ♆
inventor ☉ + ☿ - ♅, ☿ + ♆ - ♅ = ☉
inventor, great M + ⯗ -⯘
investigator, researcher ⯗/⯙
investigator, successful ⯗ + ⯙ - ♃

L

land, separation from ☉ + ⯚ - ♄
landowner ♈ + A - ♄, ♃ + ♄ - ♈
  great, owns much land ♄/⯘, ♈ + ⯘ - ♄
lawsuit ☊ + ⯘ - A
lawyer ⯘ + ⯙ - ☽
leader M + ⯗- ♂, ♈ + ⯗ - ☉
leader, spiritual ☉/⯜ , ☽/⯜
lies ☿ + ♆ - M
lightning bolt ♅/⯗
location, change of ♃/♄, ♈ + ♇ - A,
  ♈ + A - ♇
loss through misdeeds ☉ + ♅ - ⯖
love, end of or very deep ♀/⯚
love, exciting, adventurous ♀ + ♂ - ♂ or M
love, happy ♃ + A - ♀, ☿ + ♇ - ♃
love, intense expression of ☉ + ♂ - ♀
love, mighty, passionate ♀/⯛
love, spiritual or platonic ♀/⯜
love, sudden emergence of ♀ + ♅ - ☿
luck M +♃ - ♅, ☉ + ♃ - M
luck, mighty ♃/⯛
luck, sudden ♃/♅, ♂ + ♅ - ♃
lucky manager ♃/⯘

M

machines ♂/⯗
machines, problems with ♄/⯗, ♄ + ⯗ - A,
  ♂ + ⯗ - ♄
magic ⯖/⯙
magic, success in ⯖ + ⯙ - ⯛
magician M + ⯕ - ♆ = ⯛
magnetism ☉/♀, ♈ + ⯛ - ♀
man, active ☉/♂
manager, success or luck as ♃/⯘
many on this day ♈/☉
man and woman ☉/☽
marriage ☉/☽, ☉ + ☽ - ♂, ☉ + ☽ - ⯕,
  ♀ + ♂ - ☽
marriage, happy ♃/⯕, ☉ + ☽ - ♃, ☉ + ☽ - ♀
marriage, legal ⯕/⯘, ☉ + ☽ - ⯕ + ⯘,
  ☉ + ☽ - ⯘ = A, M + A - ⯕ = ⯘,
  M + A - ⯘ = ⯕, M + ♈ - ⯕ = ⯘,
  M + ♈ - ⯘ = ⯕,
  ⯕ + ⯘ - M = any personal point
marriage, separation of (see divorce)
mathematically gifted ♅/⯜
media ♅/ʃ
medium (as in channeling) ☽/⯜, ♅ + ♆ - ☉ or
  ☽, ☉ + ♆ - ⯘
mental activity, influence ⯛/⯜
merchant ☿ + ♃ - ♂ = M, ☉ + ⯗ - ⯙
Meridian of the Day M-d + ☉-t - ☉-n
metaphysics ♅ + ♆ - ♈, ♆/⯜
military leader ⯗/⯘
miscarriage, abortion ♂ + ♃ - ♆ or ⯖
misery ⯖/⯙
missionary ♀ + ⯜ - ⯗
money, lack of it ♃/⯖, ♃/♆
money, lots of ♃/⯙, ♃/⯛
moment in connection with the world M/♈
moment in the place M/A
motherhood♀ + ♂ - ☽, ♀ + ♇ - ☽
moving (change of residence) ♃/♄,
  ♈ + ♇ - A, ♈ + A - ♇

mourning, connections through ☊ + ⯚ - ♈
murder ♅/⯖
danger of ♂ + ⯖ - A, ♅ + ⯚ - A
of a woman ♂ + ⯖ - ☽
ordered/instigated by government/ authorities ⯖ + ⯘ - ♅, ♂ + ⯖ - ⯘
to experience ♅ + ⯚ - M
participant in ☉ + ♅ - ⯖
quick death through ♂ + ⯖ - ♃
musician, known as ☉ + ⯙ - ♀
mystic, mysticism ☿ + ☿ - ♆ = ♅

N

narcotics ♆/⯚, ☉ + ♆ - ⯖
negativity ☽ + ♂ - ♆
nervous ☉/♅, ♅ + ♆ - M, M + ☉ - ♅
news ☊ + ☿ - ♈
news, sudden ☿/♅
nun ☽ + ♆ - ♀

O

oath ☿ + ⯘ - ♃
occult ⯖/⯙, ♅/♆, ♆/⯜
optimism ☽ + ♃ - ☉
orator, success as ☉ + ⯙ - ☿
orator, resourceful, quick ☿ + ♃ - ♅
organization, talent for ⯕ + ⯛ - M
owner (see land)

P

painter ⯕ + ⯘ - ♆, ☿ + ♀ - ☽ = ♆
great ⯕ + ⯘ - ♆ = ☽
passion ♀/⯛
pastor, priest ☽ + ⯘ - ⯜, ♀ + ⯜ - ☉
peace ♃ + ⯕ - ⯙
perseverance ♄/⯗
pessimist M + ☉ - ♄, ☿ + ⯚ - M
physician ☉ + ⯖ - A
good ☉ + ♃ - ☿
plot dirty tricks ☿ + ♆ - ⯖
police ♂/⯘
politics ⯘/⯛
poison ♆/⯚
poverty ⯖/⯙

pregnancy ♀/⯗, ♀ + ⯗ - ☽
end of ♂ + ♃ - ♄
president ☉/⯘, ☉ + ⯘ - ⯗
pride ⯛/⯜
prison ♄/⯖, ♄/⯛
production jumps sky high ♅ + ⯗ - ♇
prosperity ♃ + ⯕ - ⯙
procreation ♀/⯗, ♂/⯗
blissful ☽ + ♃ - ♅
propaganda ♅/⯜
psychology ♆/⯜
public, first times event in ♇ + ⯙ - ☽
public, happy relationship to ♃ + ⯕ - ♈

R

rash ☉ + ♅ - ☽
religion, sower or pioneer of ♀ + ⯜ - ⯗
residence, change of ♃/♄, ♈ + ♇ - A, ♈ + A - ♇
respect from many ⯛ + ⯜ - ⯙
restless ☉ + ♅ - M
retire, to retire ☉ + ♄ - ⯘, ☿ + ♄ - ⯘
revelation ⯘/⯜
revolution ♅/♆
rheumatism ☉ + ♄ - M or ♈
rough awakening from bliss ♃ + ♆ - ⯖

S

scientist, success or recognition as ⯕ + ⯙ - ☉, M + ⯙ - ☉
self-confidence, self-esteem ⯛/⯜
separation (marriage, relationship, association) ♄/⯕, ☉ + ☽ - ♆
exciting or upsetting separation for women ♅ + ⯚ - ☽
of females ♂ + ♄ - ☽
of many ♄/⯙
sex ♀/♂, ♀/⯗, ♂/⯗, ♀ + ♂ - M or ♈ or ☉ or ☽ or A
illicit, misfortune from intimate relationship ♀ + ♂ - ⯖
sickness ♄/⯖
of females ♂ + ♄ - ☽
singing artist ☿ + ⯕ - ⯘ = ♀
spiritual perception ☿/⯜, M/⯜
speaker, success as ☉ + ⯙ - ☿,

speaker continued
- resourceful, quick ☿ + ♃ - ♅
- ability to influence through ☿ ☌ ♇

speculation, speculator ♃/♆, ♃ + ♆ - M or A or ☉ or ☽ or ♈ or ☊

stamina, lacking in ♅ + ♆ - M

sterility ♀ + Zeus - ♆, ♆/Zeus

stockmarket
- going up ♂/Apollon, ♂ + Apollon - ♈, Kronos + Apollon - ♅
- going down ♂/Admetos, ♂ + Admetos - ♈

stoic ☽/Admetos

structural weak point of body ♄/♆

student A + Apollon - Kronos

success ☉/♃, ♂/♃, ♃ + ♇ - M or A or ☉ or ☽ or ♈ or ☊
- as author or orator ☉ + Apollon - ☿
- brilliant ♂ + ♃ - ♇
- in art or associations ♃/Cupido
- in commerce or science ♂ + Apollon - Vulkanus, ♂ + Vulkanus - Apollon
- in connections ☊/♃
- in management ♃/Kronos
- in surgery: any surgery formula contacts ♃
- in work, activity ☉ + ♃ - ♂, M/A = ♂/♃
- sudden ♃ + M - ♅

sudden event ♃ + M - ♅

surgery ♂/♅, ♂ + ♅ -☉, ♂ + ♅ - ☽, ♂ + ♅ - ☿
- skill of doctor in ♂ + ♅ - ☿
- successful: any surgery formula that contacts ♃

T

teacher ♄/Apollon

technician ☉ + ☿ - ♅, ♂ + Apollon - Zeus

television ♆ + Poseidon - A = M

tension ☽/♅

test cases ♇ + Apollon - ☽

thinking, connections in ☊/☿
- creative, stimulating ☿ + ♃ - ♅
- exchange of thoughts with many ☊ + ☿ - ♈
- general ♈/☿
- limited or profound ☿/Admetos
- powerful and/or influential ☿ + Poseidon - Vulkanus
- spiritual ☿/Poseidon

torment ☉ + ☽ - ♆

U

unconscious ♅/♆, ♅ + ♆ - M

unemployment ♈ + ☉ - Hades, ♂ + Hades - Admetos

upset ☉ + ☽ - ♆

upset in relationship, marriage ☉ + ☽ - ♅

V

vacation ♂ + ♄ - ♃, ☿ + ♄ - ♃

verdict A + Kronos - ☿, ☊ + Kronos - Zeus

vocalist (see singing artist)

volcano erruption ♅ + Zeus - Hades, Zeus + Admetos - Vulkanus

vulgar, evil acts of others ♂ + Hades - A

W

war ♅/Zeus, ♅ + Zeus - Kronos, Zeus + Kronos - ♅

weak point of body ♄/♆

wealthy ☉ + ♃ - M

widow ☽/♄, ☽/Hades, ♈ + ☽ - ♄, ☽ + ♄ - ☉, ☽ + Hades - ♆, ☽ + Cupido - ♄, ☊ + ♄ - ☽
- with children ☽ + ♀ - ♄

widower ☉ + ♄ - ♂, ♀ + ♄ - ☉

wife ☽ + ♃ - ☉
- happy with husband ☽ + ♃ - ☉

will ♅/Zeus

wisdom, one who is wise Kronos/Poseidon

wise man for many, widely spread culture Kronos + Poseidon - Apollon

woman
- active ☽/♂
- deceived or deceptive ☿ + ♆ - ☽

worry ☽ + ♂ - ♆

work, in the world ♈/♂
- obstacles or restrictions in ♂/Admetos, ♄/Zeus
- the professional activity of the native M + A - ♂
- professional activities are known to the public M + A - ♂ = ♈

writing, ability to influence through ☿ ☌ ♇ (see also author)

No configuration has only one possible meaning. I will leave it to you to think of alternatives for the "good" planetary pictures that were presented in the text. Look them up in Rules for added ideas, or make up your own by combining the meanings for each factor.

For the "grim" ones, however, the list below will help you look at possible alternatives. Some of these have alternative meanings in CSI or Rules, but some are given no "good" meanings at all. For example, CSI and Rules are very hard on ♆. But ♆ can also mean art, music, poetry, spirituality, imagination. . . In my experience ♆ configurations that are given "grim" meanings in the books often work out quite differently and positively in the charts of people involved in the arts or in metaphysics.

Suppose you are doing the directions and transits for a person whose life is relatively satisfactory and productive. In the midst of configurations that reflect a generally "normal" time period, you find that directed is moving into the ♂/♅ midpoint. Are you going to speculate on the possibility of a treacherous murder? I hope not! Within that context such a delineation is extremely unlikely. So what else might it mean? Read on! Many of the delineations you'll find here are my own suggestions for how the key words for the individual factors might be combined to create more positive interpretations. I encourage you to add your own ideas and try them out. More importantly, observe! Observe what is active in charts and what is actually going on with the people.

Immediately after each planetary picture, in italics, is the "grim" delineation that caused its place on this list. On the lines that follow are alternative meanings.

M

M + ☉ means the "I"

M + ☉ - ♅ *nervous*
"I" am restless or excited

M + ☉ - ♅ *pessimist*
"I" am reserved, or "I" must make a difficult decision, or "I" work hard to be noticed.

♈

♈ + ☉ - ♇ *unemployment*
Rules also gives illness, deficiency and poverty for this one. ♈/☉ is the body, daily life, or persons in the public. ♇ can

be secrets. So, let's try secrets of the body, or secrets one keeps from the public– or perhaps, even, if we considered that the Sun, our vitality, shines, this configuration could be ancient artifacts, antiques–or secrets! (♇)–on display (☉) in public (♈).

♈ + ☽ - ♄ *widow*
an elderly woman, a separated woman, a woman who lives alone

♈ + ♃ - ♅ *earthquake*
a difficult problem is tackled

♈ + ☿ - ☽ *death of the mother*
to be present at a death, resistance in the public, concentration without emotional distraction

A

A + ♃ means officials; things that come to us from above, or the employee

A + ♃ - ♄ *to lose one's job*
a change in employment, the employee says "no" to the authority, employee is given added responsibility

A + ♃ - ♆ *to quit one's job*
disappointment or deception in employment, employment as a musician, or employment that requires much imagination or illusion

☉

☉ + ☽ - ♄ *divorce*
Rather than divorce I have seen cases where this configuration was active at the time of a marriage. Responsibility and structure (♄) came into what had before been live-in arrangements. Or, one might say that an individual, in body (☉) and soul (☽), is serious, reserved, or responsible (♄).

☉ + ☽ - ♅ *upset in relationship or marriage*
in body and soul a rebel, innovative, freedom-loving; a relationship or marriage in which freedom, originality, excitement are important

☉ + ☽ - ♆ *divorce*
in body and soul poetic, artistic, mystic; inner feelings of discontent, or illusion; a relationship or marriage in which illusion, the arts, or spiritual pursuits are important

☉ + ♄ - M or ♈ *rheumatism*
an older person, one who retires, or a day when one could catch a cold. Perhaps also: the effort (♄) one makes to be recognized ☉, M, ♈).

☉ + ♄ - ♂ death of the father
Through one's own actions one successfully overcomes a problem or hindrance.

☉/♅ heart attack
excitement, tension, sudden event, creative, inventive, freedom urges

☉ + ♅ - M emotional upheaval
a sudden event, excitement, "I" see new possibilities

☉ + ♅ - ⯡ participant in murder
energy, excitement, sudden event involving disagreeable tension, garbage (trivia), illness, antiques–or perhaps striving to attain freedom from want

☉ + ♅ - ⯥ heart attack
the excitement stops, an exciting or sudden event with disturbing consequences, excitement intensifies

☉ + ♆ - ⯡ narcotics
damage from water, susceptibility to illness, sensitivity in occult matters, ancient arts

☉ + ⯥ - ☽ death of the mother
deficiency in glands, emotional connection to the homeland, emotional persevance

☽

☽ + ♀ - ♄ widow with children
mother is ill, one is separated from mother, the loving woman takes on a responsibility

☽ + ♂ - ♆ negativity
irregular working time, giving up something, one who is works with music, poetry, dreams, mysticism

☽/♄ or ☽ + ♄ - ☉ widow
also means divorced woman, moody or depressed, hours one spends alone, evening hours, a person with strong self-control, or who is very conscientious

☽/⯡ or ☽ + ⯡ - ♆ widow
worries for the future, resignation, emotionally sensitive

☽/⯥ death of the mother, dying populace, hour of death
inner contemplation, a stoic character, narrowminded, a locked room, feeling crowded, emotional probing

☊

☊ + ♄ - ☽ widow
separated wife, emotional restraint in unions, emotionally attached to one who is older or more experienced, a resonsible caretaker

☊ + ⯣ - A lawsuit
employment contract, others have difficulty with authority, to be connected to leaders

☊ + ⯣ - A lawsuit
employment contact, others have difficulty with authority, to be connected with leaders

☊ + ⯣ - ♂ to be arrested
to take action to make contact with authorities, to work in connection with authorities, government, leadership team

☊ + ⯣ - ⯡ corruption
a connection with authorities on account of crime, garbagem dirt, secrecies, matters from the past, muck-raker

☊ + ⯥ - ♈ connections with others through death or mourning
a few people come together without freedom, or within a small exclusive circle, a member of a clique

☿

☿ + ♆ - M deception of self
"I" am gifted with intuition, imaginative. "I" may blend fiction and truth, poetic language

☿ + ♆- A deception by others
Others (in this place) are intuitive, imaginative. graceful

☿ + ♆- ♄ pessimistic
imagination is inhibited, or practical, responsible use of intuition. Rules suggests "collection mania."

☿ + ♆- ⯡ to plot dirty tricks
unclear thinking causes unpleasantness, misuse of psychic ability, intuitive thinking about illness or matters of antiquity

☿ + ♆ - M pessimist
to think about a matter thoroughly, to be serious, to be a realist

♀

♀ + ♂ - ⯡ illicit sex, misfortune through intimate relationships
This formula could also be interpreted as having to do with servant relationships. The "Illicit" (unmarried) sex no longer necessarily implies misfortune. Perhaps an unequal relationship could be reflected by this combination. Some level of unpleasantness is likely implied. According to *Rules* ♀/♂ applies to blood relatives, in addition to sex partners. "Intemperance" is given as an alternative meaning, and also delayed (⯡) attraction or sexual yearning.

♀ + ♄ - ☉ widower, loved ones who are transiently separated, a cautious love

♀ + ⯢ -♆ sterility, efforts of love in vain, lacking in ambition or desire,intuition or imagination used in devoted activity, artistic creativity, leadership in arts

♂

♂ + ♃ - ♆ abortion, miscarriage
a promise, understanding, intention that dissolves, a relationship or a happy activity that goes nowhere, the active pursuit of dreams, ideals, spirituality

♂ + ♃ - ⯡ abortion, miscarriage
a betrothal with difficulties, work where the results are mediocre or unsatisfactory, working with raw materials from the earth or with very old materials

♂/♄ is included in "death" formulas, but has many other possible meanings. Mars (action) has a conflicting energy with Saturn (stability), so can be interpreted as inhibited vitality or separation. Authority (♄) hinders action (♂), causing frustration. But ♂/♄ combinations also mean to overcome difficulties (♄), act responsibly (♄) act with endurance or stubborness, and be forceful in performance of duty.

♂ + ♄ - M one's own death
"I" am persistant, stubborn, must overcome a diffjculty, am able to bear my burdens with dignity, am energetic in my disciplined pursuit of accomplishment.

♂ + ♄ - ☉ death of a male
illness or separation of a male, weak vitality, the power of resistance to overcome illness or difficulties, concetrated energy to lead

♂ + ♄ - A death in the family
frustrations or inhibitions caused by one's reactions to others or to the environment, on persistently advances through learning to work with others in the environment

♂ + ♄ - ☽ death of a female, death of public interest
illness or separation of a female, a frustrated or inhibited mood, emotionally inhibited, persistent or stubborn, a need to balance freedom, dependency and control issues

♂ + ♄ - ⯠ death in the family, divorce
frustration, quarrel in a family or community, interruption of activities, a community is persistent in its activity, work within community sanctions

♂ + ♄ - ⯡ unusual death, murder
illness through overexertion, responsible action to alleviate waste, the "war on poverty" (I wonder if this would also work for an archeologist: persistent and disciplined (♄) work in old ruins (⯡)

♂ + ♄ - ⯣, ♂/♄ + ⯣ death of the father
death of a leader, quarrel with an authority figure or with the government, the concentrated energy of the leader

♂/♅ basic for accident and surgery configurations, but it can also be given such delineations as impulsiveness, sudden events, exciting actions, very energetic actions, unusual effort or the urge to be free. Accidents can happen when one lacks awareness of these energies or overdoes. It represents energies that need an outlet.

♂ + ♅ - ☉ accident, injury, surgery
a very energetic and vital person, a sudden action, a person who acts quickly or who must suddenly adjust to a new circumstance in life, inventive

♂ + ☿ - ☽ accident, injury, surgery
a very excited mood, the actions or enegies are motivated by emotions, an ambitious person

♂ + ♅ - ☿ surgery, the skill of the doctor in
sudden surprising news, an excited debate, an unusual or inventive work that is carefully thought out

♂ + ⯡ - A danger of murder
others cause problems or make mistakes that one has to set right, vulgarity in the environment, fatique or illness in the environment, others work with old or junk materials

♂ + ⯡ - ☽ murder of a woman
one whose actions are unpleasant, mean, vulgar; an emotional involvement in work with the poor, sick or oppressed, cutting the ties (umbilical cord) to mother

♂ + ⯡ - ♃ quick death through murder
Since fl in similar configurations means one is fortunate in accidents (♂/♅) I don't see why this one could not also be the escape from atrocity, damage, attack, or whatever else ⯡ might represent.

Or let's go back to our archeologist and speculate on fortunate accomplishments (♃) in working (♂) with ancient artifacts (⯡). Could also mean that one's faith or confidence (♃) is delayed (⯡).

♂ + ⯡ - ♆ unusual death through treachery
The mildest ***Rules*** delineation for this one is "cheated out of earnings." This ♂ section is becoming quite a challenge to re-interpret! How about: working (♂) with the sick (⯡) intuitively (♆)? Perhaps also, hidden actions.

♂ + ⯡ - ⯢ death in an automobile accident
Rules has that this also means "to be a soldier," and it can also refer to the "end of procreative ability."

♂ + ⯡ - ⯣ murder instigated by the government
mean acts by leaders or the government, the government influences work with the poor or sick

♂ + ⯡ - ⯥ unemployment
working conditions are difficult, catching cold, damages because of the cold, very intense work with the sick, active in projects to alleviate poverty

♂/⯢ fire, flames
creative activity, leadership, procreation, machines, technical sciences, the military

♂ + ⯢ - ♄ problems with machines
creative activity that is hindered, interrupted or performed with great discipline, forceful leader demands discipline

♂/⯦ stockmarket goes down
suppression, fear, crudeness, rocks, the specialist, special work, the work decreases, endurance

♂ + ⯥ - ♈ stockmarket goes down
mundane: a depression, terrorism; or personal: bankruptcy, one's field of activity is limited, or one is known to the world as a specialist in one's field

♂+ ⯥ -♆ failures in business
to explore unknown fields in science or business, a master in music, poetry, dance, mysticism, etc.

♃

♃ +♆- ♄ failure in speculation
to worry about money, the realization of carelessness, grandiose dreams need grounding

♃ + ⯠ -♆ failure of banks
a happy marriage or partnership that involves deception, illusions, or secrets, or where each encourages the others dreams

♃/⯡ lack of money
happiness in secret, luck with raw materials or antiques, idealizing poverty

♃ +⯥ - ⯡ failure in speculation
losses of money, wrong time to speculate, money through raw materials, old things, garbage, crime

♄

♄/♆ structural weak point of body
cautious, restrained, ascetic, habits, giving structure to dreams, disciplined work in music, poetry

♄ + ♆ - ♀ diabetes
disappointment in love, or artistic vision is given form, a balance between idealism and realism in love

♄/ ⯠ divorce
necessity, a slow separation, hard work, self-discipline

♄ +⯠- ⯠ divorce
adapting slowly, a necessary change in the family, a change in the family/community that takes form, art work that requires great self-discipline

♄/⯠ divorce
a separation in the family or in a partnership, family responsibilites, family discipline

♄ +⯠ -⯠ divorce
the start or the end of a separation of partners, a development or change within a family/community/marriage

♄/⯡ sickness, prison, fugitive
sadness, obstacles or problems, holding on to secrets, remaining in isolation, history, caution

♄/⯢ anxiety, anguish
perserverance, structured and disciplined creativity

♄ + ⯢ - A problems with machines
loss from a fire, others hinder activity, others persevere

♄/⯤ prison
supervision, on guard, vigilant, custody, preservation

♅

♅/♆ death, crisis, revolution, unconscious
transition into another world, the unconscious, mysticism, inner vision, psychic states, inspiration, idealism

♅ +♆ - M unconscious, nervous
not able to think or act clearly, in mourning or under anesthesia, growth in ability to meditate or enter altered states of consciousness, mysticism

♅+ ♆ - ☊ death
connections dissolved, shared grief, together with others of the same sensitive disposition

♅ + ♆ - ⯡ = ♄ assassination
Rules gives only "assassination" as interpretation. But the formula may "work" in a chart when no assassination takes place. For the first 3 factors the suggestion given is to see or not see through treachery, or one who deals with the dead professionally (mortician, pathologist).

Positive interpretations of Hades (antiquity, secrecy) with ♅/♆ could be mysticism. With Saturn, a meaning could be a disciplined study of past life regression, or a career that involves other-wordly matters.

♅/⯡ murder
disgust, sudden mean acts or damages, tension over secrecy, tension between innovation and old ways

♅/⯢ sudden fire, lightning bolt, war
the will, electric motors, dynamo, sudden leadership

♅ + ⯢ - ⯡ volcanic eruption, earthquake
forces that bring destruction, powers of nature, thunderstorms, sudden creation in secret

♅ + ⯢ - ⯣ war
a leading model in work, a master of creativity, the will of the leader or government

♅ + ⯢ - ⯦ earthquake
explosive materials or dangerous fuels, the explosion or other force is stopped, blocked, intense will-power

♅ + ⯣ - ⯡ corruption in government
crime, secrecies, illness, delays; strong tension, secrets sion, need to balance stability and risk

♅/⯥ earthquake
shock, something broken or torn, profound tension, need to balance stability and risk.

♅ + ⯥ - M to experience murder
to experience great commotion, profound change

♅ + ⯥ - ☽ murder of a woman
exciting, tense events in public, need to balance security and freedom or stability and change

♅/⯦ explosion
mighty tension, sudden force, thunderbolt, a great display of strength, electricity, outburst

Ψ

Ψ/⯡
begins the "drowning" formulas—associated with water or water catastrophes, but also damage through error, deception, decay, lack of air. If we are also to allow for positive interpretations of Ψ and ⯡, keyword combinations might be music from antiquity, or secret dreams.

Ψ+ ⯡- ☉ death by drowning
danger of infection, a voyage by sea

Ψ + ⯡- A death by drowning
others feel disappointed or deceived, others go to sea

Ψ - ⯡- ♂/♄ death by drowning
errors cause separation or frustration, endurance to overcome errors or damage

Ψ/⯢ sterility
wasted energy, creative imagination, liquid fuels, steam, without direction, spiritual or artistic leadership

Ψ + ⯤ -♈ corruption
the general (mass) uncertainty about the future, noted for "lots of" deception, escapism, daydreaming, music, dance, poetry, imagination, spirituality

Ψ + ⯤ - ⯥ the dying economy
economic problems in general, large scale illusion, deep interest in occult science or chemistry

Ψ/⯥ narcotics, poison
also alcohol or any substance abuse, decline, ice, cold air, one substance or condition changing to another, intense visualization

Ψ/⯦ mighty disappointment
deception, to resign, mighty sensitivity, power one cannot hear or see, mighty idealism, powerful dream

♇

♇ + ⯢ - ⯥ difficult beginning for a business
efforts are met with obstacles, creating art with primary or raw materials

⯡

⯡ + ⯢ - M to hate
to refuse or to be negative, idleness or compelled to be inactive, paralysis, a personal connection with industry (⯡/⯢ is related to industry or strikes)

⯡ + ⯣ - ♃ finance scandal
"to escape with a black eye" (get away with it), inflation

⯡ + ⯣ - ♅ murder ordered by government
an event where lives are lost, a sudden event involving police action,

⯡/⯤ garbage, misery, poverty
lacking in experience, knowledge of history, occult science, secret science, magic

⯡/⯦ great danger
capital crime, vice, raw force, (This one is really a challenge!) ⯦ is mighty, powerful, energy: a powerful secret, the energy that could be produced from garbage

⯡ + ⯦ -⯤ failures in business
success in history, occult sciences, magic

⯢

⯢ + ⯣ - ♅ war
to act suddenly, by surprise, large technical products

⯢ + ⯥ - ⯦ eruption of a volcano
the efforts are greatly concentrated toward one goal, forces long held back are suddenly released

⯢ + ⯦ - ♅ atomic energy, explosion
to suddenly become very busy, to apply force

⯤

© + ⯦ - · corruption
inflation, deterioration, contagious infection, a mighty success in music, poetry, art, mysticism

⯥

⯥/⯦ destiny, fate
compression, hardening, mighty hindrance, powerfully profound, primal energy

⯥ + ⯦ - ♇ destiny, fate
basic developmental changes grow out of life events that one did not initiate or over which one had no apparent control, an obsession

⯦

⯦ /M spiritual, emotional force, personal influence
⯦ + ⯧ -M self-assurance, pride, honor, dignity

⯧

⯧ + ⯧- M one's own spiritualization
⯧ + ⯧- ☿ thoughts, ideas, talks about mental or spiritual matters, to propose or present ideas.

It was never my intention to make this book a complete text on Uranian Astrology. For that I'd double–or more likely triple– it's size! There are many aspects of Uranian astrology that I don't regularly use. I've read about them, tried them out, but have not made them part of my "standard repertoire." The 90° dial techniques that I've shared with you in this book give me all the information that I need in most cases, and there's only so much time I'm willing to spend on any given chart. I am admittedly an "eclectic" astrologer, rather than an orthodox Uranian! But if I've sparked your interest in Uranian Astrology, I'm sure you'll want to expand your knowledge by attending lectures and classes on the subject whenever you get the opportunity.

There are a few techniques that I haven't covered in the **Dial Detective** case studies that are likely to be a part of even the introductory lectures by some of the best-known Uranian teachers. On these final two pages I'll briefly define them for you, so you'll be better prepared to get the most out of those lectures. First , a few alternative 90° dial techniques:

Color-keyed Dial

The alternating black and white bands that indicate each five degrees on the 90° dial offer the opportunity to color-key so that symmetry is more easily spotted. You might color the 5° white bands on either side of Aries red, the next white band in either direction (from 10° to 15° from Aries) blue, the next set of white bands green, and so on. I don't do this, but some people find that it really helps them more easily find factors that are equidistant on each side of the pointer.

Double Dial

Some people like to make a paper circle that is just a little larger than the laminated dial and mount it between the dial and the paper on which the chart is drawn. A duplicate chart is drawn on the paper circle. The circle can then be rotated according to a given solar arc. All factors, in that one motion, can then be seen in their directed positions in relation to the natal chart. Personally, I think this is unwieldy when I'm looking at a specific event, and would rather just pencil in the directions or transits, or mark the dial. For a quick scan of a whole lifetime, the double dial

technique is very valuable. You see multiple "hits" at once that you might not otherwise see. I've sometimes scanned a person's chart in this way and made some pretty accurate guesses about the nature of important times in their past.

Transparencies

Suppose you want to look at how the chart of a business compares to the charts of several individual employees. You could set up the business chart as a transparency. You can then put the transparent chart right down over each of the individual charts, mount your laminated dial on top, and presto! Instant contact chart! It's better yet if you've been able to do each chart in a different color—you could then overlay multiple charts and keep track of which is which. For computer charts printed in black, I sometimes go over the planets with color high-lighters, if I plan to use multiple charts on the dial.

It's handy to make a transparency of the current outer planet transits. Mark the positions at the beginning of the year, at the stations, and at the end of the year. Then whenever you're doing a chart you can very quickly overlay the transits. This is a real time saver. Think how often you won't have to look up the transits any more!

Half Solar Arc and Double Solar Arc

Even though I did not need to use half solar arc or double solar arc to demonstrate any of the points I wanted to make in this book, these arcs are quite commonly used by Uranian astrologers, and you're sure to hear about them in some of those lectures you'll attend.

The calculation is simple and obvious: if the solar arc is 30°, then half solar arc is 15° and double solar arc is 60°. Half solar arc would be at the midpoint between the directed factor and its own natal position. So, for example, suppose that half solar arc ♀ is on ♂. That means that ♀/♀ = ♂, or the midpoint of natal ♀ and directed ♀ =♂. (And **that**, as I'm sure you've guessed, is sexy!)

When double solar arc crosses over a factor, "regular" solar arc will be at the midpoint of the two natal factors. For example: double solar arc ♀ comes to ♂. "Regular" solar arc ♀ is at the midpoint ♀/♂.

In any case, if a half solar arc or a double solar arc factor comes to another factor it is considered a valid "hit." Personally, I don't use them very much. I usually find plenty without them, and I suppose it's part of my inclination to simplify, in spite of my admitted use of those eight hypothetical planets.

The 360° Dial

Some may criticize me for doing a book that introduces Uranian Astrology with the 90° dial alone, because the 360° dial is considered basic. Some Uranian teachers will say you should do the chart pretty thoroughly on the 360° before you even **look** at the 90° and if you have a tendency to become fascinated with little details before you have looked at the overall picture, they may be right. (But I **have** warned you about that.) I've found I prefer to look at the overall picture with a Koch chart, and then go to the 90° dial. But, if you want to do "pure" Uranian, the 360° dial is an important part of the system, and so you should be familiar with it.

The setup for the 360° dial is fairly obvious. You enter the planets in the proper sign and degree. The illustration below shows Shannon's chart (data on page 95). All the signs are marked on the dial, and the lines around the edge show each degree. The first thing likely to puzzle you is that the wheel seems upside down. Libra is in the usual place you expect to find Aries in a natural zodiac chart. Cancer is on top, rather than Capricorn. This format is called the "Horoscope of the Earth" in the Uranian tradition, and it forms the "Earth Houses" (I'll tell you about the houses later). One line of reasoning for this setup with Cancer at the top is that the Sun is in Capricorn at the time of the longest night, the nadir of the year, the ending and new beginning. The ancients considered Winter Solstice to be the "birth of the Sun" (which became the "birth of the Son" when the early Christians needed a suitable substitute for popular pagan solstice celebrations). From the time of Winter Solstice the Sun increases in light. In (apparent) daily motion, the Sun is at its darkest point at midnight, then it begins to rise, it culminates, sets and returns again to its House 4 midnight position.

360° Dial as an Aspectarian

The 360° dial makes a great aspectarian. All the major aspects are marked around the edge, in this case reading from the 0° Aries point. You can put the pointer on any factor and immediately see all the close aspects much more easily than you could on a traditionally drawn chart wheel. Notice that the Aries point (see the conjunction glyph on the arrow pointing to ¡) is conjunct M by 2°, Ï (sextile) ¤, 7 (septile) fl, ♂ (opposite) ♅, and so on. If you want to know the aspects to any factor you just point the "conjunction arrow" to it and there you are!

You can also see which are the direct midpoints and which are indirect. Direct midpoints are those where a factor aspects the midpoint by a either a conjunction or an opposition.

Then you can see which are the direct midpoints and which are indirect. Direct midpoints are those where a factor aspects the midpoint by a conjunction or opposition. Indirect midpoints are those where a factor aspects the midpoint by a square, semi-square or sesquiquadrate. Direct midpoints are said to be stronger. Find ♅ on the page 112 illustration (near ♎). Notice that it is on ♃/☋. That is a direct midpoint. Now notice that ♇ and ♄ form equal arcs looking upwards on the dial. ♅ = ♄/♇ is an indirect midpoint configuration, ♅ square ♄/♇.

Antiscia or Solstice Points

The 360° Dial also makes it easy to find antiscia. An antiscion (the singular of antiscia) is a point that is equidistant with a given planet from either of the solstice points, 0° Cancer or 0° Capricorn. If a planet is in the antiscion degree of another planet, natally or by progression, direction or transit, the two have a relationship that is of the nature of an aspect. Antiscia, then, are considered like sensitive points. Though I'm aware of them, I don't use them much. Largely, it is a matter of time–I don't have enough of it to look at everything—and again, a need to simplify. But if one of those Uranian lecturers starts talking about them, I want you to know what they are and how to find them!)

Look again at the illustration on page 112. (This should be **eas**y now that you know how to find the sensitive points for planetary pictures.) The Moon is at 0° Gemini. What is the antiscion? Look exactly the same distance in the other direction from the Cancer point. That would be 0° Leo, right? That is the antiscion of Moon for Shannon's chart This means that a planet that comes to 0° Leo (by direction, progression or transit) would, by contact with its antiscion, also contact her Moon. In this chart, Pluto and Saturn are each only one degree from being the exact antiscion of the other.

In looking at a broad overview, the 90° dial is like a magnifying glass. It can help you to see the details. But, as I have pointed out in a number of ways, there is a danger of getting hung up on details and missing the main issues. An advantage, then, of the 360° dial (if you don't clutter it up too much!) is that you clearly see the most important things—and all the aspects.

With a classic unequal house chart wheel, you have to look at the degree numbers and **think** to figure out the aspects. With the 360° dial you immediately see aspects, and which ones are "right on" and therefore the most significant. You also see the most important directions and midpoints.

Here is one example that I can cite for you:

Shannon was married toward the end of her senior year in college, when she was at the age of 21. In looking though, one day, at the things I had kept and written down when she was still just a small child, I saw that I had noted on a copy of her birth chart that she would likely marry at about the age of 21.

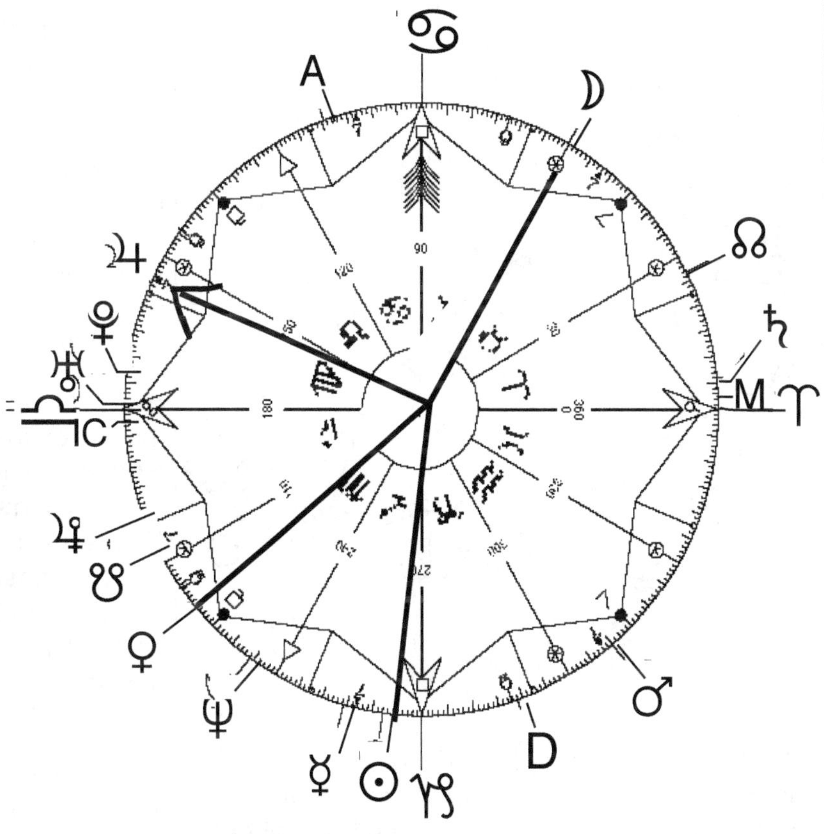

When might Shannon marry?
With the pointer on Moon I noticed the direct midpoint ☉/♀. ♀ would direct to ☽ in about 21°. This strongly suggested a love relationship. So, ☉/☽, I then reasoned, should surely be active if this is her possible time of marriage. So, I then turned the dial to the ☉/☽ midpoint....and there was Jupiter!

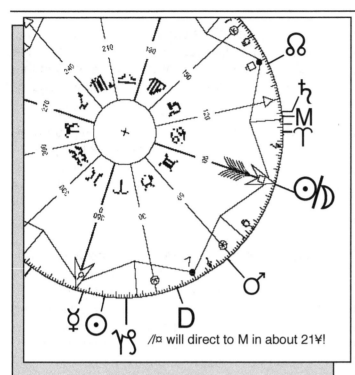

//¤ will direct to M in about 21⋎!

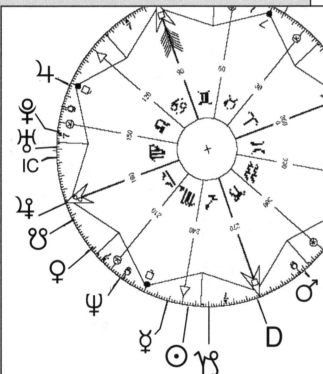

What's one more thing I could look at to confirm this idea? Of course! Cupido! (I hadn't looked at the Uranians until this point). ⯲ and ♀ are about 21° apart, too. And ♀ is 19° on the other side of ⯲... the start of the love relationship? About two years before? As it turned out, Shannon did indeed begin dating her husband-to-be two years before they married.

The illustration on page 113 plus the two at left show the step-by-step reasoning that, in this case, turned out to be right.

Each of the illustrations of Shannon's chart demonstrate very direct solar arc "hits." You see clearly, with the 360°, the things that are most important. It's not as easy to see the details, so you are less likely to clutter your mind with them before you've seen the larger picture.

The Uranian House Systems

The Uranian houses all relate to the personal points and there is a different set of houses for each one. You rotate the dial so that the proper house cusp is on its corresponding personal point and equal houses are then formed by the 30 degree dividing lines on the dial. You "read" the planets according to which house they fall in. Traditional house interpretations blend with the meaning of the personal point.

The **Earth Houses** (Libra on the left, Cancér at the top, as first illustrated on page 112) show the natives connection to the world in general. For example, in Shannon's chart one might say that she is known to speak her mind and to be a good communicator (☉ and ☿ in the 3rd), or that her work in the world (♂ in the 5th) might involve children. (She is currently very involved in raising two daughters, and she also teaches preschool part-time.) She is also known for creativity in all of her work activities.

Sun Houses are found by placing the 0° ♑ point of the dial on the Sun's position of the 360° chart. **Moon Houses** are found by placing the 0° ♋ point of the dial on the Moon's position of the 360° chart. For **Meridian Houses** you place the 0°♑ point on the Midheaven, and for **Ascendant Houses** the 0° ♎ point is placed on the Ascendant. For **Node Houses** place the 0° ♎ point on the Node. It is a complicated system, and I am not even going to attempt to explain it in much more detail here.

After numerous experiments I found these houses interesting, but was not totally convinced that a consideration of all their possible interpretations added enough to justify my time, when I can find out what I need to know more quickly in other ways. Ebertin dropped house interpretations completely when he formulated the Cosmobiology system, and it wouldn't surprise me if this very complex system of houses was not a good part of his motivation!

On the other hand, I will tell you one of my little experiments with Uranian houses. I did it primarily to demonstrate to my class that a good reading of a horoscope could be done without signs—that the relationship of planets to each other and to the angles was the most important. I gave them a chart of someone they knew personally, but I did not tell them whose chart it was and I gave them all **sidereal** positions (which means, of course, that everything was around 27° behind its position in the tropical zodiac). I allowed them to think that the chart was tropical, so of course they didn't recognize whose chart it was. They were asked to set up the chart on the 360° dial and read it according to Meridian houses. That means, as I said above, the cusp of the 10th house (0° Cancer) is pointed to M, and all other factors are interpreted according to their positions in the equal houses that are thus formed. The class members were allowed to consider house positions in relation to M, and aspects and midpoints to M, but no sign positions—don't even write them on the dial. (And, of course, since the positions were sidereal they weren't what they would have expected anyway—but every planet was still the same distance from the others as it would have been in a tropical chart.) With their 360° dials rotated to put 0° Cancer on M they did a strikingly accurate personality profile of the person, and were quite surprised to find out later whose chart they had—and that they had been "reading" sidereal positions.

More about the various Uranian houses can be found in **The Language of Uranian Astrology** by Roger A Jacobson. Essentially, the meanings of the houses derive from the meaning of the personal point, e.g.: M houses refer to the "I", the soul; Sun houses refer to physical vitality; Ascendant houses to the environment and others within it, etc.

The Personal Points

In bringing up the houses I realize that I should have given more information about the meaning of the personal points than I did in the text. Three of the personal points are primarily considered as symbolizing the self, the "I": M, ☉ and ☽, while the other three are considered as relating to the "not I": A, ♈ and ☊.

M (Midheaven), in classical astrology, is used mainly as a special point that begins the cusp of the 10th house (status, career, public image). In Uranian Astrology M is the most important point in the horoscope. It is "I",

the ego, the inner life of soul, the minute. Consider this: The Sun, referred to in many texts as the ego, is in the same degree for everyone born the same day. It is a personal point but not quite so individually personal as M, which is different for every longitude and every 4 minutes of birth time. Consider also the symbolism of the cross of matter: the vertical line (think of longitude) represents the descent of the soul into matter, which is represented by the horizontal line (think of latitude, or Ascendant axis). Configurations involving M can be read as I, the soul who has descended into this body, this environment, am, do, think, feel... depending on what other factors relate to the point of M. Think of that, and you'll find extra meaning in the numerous examples of planetary pictures involving M, as seen in the text and appendices.

☉, **Sun**, is the body, the physical life force, the vitality, the objective, the day. In the Uranian system it is seen as the male body, in terms of health or males in one's life. For anyone, though, it refers to how one functions, objectively, within one's environment—how the ego expresses itself in physical action, in manifesting goals, in using energy.

☽, **Moon**, as body or others in the life, is primarily associated with females. For everyone, it represents that which is responsive and changeable. It is the subconscious, in contrast to the Sun as conscious objectivity. Where Sun is the day, Moon is the hour. Moon is emotional and subjective. It shows moods, attitudes and emotional patterns. Beyond the individual, it represents the fluctuating moods or attitudes of many, thus the public.

Ebertin **Cosmobiology** modifies the above three personal points somewhat by calling M "ego-consciousness and spiritual awareness. ☉ is "spirit, mind, the living being" and ☽ is "soul, the female principle."

A, Ascendant, is the place, the other, the environment. Here is where you might find another apparent difference with "classic" astrological interpretation, but it's not quite so different as it may seem. If the Ascendant symbolizes the personality, we are still really dealing with how you seem to **others**, rather than how you might feel about yourself inside. So A does relate more to "you" in connection with "me" rather than "me" alone. Significant to how A works is the "place," and also to how you relate to the situations in which you find yourself, and in your relationships to others.

♈, **Aries**, is the world in general and how the native connects with it. This has been covered in numerous ways in the text. Among the personal points, it is the one that is unique to Uranian Astrology.

☊, **Moon's Node,** means connections. It, therefore, figures in unions with others (of a less personal nature than A). It means connections with anything: ☊/♅ connections with machines, ☊/♆ connections with art, for example. Uranian astrology does not use the popular interpretation of the Nodes as relating to karma (South Node as the past, North Node as what one is striving toward). Usually only the North Node is considered, implying the nodal axis.

Dial Games

Egon suggested a variety of dial techniques for our class to try. Here are two "games" that I'd like to share with you, in closing, because we found them to be particularly enjoyable.

Predicting the Birth Date of a Baby

Egon told us that this technique is supposed to be about 85% accurate. First you enter the Sun degree of every member of the immediate family on a 360° dial. The baby will be born on a day in which the Sun degree is the midpoint between any two Sun degrees of other family members—parents, siblings, grandparents. Our class, in trying this on our own families, found that the system worked a little better than 85%, although we did add aunts and uncles to make a few of them "work." Since I was pregnant at the time, of course, I tried to predict the date!

My dilemma was that so many in my family were born in the late fall and winter months that there were multiple possibilities within the range of possible times! One possibility was the exact date that the doctor had picked, and since it was also the **earliest** possibility, of course I zeroed in on it wholeheartedly. What pregnant woman wouldn't?

I was **very** wrong. Elizabeth was born on the **last** of the possibilities–three **long** weeks later. The degree of the Sun on her birthday, October 13, 1978, is right at the midpoint between her grandfather's Sun (my father), who was born on September 26, and her eldest sister Lorry's Sun (my stepdaughter), who was born on October 31.

Running "M"

During social evenings many years ago in Germany, Egon told us, he and friends would set up a dial chart for the moment the party was beginning. When the conversation led to a major change of subject, or anything eventful happened, they would check the chart to see where M was. (M moves 1° for every 4 minutes of time.) It was fascinating how often M would be on a midpoint that appropriately described the new change of subject or whatever else may have happened.

My class tried playing "Running M" a number of times and the results were quite interesting. I no longer have the documentation, but it was fun to do. I remember that once we watched the President's State of the Union address and just as he began a major new topic an appropriate midpoint would be hit, such as the ☽/☊ midpoint for women's rights.

Another time Tom Canfield, the one in my class who was always so good at finding interesting bits of "trivia," suggested that we listen to a tape of the original Orson Welles broadcast of the "War of the Worlds." We used the transits for the night of the first broadcast (Oct. 30, 1938 at 8 PM in New York City) when so many people took it seriously and mistakenly thought they were listening to an actual news report of an alien invasion instead of fiction. Not surprisingly, M/A at the beginning of the broadcast, was on ♆/♆ (mighty deception). I remember that a goodly number of the most dire Uranian midpoints were "hit" by M during the course of the broadcast. ☽/♇ (a great surprise, mighty sensation) was activated at the moment that the broadcast was interrupted for the announcement that it was only fiction.

And so . . . happy "Dial Detecting," my friends!

If you are still "with me" at this point, you have acquired some quite advanced skills in 90° dial technique, and should be able to readily understand lecturers, or other books on Cosmobiology and Uranian Astrology. In the Bibliography you will find, in addition to the books that were referenced in the text, other books and resources that will help you expand your knowledge.

My best wishes to you for many successful investigations!

Bibliography

This book list includes those cited within the text of this book, and other recommended books.

Bertucelli, Penelope, **Friends, Family, Romance and Uranian Astrology Pictures**, Weston, Florida: Penelope Publications, 1996.

Ebertin, Reinhold, **The Annual Diagram as an Aid to Life**, Aalen Germany: Ebertin-Verlag 7080, 1973.

Ebertin, Reinhold, **Applied Cosmobiology**, Aalen Germany: Ebertin-Verlag 7080, 1972.

Ebertin, Reinhold, **Cosmic Marriage,** Aalen Germany: Ebertin-Verlag 7080, 1974.

Ebertin, Reinhold, **Combination of Stellar Influences**, Aalen Germany: Ebertin-Verlag 7080, 1972.

Ebertin, Reinhold, **Rapid and Reliable Analysis**, Aalen Germany: Ebertin-Verlag 7080, 1970.

Ebertin, Reinhold, **Transits**, Aalen Germany: Ebertin-Verlag 7080, 1971.

Encyclopedia Americana, Vol. 9, Danbury CT: Grolier, Inc. 1987.

Hackett, General Sir John, **The Third World War–August 1985**, New York: Macmillan, 1978.

Hand, Robert, **Horoscope Symbols**, Rockport, MA: Whitford Press, 1981.

Henry, William, **How to Use Dials**, San Diego: ACS Publications, 1986.

Howse, Derek, **Greenwich Time and the Discovery of the Longitude**, Oxford University Press, 1980.

Jacobsen, Roger A., **The Language of Uranian Astrology**, Franksville, WI: Uranian Publications, Inc., 1975.

Kimmel, Eleanora, **Cosmobiology for the 21st Century**, Tempe, Arizona: American Federation of Astrologers, 2000.

King, Stephen, **The Stand**, New York: A Signet Book, New American Library, 1980.

Lefeldt, Herman, **Ergänzungen zur Methodik der astrologischen Häuser und zum Regelwerk für Planetenbilder**, © 1977 by Herman Lefelt, D-2351 Bornhöved/Holstein, Federal Republic of Germany. Collected by Institut für Astrologie, Bertoldstr. 27, D-7800 Freiburg, Federal Republic of Germany.

Niggemann, Hans, **Key to Planetary Pictures**, New York: published by the author, 1969.

Niggemann, Hans, **The Principles of the Uranian System**, New York: published by the author, 1961.

Niggemann, Hans, **Rules for Planetary Pictures**, New York: published by the author, 1959.

Niggemann, Hans, **Uranian Astrology**, New York: published by the author, 1971.

Michelsen, Neil F., with revisions by Rique Pottenger, **The American Ephemeris for the 20th Century 1900-2000 at Midnight, Revised** Fifth Edition, San Diego: ACS Publications, 1995. (also available in Noon version)

Michelsen, Neil F., with revisions by Rique Pottenger. **The American Ephemeris for the 21st Century 2000-2050, Expanded Second Edition**, San Diego: ACS Publications, 1997 (also available in hard cover, and in a Noon version)

Michelsen, Neil F., **Uranian Transneptune Ephemeris 1850-2000**, Franksville, WI, Uranian Publications, 1978.

Munkasey, Michael, **Midpoints: Unleashing the Power of the Planets**, ACS Publications, San Diego, 1991.

Patterson, James, **The Virgin**, Bantam Books, 1981.

Pottenger, Maritha, **What Are Astrolocality Maps?**, San Diego: ACS Publications, 1983.

Rodden, Lois, **The American Book of Charts**, San Diego: ACS Publications, 1980.

Rudolph, Udo, **Articles Uranian Astrology Concepts**, Weston, Florida: Penelope Publications, 1998.

Rudolph, Ludwig , Witte-Lefeldt **Rules for Planetary Pictures: The Astrology of Tomorrow**, Hamburg, Germany: Witte-Verlag, 1st edition 1928, 5th Ed. 1959. English Publisher: Weston, FL: Penelope Publications

Rudolph, Udo, **The Hamburg School of Astrology**, The Astrological Association, England, 1973.

Schnitzler, Ilse and Herman Lefeldt, **Lexikon für Planetenbilde**r © 1957 Ludwig Rudolph (Witte-Verlag) Olenland 24, D-2000, Hamburg 62, Federal Republic of Germany

Scofield, Bruce, **The Timing of Events: Electional Astrology**, Orleans, MA: Astrolabe, 1985.

Starr Report, Public Affairs paperback, 9/15/98, and Library of Congress web site: icreport.loc.gov/icreport/

Vohryzek, Mary, translator, **Anatomical Correspondences to Zodiacal Degrees** (from **Anatomisch Entsprechungen der Tierkreisgrade** by Elsbeth and Reinhold Ebertin) **NCGR Journal**, Winter 1985-86, Vol 4. No. 2.

Resource Guide

Author's note: Internet references and contact information contained in this guide are current as of publication of this book, but cannot be guaranteed for the future.

Sources for Cosmobiology and Uranian books and tools:
Penelope Publications, 937 Crestview Circle, Weston, Florida 33327. Phone: 954-349-0141; Fax: 954-349-0142, www.uranianastrologer.com. Penelope has the most extensive list I know of for Cosmobiology and Uranian in the USA: books, tools, software.

American Federation of Astrologers, 6535 S. Rural Rd., Tempe, Arizona, 1-888-301-7630, www.astrologers.com. Huge book list includes many Cosmobiology and Uranian titles and tools.

Astrolabe, 350 Underpass Rd., Brewster, MA 02631, 1-800-843-6682 *www.alabe.com*

Recommended Software

Nova Chartwheels, by **Astrolabe**, and **Solar Fire**, by Esoteric Technologies of Australia, published by **Astrolabe.** *www. alabe.com,* Brewster, MA, 508-896-4081 or 1-THE-NOVA. Both of these programs include dials, a moveable pointer, screen display of "trees" and other reports useful for Cosmobiology and Uranian. **Chartwheels** is a DOS program, but an easy one that affords a great deal of flexibility in working with a dial on screen, more so than anything I've seen currently available for Windows. **Solar Fire**, in Windows, is a full service calculation program, easy to use, and very popular.

AstrologicPC, Hamburg School. This premier DOS program of the Hamburg School of Astrology is exclusively for the Uranian Astrologer. It calculates every procedure used by Uranian astrologers. An additional module containing *Rules for Planetary Pictures* can be included at a discount when ordering AstrologicPC. The English version is distributed by *Penelope Publications* of Weston, Florida. (See contact information above under Sources for Books.)

AstroDatabank, software for research by Mark McDonough with Lois Rodden. An enormously helpful tool for any astrologer. *www.astrodatabank.com*, **AstroDatabank Co.**, Manchester, MA, 978-526-864

Special Interest Group Specializing in Uranian Astrology

The Uranian Society is a SIG (Special Interest Group) of National Council for Geocosmic Research, Inc. This group holds lecture meetings in New York City, but has members all across the country. They publish a journal, a newsletter and lecture tapes. For informtaton: www.geocosmic.org Click on Special Interest Groups. To join, contact Membership Secretary, Meira B. Epstein, 119 E. 83rd St., Apt. 6B, New York, NY 10028; MeiraBE@aol.com.

Recommended Internet Sites for Information and Study

International Uranian Fellowship: *www.i-u-f.com*

Astrologer's Memorial information on Uranian: *www.solsticepoint.com/astrologersmemorial/uranian*

National Council for Geocosmic Research, Inc. *www.geocosmic.org*

Online College of Astrology *www.astrocollege.com*

The Uranian Beacon *finblake.home.mindspring.com/UranBeacon*

Starcrafts LLC, 68-A Fogg Rd., Epping, NH 03042 • 603-734-4300

www.starcraftspublishing.com • *www.astrcom.com* • *www.acspublications.com*

Author queries: Maria Kay Simms, 260 N. Haverhill Rd., Kensington, NH 03833.

mariasimms@comcast.net   or   maria@astrocom.com

About the Author

Usually the author page is written by someone other than the author. More often than not, I write it from whatever biographical information I've received from the author of a book that we are in the process of preparing for publictation. Since I wrote this book, this page will be a short autobiography.

My background, in brief, includes that I grew up in Buda, a very small Illinois town, population 750, although all kids from the surrounding farms also came to the school by bus. I graduated from high school at age 18 then went to Illinois Wesleyan University where I majored in art, graduatiing in 1962 with a BFA degree. I then taught public school art for several years, mostly in junior high school, although some year involved both grade school and junior high.

I began studying astrology in the 1970s after meeting two friends who were astrologically knowledgable, first a woman friend and then later a man who worked with my first husband

Over the years astrology gradually became a major interest for me, although art remained important. In 1986, I moved to San Diego to become Art Director for ACS, after my first book had been accepted for publication. That book is **Twelve Wings of the Eagle**, which is largely a story of the processional ages, with of course the astrological background of the ages, each of which was named for a sign of the zodiac. (If anyone has missed the song, which I doubt, we are in the **Age of Aquarius**, although now fairly close to the end of it. My estimate for when the Age of Pisces will begin is about 2025.

I am owner of Astro Computing Services and ACS Publications. I firsr went to the company as art director back in 1986, when it was in San Diego. Later, I married Neil F. Michelsen, the founder and head of ACS. Sadly, he became ill and passed away in 1990, leaving me to see that the company continued. It is now located in the seacoast area of New Hampshire, in the town of Epping in a building owned by James L. Jossick, who is my husband.

Although astrology is dominant in my work, art remans very significant, both for the production design that I do for ACS on a Macintosh computer and the oil paintings and drawings that I do at home just because I enjoy doing them—and it is a good release from the more exacting computer design work I do for my business.

As for my fine arts work, I continue with my drawings and oil paintings, exhibiting them in a gallery store that we've added in the front rooms of my business location and by entering art shows held in the general area where I live. Jim and I are both well past what is generally considered to be "retirement age" although we are both still working, not because we have to—we just prefer to keep busy, doing the type of work that we each like to do. We love our rural home in Kensington, NH, surrounded on three sides by forest with lots of beautiful trees, and occasional visits into our yard by deer or wild turkeys.

Of course, we also enjoy visits from our grown children, their spouses and our eleven grand children!

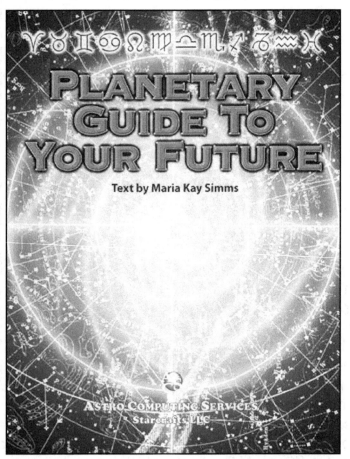

CPSIA information can be obtained
at www.ICGtesting.com
Printed in the USA
BVHW011158281119
565081BV00015B/333/P